OLD-TIME
MUSIC
AND
DANCE

OLD-TIME
MUSIC
AND
DANCE

Community and Folk Revival

John Bealle

AN IMPRINT OF
INDIANA UNIVERSITY PRESS
BLOOMINGTON AND INDIANAPOLIS

This book is a publication of

Quarry Books

an imprint of

Indiana University Press
601 North Morton Street
Bloomington, IN 47404-3797 USA

http://iupress.indiana.edu

Telephone orders   800-842-6796
Fax orders   812-855-7931
Orders by e-mail   iuporder@indiana.edu

© 2005 by John Bealle

The paper used in this publication meets the minimum
requirements of American National Standard for Information
Sciences—Permanence of Paper for Printed Library Materials,
ANSI Z39.48-1984.

Manufactured in the United States of America

Library of Congress Cataloging-in-Publication Data

Bealle, John.
   Old-time music and dance : community and folk revival / John
Bealle.
     p. cm.
   Includes bibliographical references (p.) and index.
   ISBN 0-253-34638-X (pbk. : alk. paper)
   1. Bloomington Old-Time Music and Dance Group—
History.   2. Old-time music—Indiana—Bloomington—History
and criticism.   3. Country-dance—Indiana—Bloomington—
History.   I. Title.
   ML3551.8.B56B43 2005
   781.62'130772255—dc22
                                2005004559

1 2 3 4 5 10 09 08 07 06 05

FOR ELOISE AND JOSIE

Contents

Contents

Contents

ACKNOWLEDGMENTS

On its way to publication, this manuscript has received much benefit from the comments and support of thoughtful and astute readers. I am grateful to those who took time to critique all or parts of the book: Dillon Bustin, Joyce Cauthen, Eloise Clark, Pat Gingrich, Frank Hall, Jim Johnson, Tamara Loewenthal, John McDowell, Ron Pen, and David Schloss. Others generously provided photos for the book: Bill Baus, Dillon Bustin, Min Gates, Ted Hall, Brian "Hawk" Hubbard, Teri Klassen, Laura Ley, Gary Stanton, and Dan Willens. Dudley Laufman granted permission to use his poem "Supposing you were someone else," from *A Dancing Master's Diary* (1981). Dudley's poetry and other writings can be found at his website, http://www.laufman.org. Dee Mortensen of Indiana University Press brought to the book her wisdom both as editor and also as old-time musician and participant in the Bloomington music and dance community. Countless others have offered counsel in passing, and their names are omitted only with injustice. I am grateful to all those in the community, whose memories I savor here with such fondness. What you taught me has remained with me as a beacon of wisdom, inspiration, and hope.

My parents, Ann and Rufus Bealle, have genuinely appreciated all that the music and dance community has brought to me and to others, and they are surely pleased that the long trek this manuscript has taken is finally at an end. I am grateful to Eloise Clark, my partner, for the pleasure we share as fellow travelers in old-time music and dance. At her side these ideas sprouted, and they have been nurtured to fruition with her curiosity, appreciation, support, and encouragement. My daughter Josie, now age eleven, is only vaguely aware of what all this means: it is partly my hope to give her, and the children of all those mentioned here, a clue to why we live our lives the way we do.

Acknowledgments

INTRODUCTION: CONJURING HISTORY

> To articulate the past historically does
> not mean to recognize it "the way it
> really was." . . . It means to seize hold of
> a memory as it flashes up at a moment
> of danger.
>
> —*Walter Benjamin, "Theses on the
> Philosophy of History"*

When I began this text years ago, my goal was to correct an unsettling discrepancy in the depiction of the "folksong revival," the cultural movement that has emerged in various forms throughout history in America and elsewhere. I had fallen behind this banner in my youth, and it has nourished me intellectually, politically, emotionally, and socially ever since. What I saw was a movement that at most every turn professed utopian aspirations, yet whose social and political underpinning was too often obscured by the giant shadows cast by its most prominent performers.

At the time, I was living in Bloomington, Indiana, under the euphoric spell of the old-time music and dance community there with all its nostalgic and communal yearnings. The dance group was a kind of accidental utopia, looked upon by its adherents with a wry satisfaction that over time became part of its design. There a native "history" already existed, an active collective memory that circulated in amusing stories about our common past. Moreover, this carefree vocabulary of the past belied an uncommon astuteness regarding the thorny dilemmas of folksong revival—authenticity, community, representation, the politics of culture, and so on. All I had to do was write it down, which I did, unabashedly. I identified vaguely with von Schmidt and Rooney's *Baby, Let Me Follow You Down* (1979), which seemed unique in depicting ongoing social relations and not merely the heroic achievements of star performers, as the preeminent reality of folksong revival.

This was in 1986, when I assembled the basic historical account that comprises this book. Partly as a component of an analytical study for the Indiana University Folklore Department, partly for a local history written for the group, I conducted twenty-five interviews, mostly by telephone, with the most knowledgeable veterans in the dance group. The local history I assembled was printed a year later as an attachment to the annual Sugar Hill calendar and was distributed in the dance community. Since then, this document has circulated in photocopies among those who came to the group later. My general impression was that it met with satisfaction and coincided with the prevailing historical mythos of the group.

As the years passed, I was nagged by an urgency to revise the local history, infusing it with more of the analytical material. I began tinkering with the document, rewriting it several times, trying out various formats. This urgency was fueled largely by what I saw in many places as the eclipse of the spirit that had sustained old-time music and dance revival since it emerged from the shadows decades before. Whereas the original document had been written in the fullness of the moment of the dance, I now felt the need to explain that moment to a different audience, one that no longer took its spiritual cues from those longings that brought the original dancers together.

The dance was not unique in this—few 1970s-era cultural utopias survived the unrepentant individualism of the 1980s. Postmodern culture had brought down the oppositional wall that had separated the dominant culture from all that it was not. Radical individualism and marketplace ontology made their way into the obscurest corners, appropriating culture to their liking. No one was unaffected by this, and its effects were horribly, horribly pleasant. Post-capitalist economics were particularly friendly to the smart, resourceful, and abundantly talented types who frequented old-time music and dance events. Corporate America discovered niche marketing, and suddenly things that were once the exclusive province of an underground economy—from Birken-

Introduction

stocks to Dr. Bronner's soap to Celestial Seasonings teas—could now be bought by anyone. In much the same way, old-time music and dance made its way into the cultural marketplace, where it was discovered with alacrity and enthusiasm. It may have seemed we'd won a war we set out to win long ago.

But as a part of the underground, these materials had been part of a worldview linked to Vietnam-era culture and politics. For those of us who felt we were enduring a bitter world, with too much hatred, hunger, and self-centered ambition, the materials of the cultural underground were powerful devices of spiritual rejuvenation. They were the essential tools of a simple and peaceful life that, we thought, could bring the madness of the world to its knees. So it was with old-time music and dance. And in Bloomington, it was the particular way dancers nurtured their miracle—the wry, inscrutable satisfaction that provided their only real source of political stability and strength—that was the key component of the empowering atmosphere of the dance. I am awe-struck to think how this could have been so bold at the time, yet ultimately so fragile.

That is why I have perceived an urgency about the need to tell this story. But this is not an easy thing to do, unraveling the cultural mischief of postmodern capitalism. For one thing, there are a great many Bloomington stories to tell, and I have chosen a particularly untriumphant thread to follow. This thread, I hope, is the one least likely to have followed its protagonists into the new century, the one least suitable to the all-too-receptive postmodern environment. It is this story whose "moment of danger" is nigh.

To make this fact apparent, I have used several devices in the book. First, I have personalized the historical stance, confirming that it emanates from a point of view and hoping thereby to shoulder any historical obligation readers might want to avoid. I have also given the story abrupt historical closure, writing decisively in the past tense and assigning an apocalyptic tone to the outcome. These voices—along with the uncontroversial historical material that had been brought forward—are interwoven throughout the narrative and should be readily apparent.

This book is structured as a sequence of short essays, following a vague chronology, on subjects that were the definitive concerns of the group. The first few chapters cover the historical context, addressing old-time music, contra dance, the town of Bloomington, and the landscape of southern Indiana. From there the book turns to the substance of the dance group, in many cases focusing on themes peripheral to the dance event itself. Chapter 29 is a snapshot of a "typical" Wednesday night dance, taken sometime in the mid-1980s when the original manuscript of this book was drafted.

Ultimately what I found that I produced was a vivid historical otherness—a past just beyond the reach of palpable memory, accessible only to believers by way of some ritual conjuring. In this I hope to have replicated something of the spirit of the folk revival as it was constituted long ago as a historical conjuring, as Robert Cantwell has described it. One never truly receives history; it must be pursued. It is this urgency which unites on common ground the most vigorous traditional cultures with the most responsible cultural revivals. And it is with this thought that I now direct readers to a rather arbitrary and trifling moment in 1972, yet one from which much was said to come.

Introduction

Supposing you were
someone else

& we met
in the reel

What would you
do if I

squeezed your hand
on the ladies' chain,

& on the return
squeezed it again?

—*Dudley Laufman,* A Dancing
Master's Diary

OLD-TIME
MUSIC
AND
DANCE

1 AN APOCRYPHAL STORY

Among those who participated in the old-time music and dance group in the town of Bloomington, Indiana, in the 1970s and 1980s, there circulated an apocryphal story of the group's origin. The story is all but forgotten now, but at the time it was a well-known point of historical reference for the group. The narrative itself is of some concern to me here, but more important is the weekly Wednesday Night Dance and the social entity surrounding it, both of which had the extraordinary circumstance of having been organized under the auspices of a story.

In this story, Dillon Bustin, an Indiana native familiar with contra dance, was said to have serendipitously come upon old-time fiddler Miles Krassen while wandering through the Indiana University campus area known as Dunn Meadow on a summer day in 1972. Some recalled the site as the Monroe County Courthouse square, and one account had Miles sitting on a stump as he fiddled. Some attributed to Dillon the conversational opener, "That's a fine 'Red Haired Boy' you're playing." Dillon has confirmed the story, stump included, citing "Rights of Man Hornpipe" as the proper tune and the old quadrangle area near Lindley Hall as the location. This auspicious meeting, it is said, led to the convening of weekly dances with Dillon calling and Miles fiddling.

Whatever the actual facts, the story of this meeting would come to personify the marriage of intricate northern dance and reckless southern music, long to be the cultural fabric of the Wednesday Night Dance. It was the origin of this "group" that the unusual story served to explain.

There was never much concern over the truth of the story, perhaps instead a wry satisfaction that even the story had no authoritative origin, or even a vague awareness that the story was the consequence and not the origin of the group. Nor, at the time, were there models for what are today called "dance groups"—a term later used to describe the local groups affiliated with the post–World War II music and dance revival. The term "dance crowd," suggesting less formality than "dance group," was also common during the early Bloomington years. Nor was there any other device that might have served as a premeditated point of origin—a founding or a charter, for example. This quasi-myth seemed designed instead to constitute the group as a kind of providential event, its existence having been received as a circumstance. There was certainly not, in those early years, any institution separate from the experience, separate from the re-creation that those dancers who showed up each week were inspired to enact. The dance seemed almost a social archetype, arising perfectly and naturally from the needs of the dancers. There was no membership and at the time no communal property: to belong required no more and no less than presence and affirmation sufficient to one's expectations. Consequently, many dancers first experienced the dance as something of an epiphany, as the discovery of some long-submerged inner desire.

The cultural aspects of the experience seemed equally providential. Most participants knew that southern old-time music and northern contra dance arose from different historical origins. Old-time musicians knew that their tunes and styles were based primarily in the South, and contra dance callers knew their dances were based in rural New England. But they also knew that their blending in Bloomington was a circumstantial necessity, not a clever idea, and that both, in their separate historical contexts, were fundamental rituals of community social experience. They seemed naturally compatible, as if the particular features each offered were uniquely suited to the social needs of the group, as if history had unnecessarily thrown them apart.

Old-Time Music and Dance

The foundations for this experience and for the group are to be found in some particular strains of American culture that were especially prominent after World War II. At the time the Bloomington dance began, southern folk music was experiencing a widespread renaissance. In the early 1970s, the burgeoning popularity of folk festivals, the widening accessibility of bluegrass music, the growing success of "acoustic" music stores, the interest in southern music by such recording artists as Bob Dylan and the Byrds, and even the film *Deliverance* (1972) were all drawing uncommon attention to traditional southern music. The three-disc recording *Will the Circle Be Unbroken?*, released by Capitol Records in 1972, was a milestone in bringing traditional music to popular audiences and also in establishing the folk revival as a component in the "circle" of generations that foster musical traditions. Yet, in certain enclaves, this was more than simply a shift in taste in musical style. It was part of a folksong revival movement, whereby a music with roots attributed to rural America, especially the South, was sought after, nurtured, and re-created as if to extract existential qualities the music was thought to have accumulated in its authentic native habitat.

As is so often the case with folk revivals, these musical tastes and their attendant spiritual strivings were tied to particular socio-political causes. In the postwar folksong revival, traditional culture was seen as an attractive, viable, and historically grounded alternative to the postwar modernism that had fostered unbridled consumer capitalism, racial intolerance, social alienation, environmental degradation, the military-industrial complex, and, notably, the Vietnam War. As I suggest throughout the book, the particular strain of old-time music and dance revival that blossomed in Bloomington had its roots in the historical movements that sought alternatives to the ills of modern life.

But the dance group did not arise, the origin story tells us, as a deliberate articulation of this cause. Rather, it emerged spontaneously as a circumstance framed by it. The sites mentioned in the story formed its cradle of significance, the place where local old-time music and dance revival took its cue from the social and political context. The courthouse square is the symbolic center of civic life and is a ubiquitous presence in Indiana county seats. On the south side of the square is Kirkwood Avenue, and running east from that point is a bustling "strip" with many

An Apocryphal Story

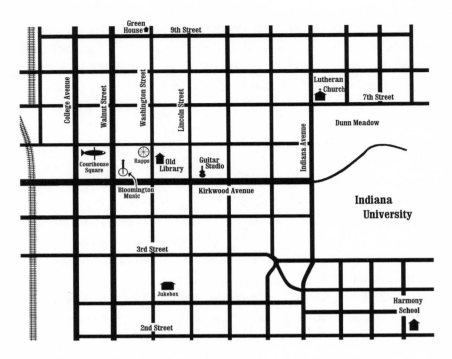

Layout of the Bloomington town-gown corridor showing sites important in the history of the old-time music and dance group.

student-oriented businesses. At its terminus, a mere five blocks from the courthouse, is the arched "entrance" to the Indiana University campus. Most all college campuses have these fringe areas, where economic and cultural access to academia fosters a kind of free-spirited organic intellectualism. But the close proximity in Bloomington of the twin archetypal institutions, town and gown, as I suggest throughout this book, lent salience and visibility to the kinds of expressive discourse that either, alone, would not or could not embrace.

Moreover, the availability of land forced the campus to grow toward the east, leaving the traditional campus center concentrated on its western edge. Dunn Meadow and the Lindley quadrangle are on this western edge, accessible both to Kirkwood Avenue and to the student union. Both are important locales for social and political gatherings; Dunn Meadow, in particular, has been the site of important protests and rock concerts. Thus all of these story settings are outdoor locales where expressive culture asserts its significance, sometimes spontaneously, against the backdrop of conventional civic and academic institutions. They are settings where playing a fiddle in 1972 would have been seen as a public act, possibly meaningful, possibly subversive.

And just as these locales provided a meaningful setting, so also did the chance meeting of Miles and Dillon. The chance encounter—the play of meaningful serendipity against meaningless chance—was a common motif in folk revival narrative and experience, validating the atmosphere of effortless discovery that impelled so much of dance group social experience. In fact, encounter experiences had much to do with the geo-social disposition of the movement: music and dance life was punctuated by frequent travel, gravitation toward the same kinds of places, and visible displays of expressive culture. Life seemed enchanted by serendipity, but, in fact, old-time musicians and dancers fostered the kinds of encounters that made them seem several degrees of separation closer than the norm.

There were other reasons the folk revival found an especially auspicious reception in Bloomington. Notably, it already had deeply rooted connections with Indiana University. Under the guidance of president and later chancellor Herman B Wells, the university had established itself as a center for international studies, situated amid conservative heartland tradition where this approach would not have been readily anticipated. Within this environment, the Folklore Institute had emerged during the postwar era as a research center for international folklore study.

During its founding era, however, the institute explicitly excluded folk revival concerns from its purview. Its longtime director, Richard Dorson, was a well-known opponent of folksong revival, even coining the term "fakelore" as a pejorative label that would come to embrace the kind of conscious imitation or display of traditional forms that was common in folksong revival. Not all faculty members shared this prejudice, however, and those sympathetic to the revival became valuable allies to students who were struggling with its political, aesthetic, and intellectual dilemmas.

Even with this mixed reception, the Folklore Institute attracted mu-

An Apocryphal Story

sicians, who came with a balance of intellectual and artistic ambitions. Some students from this period—such as Joe Hickerson, Richard Blaustein, Richard Reuss, and Neil Rosenberg—persisted and earned degrees working on revival-related subjects. Others, such as Peter Gold, came to work with the Archives of Traditional Music, which held collections of recorded traditional music from throughout the world. There were scores of others who came to the institute or to the archives with musical interests shaped in part by popular folksong revival.

Surely popular culture did foster some misconception of folklore scholarship. Even a sympathetic figure like Richard Reuss, who was to become a leading scholar on political folksong, felt the need to write an article for the folksong revival magazine *Sing Out!*, "So You Want to Be a Folklorist?" (1965). The article sought to explain to prospective students that the program was not designed to promote folk music performance. Nowadays, of course, there are public folklore components in most every academic program, and folklore revival, through the subject of authenticity, has become an accepted research area.

Although campus fringe areas were important sites for folksong revival performance, there was also much activity on campuses themselves. In the mid-1950s Bruce Buckley began a weekly folk music radio program on what later became the local National Public Radio affiliate station. It ran continuously until the mid-1980s, passed on through a succession of folklore graduate students. The most important university-affiliated venues, however, were campus folk clubs, which had become common nationwide in universities where folklore had some presence. One of the most ambitious clubs was founded in 1961 at the University of Illinois, in nearby Urbana, and remained active until 1970. Its driving force was folklorist Archie Green, who intently kept the club focused on its mission to bring to campus artists from marginalized culture groups—even though some club members had little other interest than promoting themselves as folk-pop performers (Green 1993).

In Bloomington, the Indiana University Folk Club was established in 1962 with official campus affiliation. It became a component of a campus folk scene that already included a local coffeehouse (Phase Three), radio shows, and hootenannies. According to Neil Rosenberg, the club was founded on the campus side of a deep town-gown cultural chasm, with little evidence of interest in local or regional folk culture (1995b: 279, 285 n5). This divide was typical of college towns, but in Bloomington it was amplified by other facets of local history.

In 1854, the New Albany and Salem Railroad extended its tracks through Bloomington, just west of the courthouse square (Madison 2002). This spurred growth both for Bloomington industries and for Indiana University, and by century's end the west side was the industrial area, while the east was residential. West-side industrial growth was an important facet of Bloomington life until the 1970s, when economic stagnation and quest for cheap labor began the steady decline of Bloomington industrial economy. Nonetheless, the east-west pattern is still woven deeply into Bloomington's cultural fabric, influencing the disbursement of architectural styles, churches and worship styles, and suburban development.

To the east, Indiana University, founded in 1820, struggled to survive during its early years. In 1884, after a fire, the campus was moved from College Avenue to the area called Dunn's Woods bordering Indiana Avenue. It became Bloomington's definitive institution largely as a consequence of the postwar education boom, punctuated by the signature international programs developed under Herman B Wells's presidency. Novelist Larry Lockridge, who assessed the Bloomington of his 1950s childhood, could see the roots of a long-standing cooperation between town and gown. "Still," he wrote, "much of Bloomington, with its practical-minded and laboring classes, was worlds apart from academe" (Lockridge 1994: 70).

Although one might have expected folk clubs to have routinely transcended this barrier, most often the clubs sought out seasoned performers well known on the festival-coffeehouse circuit. Local traditional culture was of lesser importance in the 1960s folk revival, as illustrated by Joe Hickerson's comment in *Sing Out!* in 1960 that "folk music has reached the Ivory Tower and can be heard live at the Quiet Answer Coffee Shop in Bloomington" (quoted in Tyler 1991–92: 32). Ironically, at the same time, local high schoolers involved in the revival were attending bluegrass sessions at the Brown County Jamboree in nearby

An Apocryphal Story

Bean Blossom. Some of these Bloomington natives later became active in music and dance in Bloomington and elsewhere, providing evidence of distinct strains of influence in local-based or campus-based culture.

The Folk Club's constitution expressed as its goals "to promote interest and participation in folk music activity in Indiana University, and to encourage the appreciation of folklore and its studies." According to Neil Rosenberg, who was involved in the club throughout its run, its activities were "both recreational and educational, including folk sings, lectures, symposia, films, concerts, and instructional workshops" (1995a: 73). The club sponsored performances by traditional performers such as Doc Watson, the Stanley Brothers, Mance Lipscomb, the New Lost City Ramblers, Jesse Fuller, Dave Van Ronk, the Reverend Gary Davis, Ramblin' Jack Elliott, and Frank Proffitt. But club members and institute students also gave performances, including Joe Hickerson, Frank Gillis, the Jordan River Ramblers, and the Pigeon Hill String Ticklers. The club did not promote dancing but did serve as a kind of institutional hub that would have attracted people interested in both music and dance.

In Neil Rosenberg's personal recollection, the club's abrupt decline and disappearance by 1967 was related to two factors. The first was the cultural and political climate nationwide. The postwar folksong revival had been nurtured by leftist ideology, based partly on the notion that folksong performance was in itself a political act. But the growing urgency of the Vietnam War had led many away from the folksong movement toward a more explicit anti-war discourse. And rock music by this time had absorbed the leftist and anti-war influences that had originated in folksong revival, thereby drawing political energy away from the revival.

But a second factor may have had more significance locally. The Folk Club was almost wholly a campus-based institution, with little interest in folk culture in the Bloomington area. For those, like Rosenberg, who were most deeply involved in the club, its decline went hand in hand with a turn toward the burgeoning autonomous networks that were forming around folk musical styles or toward traditional performance settings or institutions. In Rosenberg's case, he was led by local folksong revivalists to the Brown County Jamboree in Bean Blossom and later to

Old–Time Music and Dance

other "country music performance venues, weekly jam sessions, square dances, and individual homes" (1995b: 279). He recalls a rather deliberate decision to "turn off" his ethnographic consciousness and plunge headfirst as a novice into a culture he considered entirely alien to his own (281). When asked in 1967 to participate in a bluegrass recording, Rosenberg considered it a "granting of naturalized citizenship" into the nation of bluegrass (283).

In retrospect, knowing the profound significance of nearby Bean Blossom in bluegrass tradition, it seems odd that this did not happen sooner. Bean Blossom is a small community about an hour's drive east of Bloomington. Its significance rests partly in its location in Brown County, an area promoted by residents as a repository of homespun traditional culture and as a center for arts and crafts. This has given rise to various country and folk music venues over the years. But most important here was the purchase of land near Bean Blossom by the family of legendary bluegrass musician Bill Monroe, and the development of a performance venue there as early as 1951.

Yet this is not merely to say that Indiana folklorists might have visited Bean Blossom sooner. Rather, when they did, bluegrass itself had much to do with the subtle shift in folkloristic consciousness toward local traditions and indigenous performance settings. Bluegrass was not at all a "survival" on the precipice of decline, as much folk tradition was thought to be, but a new postwar form with an active, energetic, and tradition-minded constituency. It had been introduced to the folk revival a decade earlier as a living tradition. It was a "new kind of orchestra," as Alan Lomax put it, "folk music with overdrive," a popular country music style with a self-motivated affinity for traditional music forms (Lomax 1959).

Moreover, whereas bluegrass sometimes received mixed reviews in folk revival performance circles, the reverse was not true: more adventurous musicians like Rosenberg were eagerly patriated into the emerging institutional apparatus that constituted this folk "nation." Bluegrass promoters were keen observers of American culture and had already incorporated folk revival elements—particularly outdoor festival venues and the use of antimodernist descriptive rhetoric—into bluegrass culture. With its own authenticating machinery, performance venues, and

An Apocryphal Story

recording industry, bluegrass and similar living traditions could penetrate locality with the kind of significance that Rosenberg and others discovered in Bloomington and its environs. Now, everywhere, in boundless quantity, locality was infused with authenticity, providing an alternative to organized folk clubs in the search for the elusive qualities of performed folksong. For the next two decades, folksong and folksong revival were increasingly manifested as authentic localized discourse, juxtaposed with "official" local culture. It was this fundamental structure that prepared the way for the serendipitous meeting of Dillon Bustin and Miles Krassen.

2 OLD-TIME MUSIC REVIVAL

The institutional machinery of bluegrass may have been influential in the emergence of localized folksong revival, but in Bloomington and elsewhere there was another vivid and influential model—the pre–World War II country music style known as "old-time music." This musical form is generally associated with acoustic string band music, with fiddle as the lead instrument combined with some arrangement of other instruments such as banjo, guitar, mandolin, and bass. Presentations of this style ordinarily featured both instrumental and vocal performance, but there was also a strong link to rural social dance. Old-time music was a pervasive component of rural music tradition in most areas of the U.S. and provided abundant opportunities for local engagement of tradition during the postwar revival years in most areas of the U.S. The earliest interest in old-time music revival, however, was not in living tradition but in 78 rpm commercial recordings made during the prewar era.

The term "old-time music" was used, along with other terms, in 1920s recording industry marketing materials, but its symbolically loaded association with a specific style was negotiated in the pages of *Sing Out!* magazine following the 1959 emergence of the influential band the New Lost City Ramblers (see Rosenberg 1985: 173). Mike Seeger especially credits the marketing philosophy of Frank Warner of Columbia Records, who avoided disparaging terms such as "hillbilly" in the recordings he produced (Seeger 1964: 27). In particular, the term incorporated a crucial distinction between prewar "old-time" music from postwar forms such as bluegrass. In effect, if not intent, this distinction established for old-time music more prestigious antimodernist credentials and the potential for authentic experience as a key performance component. Old-time music revival's fundamental tenet, which Robert Cantwell (1996) and others have traced to Harry Smith's *Anthology of American Folk Music* (1952), was the fetishization of aural style. According to the model derived from Smith, the old-time revival looked beyond more contemporary and more accessible forms of southern music to embrace meticulously the austere prewar style captured and preserved on prewar 78s.

Smith's *Anthology* was a boxed three-volume set of 33 rpm LPs that contained recordings from the 1920s and 1930s originally released as commercial country music on 78 rpm discs. Smith assembled the eighty-four performances under the general rubric "folk music." By all accounts, this taxonomy had a substantial influence on the early years of the revival and on American musical culture. An accompanying booklet provided the minutiae of the circumstances of the original recordings along with an over-condensed headline-style summary of the narrative "Zoologic Miscegeny Achieved in Mouse-Frog Nuptials, Relatives Approve" for 'Froggy Went a-Courtin'." Arranged numerically with scant contextual documentation, the *Anthology* deliberately effaced the stereotypical categories "which had lain over folksong collections like lines of latitude and longitude"—not even the race of the performers was given (Cantwell 1996: 193). Instead, Smith's "memory theater," as Cantwell has put it, alluded to a cultural architecture in which its "folk music" reached to the primordial origins of the musical cosmos (Cantwell 1996, esp. 192–94, 204–206). On the cover, Smith reproduced a seventeenth-century drawing depicting God tuning a celestial monochord, suggesting the restoration of human consciousness "to its Adamic state of pure unmediated apprehension of the laws and powers of Nature" (205).

It is notable that the *Anthology* selections were originally commercial releases made by recording companies, not field recordings made by folklorists. Indeed, Smith deliberately excluded field recordings, favoring instead commercial products sold during 1927–32 to regional audiences. These recordings, concluded Greil Marcus, "at least some people thought were worth paying for" (Marcus 1997: 102). The performers were "contingent individuals," uniquely aware of their desperate circumstances, uniquely driven by this awareness to seek out recording contracts. They performed "as if they knew their neighbors would hear, but also as if they imagined the nation itself might actually acknowledge their existence" (123). Theirs was "the folk music of people attempting to connect to other people" (122). It seems scarcely necessary to note how extraordinary was Smith's reasoning. During a time when Marxist theory was deeply influential in folksong revival and study, when commercialism was thought to taint the value of folksong as authentic, Smith implicated commercialism as almost a test of purity.

By the 1970s, the *Anthology* milieu had given way to a much larger "reissue" market of similar prewar 78 rpm records released on 33 rpm LPs. Where the *Anthology* was comprehensive in scope, the later reissue LPs were the province of a growing number of specialty record labels, each devoted to a particular style of music. It was largely in this transition that Smith's general rubric "folk music" gave way to more specific stylistic categories and to what Neil Rosenberg (1993) has called "named-system revivals." It was in this environment that "old-time music" began to take shape at the convergence of a particular style of music and the separate institutional means to promote it. It behooves us to examine how this transition happened.

Among the earliest to associate 78s with prewar antiquity were record collectors. Initially, collecting 78s was at most an obscure hobby—surely the least celebrated element of the folk revival. Operating in the shadows of the folk boom (in 1962 Joan Baez was featured on the cover of *Time* magazine), collectors scoured antique stores and sometimes went door-to-door in search of rare recordings. Collectors drew upon unique skills as antiquarians and not as entrepreneurs. Indeed, the trauma of the war and the delirious modernism of the postwar years had left an abundance of prewar artifacts—including recordings and musical instruments—whose value could be comprehended only by those with a keen sensitivity to the past.

Smith himself was an obscure collector before he assembled the brilliant *Anthology*. Few collectors were as ambitious as Smith, however. Most were pleased with any interest in their obscure hobby and generous to genuine old-time music enthusiasts. Fiddler and folklorist Richard Blaustein, who grew up and discovered old-time music in New York, recalled the generosity of Loy Beaver, a transplanted Georgian who had accumulated a massive collection of 78s, many later reissued on County Records (Blaustein 1994). Some collectors compiled "lists" of records they hoped to sell or trade. A few, such as Joe Bussard, were actually willing to make tape copies for a small fee (Wyatt 1999). Bussard's list grew to around a hundred pages, each with several dozen titles, and was duplicated over and over by enthusiasts after the advent of photocopy technology. Together, collectors formed a hidden network, keepers of a unified inventory of the old-time revival's most precious currency—the genuine musical artifacts from the "golden age" of country music.

The mere presence of this compelling musical inventory was enough to inspire a revival performance milieu. Initially, this consisted of staged folk revival presentations, crafted in deference to the performance on the recordings. The New Lost City Ramblers, the string band ensemble formed in 1959 with Mike Seeger, Tom Paley, and John Cohen, were the progenitors of this musical form in old–time music. In their 1964 book, *The New Lost City Ramblers Song Book,* band members outlined the sources that inspired the formation of the band. John Cohen traced the evolution of the string band through the transformations in performing ensembles during the period of commercial old-time music 78s (1964b: 17–21). Mike Seeger, who listened to commercial and field recordings as a youth, noted the significance to the band of songs that "were originally recorded by commercial companies and the Library of Congress in the Southeastern mountains between 1925 and 1935 and show the first attempts of the hill musicians to 'make a hit' with old traditional songs that had been in the mountains since pioneer days"

(Seeger 1964: 22). The Ramblers introduced a distinctive and influential component to old–time music revival: the vivid articulation of an imagined past based on its recorded artifacts.

In due time, however, it became known that some of the original *Anthology* performers were still alive, often living in obscurity in the rural South. Surely the most celebrated case was the discovery in 1963 of country blues singer Mississippi John Hurt. Northern aficionados of Hurt's recordings speculated that a line from one of his recordings, "Avalon's my hometown, always on my mind," referred to Avalon, Mississippi, and went there, going practically house to house, to look for him. There indeed he was—and his rediscovery and presentation inspired a spate of copycat sleuthing, of which one of the more bizarre was the 1964 rediscovery of bluesman Son House, conducted against the backdrop of the Mississippi voter registration drive and vividly recounted firsthand in von Schmidt and Rooney's *Baby, Let Me Follow You Down* (1979: 188–201).

The discovery, exhibition, and career management of prewar performers was a watershed in the evolving folksong revival, bringing unprecedented clarity to distinctions between revivalist and authentic performance. Most of the rediscovered performers adapted quickly to the role of folksinger, enjoying a measure of attention to their music and sometimes also of prosperity that had been absent for decades. Lightnin' Hopkins accommodated the revival famously, code-switching between electric and acoustic guitar as the circumstance demanded. One who did not adapt well was the irascible fiddler Clayton McMichen, romanticized by folksong enthusiasts for his flamboyant stint with the Skillet Lickers in the 1920s. Having once quipped that "there's 500 pairs of overalls sold to every one tuxedo suit—that's why I stick to swamp opera," McMichen actually struggled against the hillbilly stereotype for most of his career. In later post–Skillet Licker years McMichen became adept at the versatile long-bow style of fiddling and experimented with jazz and popular music. Thus the rediscovered McMichen "gradually began to tire of people who were ignorant of or unsympathetic with the later, equally significant aspects of his career, and who persisted in glorifying the five frustrating years he had spent in Atlanta" (Wolfe 1997:

96). Performing at the 1964 Newport Folk Festival the year rediscoveries were most intensely celebrated, he was reported to have complained to his audience:

> What are you people doing here? You don't know anything about the music. You're the easiest audience in the world to play for, because you don't want anything from us. I could play the worst fiddle in the world, and you'd still applaud. You just like us because we're old. (Nelson 1964: 7)

Possibly McMichen, who died in 1970, would have thought better of his folk revival experience had he lived to see the old-time music revival in full flower, where his fiddling style was widely studied and the balance of his career more generously esteemed. Possibly, given the insightful appreciation country music has received since that time, he would reassess those contributions. But in this formative period, he undoubtedly did encounter in folk revival audiences a superficial association of his music with the classic old-time aesthetic. Selections from McMichen's 1964 Newport performance have been reissued on *Bluegrass Breakdown* (1992).

The historical marks left by the rediscovery phenomenon seem profoundly ironic, but by Greil Marcus's reckoning these inconsistencies are only superficial. The *Anthology* performers had deeply personal agendas and no more genuinely embraced the utopia of the folk revival than they once did the corporate capitalism of the record companies. Marcus traces the thread of personal ambition from the desperate circumstances of the 78s to Smith's ingenious *Anthology*. From this historical imperative follow without contradiction the panoply of ornery, acquiescent, and manipulative rediscovered performers who stood with Bob Dylan at Newport in 1964. And finally, Marcus's destination: the leap to Dylan's *Basement Tapes* (recorded 1967–68), inspired directly by and modeled on the *Anthology* in the aftermath of Dylan's confrontation over authenticity at the 1965 Newport Folk Festival. For Marcus, *The Basement Tapes*—in the pure personal ambition of Dylan, in the deeply anagrammatic coding of his language, in the desperate circumstance both of America and of Dylan—constitutes the logical and genuine destination of the originary spirit of the 78s.

What now becomes ironic, and what reviewer Bruce Shapiro (1997) noted was a troubling omission in Marcus's argument, was the emergence of a communal, largely anti-entrepreneurial, old-time music revival out of character with the desperate, ambitious world of the performers that Marcus dubbed "Smithville." This is the vexing territory of Marcus's *Invisible Republic*—that the essence of the folk revival was condensed into *The Basement Tapes,* and, more vexing, that genuine folk music has no utopian aspiration. It is thus necessary to follow a different thread from the *Anthology.* Let us not reappropriate the authenticity Marcus has deftly infused into *The Basement Tapes* but merely follow the route to the reissues, where others have thought this authenticity always resided.

Clearly, in the lengthy span between the 1952 *Anthology* and the explosion of the old-time music revival around 1970, the reissue market served as a crucial intervening phenomenon that gave the emerging revival its distinctive character. Here old-time music took its cue not only from the *Anthology* but also from jazz, where record collectors, borrowing a format originally designed around the length of classical performances, had begun reissuing 78s on 33 rpm LP albums. Thus old-time reissues followed in the path of the *Anthology,* reframing music once thought to be patently inferior "as a kind of avant garde art" (Cantwell 1996: 190).

The formative period of the reissues was the second half of the 1960s, supplanted eventually by the emergence of influential contemporary old-time bands in the 1970s. During this early period, producers of reissue albums, much like Harry Smith, looked scrupulously across the chasm of World War II to the world of the 78s. But the vision they saw and amplified manyfold, their "memory theater," articulated instead a romanticist and utopian world whose definition was extracted not merely from aural style but also from the lives and social environment of the performers. As this historical world took shape, so did an increasingly coherent style of music. Both were emerging realities on which reissuers themselves—unlike Smith, who remained withdrawn from public life—exerted ongoing and evolving influence. And perhaps foremost, like the hardy performers on 78s, reissuers invested considerable time and personal finances with the hope that "at least some people thought [their recordings] were worth paying for"—engendering, however, a quite different symbolic reward.

The first old-time music reissue specialty LP label, County Records, was begun unceremoniously by Dave Freeman in 1964. Freeman, a New York City postal worker who had a small collection of 78s, decided to experiment with a modest and self-financed reissue of old-time fiddle performances on LP to see if there was a viable audience (Wolfe 1980). Modeled after jazz reissues, Freeman first pressed 440 copies of County 501, "A Collection of Mountain Fiddle Music," containing the best recordings from his own collection. For the cover he engaged his father, a printer, who sketched a log cabin for the cover design and printed the cover on a press normally used for greeting cards. The recording sold slowly over four or five years, providing enough encouragement to continue the reissue venture.

In 1965, Freeman introduced a second series of recordings, featuring living old-time musicians and numbered as a 700 series to distinguish them from the 500 reissue series. The earliest of the 700 series recordings were produced by Charles Faurot, who took an uncommon interest in the musical style popular in the Galax, Virginia, area. The implication of these strategies, still profoundly felt today, was that old-time sound of the reissues had a distinct contemporary parallel, and that the Galax style was its purest modern transformation. Even today, some in the revival associate the term "old-time music" with that style alone. From this point on, the reissue market abandoned its exclusive association with 78s, bringing together the music of the prewar recordings and of the living musicians who had inherited that style. Consequently, the "ghostly" presence of rediscovered reissue performers now contended with contemporary traditional old-time musicians whose lives were brought in vivid dialogue with the utopian aspirations of the present.

In 1965, Freeman began including written commentary with the albums, and it was here that the formative social dimensions of the "memory theater" took shape. These consisted of liner notes on the back of the albums or in a booklet inside; over time they became increasingly extensive and sometimes were crowded tightly into the space on the jacket. Freeman wrote many of the notes himself but recruited notable old-time music authorities such as Norm Cohen or Joe Wilson for others. The most extensive and influential notes were written by Richard Nevins, who must have recognized the impact these notes would have at a time when so little was published on the history of country music.

Nevins was uncommonly adept at giving dramatic structure to obscure events in old-time music history or to attributing significance to its various sites. Of Frank Jenkins and Ben Jarrell, for example, he unabashedly concluded that "it is doubtful that anywhere else in the South outside of this Surry County, N.C., region one could have found many performers whose talent and skill equaled theirs" (1972). The tunes they recorded for Gennett in 1927 in Richmond, Indiana, he called "some of the most significant music ever produced by the minds and hearts of men." Nevins introduced listeners to the turmoil surrounding the renowned Skillet Lickers and established his preference for the ensemble that appeared at their fourth recording session:

> The fiddling of the Skillet Lickers was [at that session] being led by one of America's truly gifted rural musicians, Lowe Stokes, and seconded, either just above or just below by his close friend McMichen. [Gid] Tanner retained his same self-ordained role in the framework of the band's music, filling in a little here and then a little there, mostly on the high side of the lead. (1973)

He described musical style vividly, connecting the details of a complex musical idiom to an evolving metaphoric vocabulary. Fred Cockerham's unusual clawhammer playing, he said, was "called double-noting by local musicians (referring to the amazing number of notes which can be fit in by constantly dropping the thumb down to the second string and increasing the complexity of the chording)." It emerged from the exceptional human strength and sensitivity of a man "very much in touch with the hardness of life" (1968). In fact, the rhythm and inflections that are the trademark of the great rural bands of the 1920s emerged, Nevins wrote, from deeply human characteristics—"the enduring warmth, the joyous vitality, the unyielding strength, that life, when most fulfilled, reflects" (1972).

Perhaps most importantly for the revival, Nevins made lucid reference to an old-time way of life far superior to the modern ways of his readers. Of the Ward home near Galax, Virginia, where music sessions were held leading eventually to the band the Bogtrotters, Nevins wrote:

> Frequently the furniture was moved aside to make room for dancing, and as there were no time limits imposed, the musicians played well into the night. If the get-togethers broke up quite late, there was always room for guests to stay over, and some remained for days. Such community participation in cultural affairs has long since been lost, as has the priceless art of neighbors pleasantly visiting each other, and all the TV's and Hi-Fi's and Drive-In's in America are only a poor substitution for them. (n.d.)

Nevins's writing style may later have given way to more conventional historical and ethnographic writing, but his extravagant accounts were permanently attached to the best and most influential reissue LPs. As liner notes, they penetrated the revival far more extensively than books or articles. They thoroughly supplanted the austere pastiche of the *Anthology*, replacing the unifying image of Smith's celestial monochord with fragments of a grand romantic narrative. If the reissue movement set up a parallel between the yearnings of the present and the utopia of the past, it was Nevins who best explained the moral relationship between the two.

In the defense of reissuers, it should be recalled that their romantic orientation was not cut whole cloth from the political expediencies of their day—romantic inclinations had revitalized old-time music during earlier periods also. Perhaps the most influential period was the first decade of the twentieth century, a period of tumultuous cultural and technological change during which newspapers began touting old-time music's association with antiquity and, later in the 1920s, its superiority to jazz (see Cauthen 1989: 164–65). In Georgia, even hillbilly imagery was a formidable political and aesthetic force until Depression-era politicians exploited its negative associations with poverty (Wiggins 1987: 129–30). Still, for the first half of the twentieth century, romanticism as a self-marginalizing influence on old-time music was held in check by two important trends: first, the ability of community old-time tradition to absorb most every popular musical fashion that it encountered, and second, the continuing viability of the traditional musical community until post-WWII affluence and urban migration sapped rural areas of

Old–Time Music and Dance

their most auspicious and most talented musical heirs (e.g., Cauthen 1989: 38).

Thus in spite of Marcus's entrepreneurial reading of the pre-WWII 78s, there is much to support the romanticist view of prewar tradition. A great many very good musicians, for example, declined opportunities in radio and recordings precisely because they resented the compromises to traditional aesthetics and lifestyle that were demanded. The Kentucky fiddlers that Jeff Todd Titon studied drew strength from the "affecting power" of their state's antimodernist symbolism as an "alternative to the speed, efficiency, and dehumanization of the modern industrial state" (Titon 2001: xvi). Even in Atlanta, old-time music's first urban center, a substantial contingency of those who did record did not view the event as a career benchmark (Daniel 1990: 50–51). And for the others, recording was not always the commercial epiphany Marcus describes, but rather a component of an ongoing career of professional aspiration that may or may not have been fully realized. Indeed, the gathered ironic distance drawn in depictions of some of the most extraordinary recording encounters was not invented by postwar romanticists. Rather, it emerged firsthand as a calculated marketing strategy designed to gain advantage over recordings by competing companies made in presumably more mundane circumstances (e.g., Wolfe 1989). Thus on the whole, even for the best old-time musicians, the cultural economy of traditional musical community was not at all a wasteland to escape from, but a viable and inseparable link to the musical career that was professional only in widely varying degrees. If the romanticist premise held that tradition was a nurturing and not a devitalizing muse, there is much in recent historical accounts of formative periods to support that view.

The emerging romanticization of the reissue market was reflected also in its own historical development. The *Anthology* was affiliated with Folkways Records, and thus with New York City, the cultural epicenter of the folksong revival. County Records was developed in that environment also, although its ties were more to the subculture of record collectors. By the 1970s, however, the reissue market had expanded enormously and lost any sense of cultural detachment that might have been associated with County's location in New York. By the mid-1970s, one could buy, for example, a different Skillet Lickers reissue LP from County Records in New York, from Vetco in Cincinnati, from Rounder in Somerville, Massachusetts, or from Voyager in Seattle. In 1974, Freeman even moved County Records from New York to Luray, Virginia, in part because sales to rural audiences were so strong. Reissue recordings, by then numbering in the hundreds of titles, were sold in record booths at large folk festivals or old-time music festivals, in specialty music stores, or, most importantly, through mail-order catalogs from distributorships operated by County and Rounder. The Rounder and County catalogs were extensive compilations of recordings containing an extraordinary variety of marginalized forms of American music— reaching far beyond the cultural sites within which the revival had previously been concentrated. The map they drew of cultural America was one of increasingly coherent musical styles, with historical and contemporary dimensions linked by aural association of the reissues to contemporary traditional and revivalist performers.

The reissue movement incorporated some of the revival's most important contradictions, inscribing an anti-technological message onto youth culture's most potent technological symbol, the LP. As Nevins himself put it, the recording was a transitional device, a "poor substitute" for community musical tradition. As the 1970s progressed, however, there were increasing numbers of customers who had little trouble comprehending the self-effacing medium of the reissue LP. Without much difficulty, reissue customers could place these LPs—two very profound technological removes from the values they represented—on the shelf not that far from the Beatles or, for that matter, Dylan's *Basement Tapes*. If, as Greil Marcus insists, Dylan inherited the mantle of the *Anthology*, the reissue movement claimed its legacy also, yet for an entirely different cause. Herein lies the perplexing contradiction of Marcus's claim: with Dylan, the "invisible republic" remained invisible. It was the reissue movement that, itself invisible to Marcus, brought meaningful exposure, however ironic, to the prewar performers and their kin.

It helped, of course, that reissue companies gave ample evidence that their products—in their design, production, sales strategies, and stated purpose—differed from other LPs. It is difficult to dismiss the irony of having the purest folk music on what was surely among the purest symbols of modern life, but no one seemed to mind. Instead, the old-time music revival drew away from the mainstream romantic impulse and settled into its own marginalized enclave. There, it seems, in rural settlements, campus fringe areas, and other culturally charged sites, old-time music could sustain itself. There, complex listening strategies mediated the conflicts presented by recorded musical tradition and shielded listeners from the disturbing paradoxes of technological media.

There, also, old-time music could retain its complex and often unexpressed alignment with the politics of youth culture. Indeed, in the late 1960s, as so many followers of the folksong revival veered away from folk music and toward more explicit objective political discourse or politicized subjectivity, there seems to have been a countervailing tendency in which others drifted for similar reasons toward *less explicit* discourses such as old-time music. By appearance, it seems astonishing that one could look into distant antiquity and find contemporary countercultural messages, but this is precisely what happened. Fiddler Bill Hicks, who found this refuge in North Carolina in 1967, saw in old-time music a bedrock of integrity in a world gone mad: "In a time when Vietnam made everything ironic, the music was, for me and perhaps for all of us, another country. The tunes, in their beauty and sheer independence, justified themselves" (1991: 25). Fiddler Andy Woolf reported that after flunking his draft induction physical in 1971, he went to the Country Dance and Song Society office, bought some dance tune books, and went home and began learning them. Old-time music provided him refuge, but also strength. Singing ballads, like Shakespeare's poetry, was "a more subversive act than marching in a demonstration." Like ballads, Shakespeare's songs "speak of and affirm essential human relationships that cannot be corrupted by the state" (1971: 36).

In California, old-time music was a staple musical form at counterculture enclaves in Berkeley, in San Francisco, and at Sweet's Mill Camp in the Sierras near Fresno. At the camp in the late 1960s, the pristine setting and the egalitarian spirit seemed to be wedded to the sound of old-time music and late-night dancing (Bluestein et al. 1992–93). In old-time music sessions, attention was often drawn to older musicians who had learned their craft long ago as a part of a once-noble tradition—such as fiddler and Missouri-transplant Ron Hughey and mandolin player Kenny Hall. One writer told how Izzy Young, founder of the Folklore Center in New York, had visited the camp and had presented his "Death of Folk Music" lecture (see Cohen 2002: 275). The writer contrasted this somber pronouncement with the rejuvenating reality of the Sweet's Mill spirit. Those of us who participate in old-time revival—who by word or deed claim some piece of this inheritance that is old-time music—must never forget this circumstance: that during this brief period of American history there were those who were driven by desperate circumstances into a deep psychological bonding with old-time music. If "folk music" died, it was surely reborn in the guise of community forms like old-time music.

It is also important to recall that there was another quite different old-time music revival that loomed in the cultural distance. In 1953 in Weiser, Idaho, an amateur folklorist revived an annual fiddle contest that had been discontinued in 1915 (Blaustein 1994: 206). The contest grew rapidly by word of mouth. By 1956, it had been dubbed the "Northwest Regional Oldtime Fiddlers Contest"; by 1963 it led to an organized "association," the Idaho Oldtime Fiddlers Association, the first of many modern fiddling associations linked by participation in contests and later a common affinity for competitive aesthetics such as smooth bowing and ornate melodies. By the end of the 1960s, the association movement had expanded rapidly into areas where traditional fiddling lay dormant. From Washington to Alabama to Maine, fiddling associations were the most prominent institutional means to draw traditional musicians out of retirement. In organized areas they sponsored jam sessions, but it was through fiddle contests, which could draw contestants from great distances, that they had their greatest impact.

In truth, fiddlers' associations have a lengthy tenure in fiddling tradition and have not always been associated with the ornate "contest style." In Atlanta during the second decade of the twentieth century, an old-time fiddlers' association helped the traditional hoedown style prevail until disaffected modernists formed their own group in 1921 and organized contests decided by judges, as opposed to audience appeal (Wiggins 1987: 46, 58, 92). In Alabama in the 1920s, associations sponsored contests that attracted the state's best fiddlers (Cauthen 1989: 169–70, 192–93). Contests themselves are even older, dating to 1736 by one assessment (Hulan 1969). But the unique mix of association polity, competitive protocol, and the smooth-bowing "contest style" became a distinct cultural enclave only in the post-WWII environment.

Naturally, old-time music proponents took interest in fiddling associations, but ideological and institutional differences often kept the two movements at arm's length. Like club square dancing and competition clogging, postwar fiddling associations had been shaped by the competitive values of the 1950s and not by the folk boom. Richard Blaustein, who has written extensively on the subject, concluded that while association leaders were "encouraged by the positive attention from the folk revival," their movement was genuinely independent, a revitalization led by those who experienced as personal loss the waning viability of traditional culture in post-WWII America (1994: 206). Said Blaustein, fiddling associations "selectively incorporate valued elements of an earlier culture into a formal bureaucratic structure that meets modern needs and conditions" (210).

For this reason, associations and their contests were not always appealing to those in the old-time music revival. As Blaustein observed, native revitalizations such as fiddling associations did not attempt to replicate social and cultural patterns of the rural past. Where, for example, reissues of 78s were cardinal points of interest in old-time revival, contemporary recordings were far more important in association culture. Where old-time music events employed sites that could accommodate informal activities, contests were designed around the progression of contestants across the stage. An Alabama contest organizer, for example, introduced the practice of holding contests in shopping malls, which "had replaced schoolhouses and courthouses as community gathering places" (Cauthen 1989: 198). Contest culture could be highly competitive, and frequent winners would often sport cases lined with blue ribbons or produce recordings with cover photos of the fiddler posed holding a prized trophy. To ensure fairness, contest rules became increasingly complex, and judges were often sequestered backstage so as not to know the identities of the contestants they were judging (Blaustein 1994: 212).

To old-time music enthusiasts, association-backed contests could at times seem like prototypes of retributive justice, with complex rules of style that served as both restraint from and temptation for complex melodic improvisation. Compared to the pristine rural settings of old-time revival events, contests could seem institutional in both setting and demeanor. Many old-time enthusiasts, for example, would have abhorred shopping malls for their role in the neglect of downtowns, in the over-dependence on automobiles, in the unbridled development of rural areas, and in their purposeful insulation of shoppers from the human aspects of participatory democracy.

The emerging trans-regional "contest style" seemed on the surface a modern contrivance, and few may have known or cared that it drew deeply from traditional points of influence—such as the style, championed by Eck Robertson, that developed around contests in Texas (see Wolfe 1997: 12–29, esp. 12) or the long-bow style that developed in the 1920s in Alabama and Georgia as a result of the influence of Alabama fiddler Joe Lee (Cauthen 1989: 119–24; Wolfe 1997: 84). Indeed, it was not until the 1950s that the decline of community-based alternatives made way for the seemingly unrestrained ascendancy of "contest style" as common stylistic currency.

From the outside, both the style itself and its organizational infrastructure seemed monolithic and could assault the senses of those in the old-time revival who preferred plaintive melodies, straightforward accompaniment, and the relaxed atmosphere of jam sessions. Consequently, old-time revivalists sought out those contests which catered to their tastes. Bloomington musicians were far more likely, for example, to make long journeys to Glenville, West Virginia, or to Galax, Virginia, than they were to attend the association-style contest at the Indiana State Fair an hour away in Indianapolis.

Even with distinct worldviews, parallel institutions, and different histories, however, many traditional fiddle enthusiasts moved easily throughout both worlds, perhaps without noticing any conflict. In celebrating a musical form that post-WWII America had come to neglect, powerful feelings of shared compassion were evoked, deflecting attention away from divisive differences. This, some would say, was the foremost principle of the revival. Still, there were institutional differences, and it was my hope to determine clearly what strain of thinking led to the Bloomington dance.

3

BANJO
PEDAGOGY

To determine the thinking that led to the Bloomington dance, I return to the revival of the late 1960s and examine several important pedagogical works to understand this transition from folksong revival to old-time music revival. Surely a key transitional text was Art Rosenbaum's *Old-Time Mountain Banjo* (1968), one of the many $8^{1}/_{2}$-by-11 inch softbound folk music instruction books that Oak Publications kept in wide distribution for so long. For more than two decades, New York–based Oak Publications was the primary publishing outlet for folksong revival music books. In the 1950s, Oak issued reprints of the best songs from *Sing Out!* and other song collections associated with individuals such as Ruth Crawford Seeger or Joe Hill. In 1964, just as the rediscovery movement was cresting, Oak introduced Jerry Silverman's *The Art of the Folk-Blues Guitar*, the first in its prolific run of style instruction books. This series was a key element of the burgeoning folksong revival, providing musicians with technical instruction and philosophical orientation in the most fundamental authenticating act of folksong revival. It was in this series that Art Rosenbaum's banjo manual appeared four years later.

In several key passages, Rosenbaum situated his book at the culmination of a twenty-year chronology of renewed popularity for the banjo in American musical culture. At the start of that chronology loomed, always, Pete Seeger and *How to Play the Five-String Banjo* (orig. 1948, with many reprints and revisions), which had been Rosenbaum's own initiation into the subject. Seeger's book was respectful of traditional style, but on the whole he viewed the banjo in a broader context, as an "instrument" for making folk music, and not so much as an artifact of tradition itself. For example, he included chord diagrams for 280 chords and charts for many popular folksongs, even those, such as blues, jazz, Spanish, and South American songs, that had had no established connection with the banjo. So Rosenbaum was clearly up to something different. And he said so explicitly, for example, by warning readers in "What Kind of Banjo Should You Have?" that the long-necked banjo, which Seeger had popularized, was unwieldy and unnecessary for low tunings. In contrast, nothing had signaled Seeger's limited antiquarian rigor more than his instructions on "How to Lengthen the Banjo Neck" by sawing the neck through and attaching a new peghead two frets longer. Old-time banjo players of Rosenberg's school of thought, mindful of the value of antique banjos, would shudder in horror at such desecration.

Even more generally, however, Rosenbaum's book redrew entirely the defining features of the banjo revival. *Old-Time Mountain Banjo* was a meticulous comparative study of style based on the playing of traditional performers whose playing Rosenbaum had scrutinized. Below is a typical passage, comparing the use of high fret positions on the second string (so as to leave the first string free for syncopation) in the playing of Roscoe Holcomb, Pete Steele, and B. F. Shelton:

> Here is another way a note higher than the 1st position of the 2nd string may be played in this style: keep the thumb lead patterns and carry the melody right up the 2nd string as high as need be. This is a smoother approach, very nice indeed, but lacking the syncopation and drive of Steele's or Holcomb's playing. B. F. Shelton, an old-time Victor recording artist, used this technique on "Darlin' Cora" (reissued on County 502 and transcribed in Seeger's *How to Play the Five-String Banjo*), as well as on his version of "Pretty Polly," where he treated the higher section of the melody like this. (1968: 28–29)

Repeatedly, Rosenbaum forged a driving argument that the unique "mountain banjo" style was a web of intricate complexity spun around a tradition based on restraint.

But, in 1968, how did this change the way banjo revival pedagogy was approached? Rosenbaum took care to extend the notion of style to include "intangibles" that distinguished the mountain banjo picker as not merely a technician. He noted, for example, the class of "banjo songs" identified by Alan Lomax, with their "loose succession of evocative verses," that were shaped equally by the singer's mood and the "compelling rhythms and tonality of the banjo" (5). He noted the curious yet deliberate preference among some players for the fretless banjo, valued by traditional players not for antiquarian reasons but for its subtle musical qualities (59). And foremost, he noted in banjo tradition the typical social character of the banjo player, slightly at odds with conventional social practice, which facilitated the integration of dissonant cultural influences into a coherent mountain banjo style (5–6). (With an abundance of historical evidence, this position is confirmed by Cecelia Conway [1995, esp. chaps. 6–7], who traces both the social world evoked in banjo songs and the ethnographic disposition of the learner to traditional motifs established in the earliest tutelage of Anglo-American Appalachians by African American banjo players.) These observations, Rosenbaum emphasized, emerged best from direct and deliberate ethnographic experience—from his own and others' field experiences or local observations—and less by observing the products of their commercial aspirations. The balance of Rosenbaum's career as an ethnomusicological fieldworker confirms that claim (see Gerrard 1995–96).

Consequently, learning the banjo demanded as much in empathy as it did in technical rigor. There were, in fact, "just a few basic ways of sounding the strings" (Rosenbaum 1968: 5). Through recordings or immediate contact with traditional players, the goal of the novice was to learn to think through the idiom, to reintegrate one's own world, to achieve the idiosyncrasy of the mountain banjo style while avoiding the alien worlds of unbridled improvisation and slavish imitation. If taking lessons, he said, make sure the teacher "shares your bias" (5). And no longer, in 1968, was Rosenbaum concerned that self-consciousness could corrupt the experience: "But there is little danger that the new generations of banjo pickers will assume precious attitudes toward the music, or that their playing will become stilted, so great is the vitality of the mountain banjo tradition, so tough are its sinews" (77). Rosenbaum never actually said that, in studying mountain banjo, this empathetic shift of consciousness was more the end than the means, but how close he came to crossing that line! We need wonder no longer how folksong escaped the ivory tower.

It was during this period, when old-time music was depicted as a solitary and studied encounter with traditional practice, while there was a wane in organized folksong activity in Bloomington and at the same time a motivated "opening" to local culture, that Miles Krassen came from New York, in 1967, to study ethnomusicology with Professor George List. Already, Krassen was a serious student of old-time music. Of his association with traditional fiddlers, he would say, "I have always looked upon fiddlers as people who in at least one area of their lives were a type of Western wise man. Their tunes were like incantations, a form of ancient wisdom that induced high feeling" (Krassen 1973: back cover). He left Bloomington in 1969 but returned in 1971, this time with Linda Higginbotham, to resume his studies. Later, Krassen wrote two important old-time music instruction books, *Appalachian Fiddle* (1973) and *Clawhammer Banjo* (1974). They were published by Oak Publications and followed the format established by the Oak folk music style instruction books that had proliferated throughout the 1960s. They were also widely popular, even to the extent that they were sometimes stocked with band instruction materials in mainstream music stores.

One might wonder why Oak would have endorsed a new banjo instruction book in 1974, just six years after Rosenbaum's *Old-Time Mountain Banjo* appeared. Had banjo pedagogy changed that much? Indeed, Krassen paid tribute to Rosenbaum's book (but to no other predecessors) and in this way situated his book in the lineage of banjo pedagogy. Notably, Pete Seeger was not mentioned in the book at all, and Krassen's advice on buying a banjo voiced no concern for the temptations of the longneck style. Rosenbaum had produced a comparative survey of individual styles, emerging from his comprehensive interest in performer study (see Gerrard 1995–96). For Krassen, style was a social entity, the common knowledge that formed the basis of community musical tradition. Individual style could have enduring significance only within this social nexus. Consequently, Krassen sought to explore in depth a single banjo tradition—the music of the Galax, Virginia, area and of southeastern West Virginia, the very site Rich Nevins had anointed as endemic to the term "old-time music."

Undoubtedly Krassen's decision to focus on this style was influenced by the pivotal role it was playing in the expanding popularity of old-time music in general. As he described the phenomenon:

> Interest in the old dance music of the Southern Appalachians is on the increase. In recent years people from all parts of the country have begun to take a serious interest in the old tunes. Small record companies have been formed for the purpose of reissuing classic recordings of early mountain musicians. Formerly obscure Fiddlers' Conventions have become popular meeting places for mountain music enthusiasts. (1974: 5)

Where Rosenbaum could name prominent individuals who were drawing attention to the instrument, Krassen noted an expanding market for traditional music and a newfound attraction to social events that featured old-time music. Krassen saw, as did most everyone else at the time, that this movement was necessarily drawn around a common stock of tunes and performance practices. Although attentive to traditional sources, *Clawhammer Banjo* was designed to facilitate the learning of the rudimentary skills necessary to participate as a musician in this old-time music revival.

Consequently, where Rosenbaum was concerned with the way traditional mountain banjo players organize the complexity of ideas that constitute tradition, Krassen sought to examine how a contemporary novice develops the fundamental skills needed to play a kind of synthesized version of a particular regional style. For Rosenbaum, style was a matter of the way individuals articulated the essential qualities of mountain banjo, and he organized his book in sections of similar technical features (e.g., two-finger, frailing, drop-thumb, fretless) arranged in order of increasing complexity. Krassen proceeded by musical key—the way individuals could best comprehend their own repertoire and the way social musical events with fiddlers and banjo players were organized. Where Rosenbaum described twenty-three tunings, Krassen covered only the five most common ones, which "make it possible to play just about any fiddle tune" (8). In describing these tunings, moreover, Krassen's emphasis was on how, in actual performance settings, to get from one tuning to any other tuning quickly and easily when fiddlers and other musicians must wait for the banjo player to retune. Where Rosenbaum was concerned with accurate transcriptions, at least to an extent that they could represent a player's style, Krassen only approximated the practices that were the common currency of the idiom. Rosenbaum's transcriptions even included, on a separate staff, the tune of any vocal melody; where possible, he took special note of the interaction between voice and instrument. Krassen focused on instrumental music and could presume that a fiddle, if not a dance also, might be present.

One final measure of the differences of these books was the way each treated the use of the capo. The capo is a mechanical device clamped onto the neck of fretted stringed instruments to raise the pitch of all strings so as to be able to play in different keys using the same fingering patterns. Seeger gave an unqualified endorsement of the capo to accommodate the range of a singer's voice: "If you have not already bought a banjo capo, do so now—they cost only a few cents" (P. Seeger 1961: 22). Rosenbaum's endorsement was measured against the rarity of capos in tradition, but he nonetheless deemed the capo a compatible convenience: "Capos were unknown to traditional banjo pickers in the old days and are still very seldom used by them; however, there is no reason why you should not enjoy the convenience they afford" (1968: 55). Krassen recommended capos for social settings where fiddlers don't accommodate retuning: "Usually in consideration of the banjo player's tuning predicament, a fiddler will play several tunes in the same key before switching to a new one. Sometimes keys are changed more frequently and then a capo can be quite a help" (1974: 9).

The differences in the Rosenbaum and Krassen books were dramatic and mapped the changes that were rapidly taking place in the old-time revival as the decade of the 1960s drew to a close. If Rosenbaum's approach was ethno-logical in design, reflecting solitary excursions into traditional thinking, Krassen's was pragmatic, reflecting the newfound attention to the social institutions that nurtured traditional music. Build

Old–Time Music and Dance

these traditional forms together, Krassen's functionalist pedagogy seemed to suggest, and the details of traditional thinking would fall naturally into place.

Perhaps the clearest articulation of the institutional backdrop to banjo pedagogy was in the illustrations. During the period of influence of the *Anthology*, with the over-determined significance of pre–World War II culture, it was common to use Farm Security Administration (FSA) photographs representative of the prewar period. But this strategy obscured the important distinction between the Great Depression and World War II as influential events. The old-time 78s emerged as a speculative business venture in the "commercial half-light of the Jazz Age," as Marcus has put it (1997: 101). They were artifacts of a culture of relative affluence. Their very existence depended upon customers' ability to buy them, and sales and production plummeted rapidly after 1929.

In contrast, the FSA photographers, motivated by genuine pathos and populist ideology, were a product of the national recovery effort that took place well after the effects of the Depression had begun to be felt. Marcus notes that Harry Smith carefully distinguished the two periods (1997: 103n). But in the early 1960s Folkways replaced his allegorical cover with a Ben Shahn photograph, effectively reappropriating the *Anthology* as a tool of populist discourse. It is to be understood, of course, that the poorest Americans reported having suffered equally in the Jazz Age and the Depression and that the music itself, in community settings, thrived during both eras. But the point—that juxtaposing FSA photographs with commercial recordings left an ironic misconception—should be well taken nonetheless.

In any case, Rosenbaum transformed this premise entirely by suggesting that living traditional performers were the best pedagogical resource, and he used sketches of domestic musical events or collecting sessions to illustrate these encounters. Again, this strategy affirmed his premise of old-time music as an encounter with living tradition and thus wholly undermined the notion suggested by Smith that folk music was the province of an "invisible republic."

Krassen, however, featured contemporary photographs, most of rural scenes unrelated to the music. None were landscapes; none except the few of musicians were portraits. Instead there was a roadside cabin, a barefoot child crossing a country bridge, a run-down country store, a flock of guineas in a yard, an aging porch swing. All situated the viewer/photographer up close and within the arena of involvement of the scene. Many reflected an odd sense of composition, with some subjects half in and out of the frame, as if they were composed not by the eye, but by a circumstance from which someone had briefly withdrawn to photograph. On the back cover of *Appalachian Fiddle* was a considerably more deliberate pose, with Miles Krassen playing his fiddle on a stump beside a farmhouse, flanked on either side by a pig and an uncooperative-looking goat, half out of the frame.

These images reflected a new symbolic currency circulating in the old-time music revival, one from which the revival was positioned not as an observer of tradition but as a part of a return to comprehensive traditional rural living. This movement, which gained considerable strength in the 1970s, provided the ideological underpinning for a variety of "old-time" social enterprises, one of which was old-time music. Another of these was dance, and as I demonstrate, it is not quite correct to refer to either at that time as a "named-system revival" since both emanated from a single socio-cultural template.

4

BACK TO
THE LAND

Dillon Bustin came to Bloomington in 1969. Although born and raised in Indiana—during most of his youth he lived in Cumberland, near Indianapolis—he spent two formative high school years in New England, where he began accumulating the unusual set of experiences that led eventually to the Bloomington dance. He learned contra dancing in the Monadnock region of southern New Hampshire, dancing to Ralph Page, Ted Sannella, and Dudley Laufman. He also worked at an Audubon camp in Lincoln, Massachusetts, and played in a camp dance band, called Roaring Jelly after the tune of that name. In 1972, he visited the John C. Campbell Folk School in Brasstown, North Carolina, where programs in music and dance were encouraging influential and idealistic young people to promote folk culture in their home communities. Dillon would later recall that, inspired in part by the Folk School, he and his friends "dropped out of college and went back to the land" (1990b: 7).

To understand the significance of these circumstances, consider that recreation leaders had long extolled the virtues of traditional American community dance, perhaps with the vague hope of establishing communities such as those today. Yet for most of the twentieth century,

Kathy Restle and Dillon Bustin at their rented house near Orangeville, Orange County, summer, 1974. Photo by Dan Willens.

Old–Time Music and Dance

their efforts were only sparsely rewarded. Among the dance forms encouraged by this movement was contra dance (also, "country-dance"), a once-popular social dance form that had roots in colonial America. Its essential structure consists of sets of dancers in two long lines of indeterminate length. Partners begin the dance facing one another across the set and work their way up and down, eventually interacting with all or most other couples in the set. Losing its popularity elsewhere—primarily to nineteenth-century couple dances—contra dance settled into the New England villages, where it has enjoyed an unbroken tradition on the margins of mainstream culture. Its vigor throughout this century has drawn strength from several "revivals," each a mix of community tradition, regional consciousness, promotion as recreation, and affiliation with younger generations. Undoubtedly, the sense of self-renewal that Dillon and others experienced in contra dance in the late 1960s was on the one hand an appropriation of tradition as part of the countercultural movement and on the other the experience of the cycle of tradition that had sustained contra dance for two centuries.

The particular suitability of contra dance to the needs of the post-WWII folksong revival seems to have been well established even before the war by Ralph Page. Page was a pivotal figure, not only because he was a tireless caller and dance leader into the 1960s, but even more importantly, because his vision of dance was so well suited to the egalitarian utopia of the counterculture. It was a native vision, established locally well before contra dance was "discovered" by postwar revivalists. His 1937 *Country Dance Book,* written with Beth Tolman, depicted the revival of tradition as operating in cultural "islands," of which his own rural southern New Hampshire was one (Tolman and Page 1937: 9).

Thus through Tolman and Page there was already established the importance of "place" as a vehicle for durable oppositional values. They quoted directly from vintage dancing manuals to recognize the need for "making manners," but they were also pleasantly tolerant of liquor for the fiddler, harmless pranks from locals, and irreverence toward "chiding prompters." They viewed New England tradition not as the wellspring of American culture but as local and regional components of a grand pluralist experiment. Foremost, Tolman and Page quickly grasped the insider/outsider dichotomy that would come to define post–World War II folksong revival, and used it to the locals' advantage. "The country dance picture has grown more and more encouraging," they concluded, since their rural neighbors opened up their "guest chambers" to the "summer and winter sportsters" (1937: 21). They took inspiration from the belief that "most city folks really wanted to learn the dances in a 'serious' way" and, confidently and irreverently, brushed aside considerable evidence to the contrary. Winter skiers, for example, were "harder to cope with." But this only gave locals cause to smirk: "[The skiers] are really a good bunch, with unusual vigor and a high I.Q., and with a little instruction they merged right in" (22).

Tolman and Page espoused the belief that traditional dance was so fundamental a social practice that some regions could reestablish for it the cultural coherence and integrity that had been lost by dramatic shifts in lifestyle, population distribution, and land use. In these cultural "islands," traditional dance could provide a kind of leverage whereby local interests could compete genuinely and equitably with the intractable extralocal hegemony of modern life. It was as if, with its unique capacity for repeated social interaction, set dancing could liberate moderns from the evolving cultural and social practices that cast them in increasingly debilitating isolation. "Modern country dancing," they wrote, "has been responsible for a friendship of town and country, young and old, beginner and veteran, 'high' and 'low' " (1937: 21). They called it a "workable democracy" that they often thought of, in 1937, in a "utopian light." "So," they boldly concluded, "we hereby nominate the Country Dance Plan as the first crocus in the recovery of civilization from its self-poisoning. Any takers?" (25).

In the postwar years, Page's "takers" were increasingly those who, following counterculture values, had left cities for a simpler life on communes and small farms (Nevell 1977). The most influential figure of this period, Dudley Laufman, grew up in a Boston suburb but was deeply moved by agrarian tradition while working on a dairy farm in southern New Hampshire in 1946. There he experienced contra dance as an integral component of informal gatherings of neighbors, relatives, and guests. This was the "kitchen junket" or "kitchen dance," and it remains one of the formative images of his career:

The year is 1946. The name of the farm is Mistwold. On an early fall Sunday the family invites relatives and neighbors over for a corn roast. After lunch the group sings hymns, then the men push the furniture aside. Guests crowd in. The kitchen becomes an intimate, low-ceilinged dance hall. Old couples hold hands and fall naturally into squares. A cousin shyly asks a neighbor for the first dance. In the commotion, a girl gives her beau a quick kiss. Dudley's boss nods and draws the bow across his fiddle; the boss's wife hits the keys of the piano, and music fills the house. The dancers step together. The smells of wood smoke, pies, and wool clothing mingle. (Collins 1996: 10)

In 1959, Laufman bought two acres of land near Canterbury, New Hampshire, for $25 and set about "to keep the wolf from the door on a pittance" (Laufman 1974). He still lives there in a cabin with wood heat, well water, and a root cellar for refrigeration.

From these experiences, dance became deeply etched in his psyche as something unbearably simple in its outward form yet mystically complex in its relation to agrarian tradition. When, in the decades to follow, hordes of youthful idealists began searching traditional culture for these very qualities, Laufman stood as a potent symbol and lucid mentor. In the 1960s he made folk festival and club appearances with his loosely organized Canterbury Country Dance Orchestra, including the Newport Folk Festival (Rhode Island), Club 47 (Cambridge, Massachusetts), and the National Folk Festival (Washington, D.C.). In 1972, the band began making recordings, most with extensive liner notes that included introductions of the musicians (which usually numbered at least a dozen), poetry, accounts of dances and recording sessions, and even vignettes of domestic scenes. Laufman's notes depicted contra dance as deeply rooted in simple rural life, even for those who, like himself, had once fled from urban settings. And always he wrote with a comic irony, as if to disarm the cold formality of the recording and divert attention to the land, the tradition, and the moment of dance experience that grounded it.

For Dillon Bustin, these ideas, already fundamental to contra dance revival, were wedded specifically to the principles of self-reliance through nature that were the trademark of the American Transcendentalists. The boldest was Henry David Thoreau, whose principles in-

Back to the Land

spired Bustin to experiment with subsistence living. Later he would write, making the connection between Thoreau and counterculture antimodernism: "What Thoreau, the testy individualist, was ultimately decrying was the dissolution of . . . traditional communities constituting a spacious, egalitarian society of modest means, local markets, mutual toleration, and open access" (1988: 3). Nor was he alone in this thinking: during the 1970s when contra dance was first spreading to communities of young people across the country, it very often was promoted as articulating the social forms of traditional community. As mainstream youth culture increasingly revealed its dependence on the entertainment industry, contra dance offered a refreshing alternative, a self-sustaining social form, not tangibly connected to the media or to other sources of cultural authority. As Mary Dart concluded, after interviewing veteran dance leaders from throughout the eastern U.S. in the 1980s, it was "the idea of home-made fun, as opposed to the passive enjoyment of the media" (1995: 24). In 1971, Andy Woolf put it this way: "Today in the United States, and even in England, country dancing is an eccentric activity, done by a few people. It functions as a rebellion against certain norms of this society. The country dancer does not sit and wait to be entertained. His activities require no great expenditure of money. Refusing to follow the trends of popular taste, he is connected with the past and a tradition which he helps to make" (1971: 39).

Yet the mixing of contra dance and southern old-time music was not common; even in Bloomington, its appearance seemed largely circumstantial. Since Dillon's exposure to contra dance had come originally in New England, it was contra dance he taught in Bloomington. Old-time music became prominent because of Miles's interest and because of its emerging popularity nationwide. But this circumstance was not entirely an accident. Already, old-time music revival was shaping itself around community music events, and New England styles—with tunes like "St. Anne's Reel" as prominent artifacts—were not considered outside its province. More broadly, the old-time music community was a social form of extraordinary power, accommodating a variety of other forms around its participatory, celebratory, and utopian tendencies. At one of the National Folk Festivals of the early 1970s, during Andy Wallace's run as director, I spent much of the day in jam sessions out on the

Old-Time Music and Dance

festival grounds but drifted down with a few friends to dance in Dudley Laufman's contra workshop. Structurally, old-time music was all about which forms would be able to make their way from the stage to the festival grounds, and it seems hardly unlikely that contra dance would have soon made this voyage.

Although it might have happened anywhere, Bloomington dancers recall that as time passed Dillon came to believe that southern Indiana was the right place for this blending to occur. U.S. Highway 40, running east-west through Indianapolis, was a widely recognized north-south cultural boundary not far from Bloomington. Indeed, the syncretic fiddle styles of such old-timers as John Summers of Marion, Indiana, featured on the recording *Fine Times at Our House* (Dunford and Rosenbaum 1964), seemed to suggest that the "old-time" musical culture of the region was closely related to but not entirely a part of the cultural upland South. Art Rosenbaum, who recorded Summers, reckoned that it was the recording companies and their exorbitant fascination with the South that left the impression that rural dance music outside New England fundamentally followed the southern "string band" style (Gerrard 1995–96: 25).

Moreover, southern Indiana, too hilly for large commercial farms, had always been a refuge for self-reliant and sometimes idiosyncratic people. Surveying the region's agricultural practices in 1980, folklorist Ormond Loomis described the distinctive physical qualities that seemed to suit traditional farming:

> The region is easily recognized as one traverses the southern part of the state. Its rugged, wooded hills rise abruptly from the surrounding lowlands providing a line of demarcation. Throughout the area, layered outcroppings protrude as cliffs or from hillsides and along creek beds. Hardwood forests cover much of the land. But where the land is farmed, one finds open space: a long hilltop, a wedge between creek and cliff, a gentler hillside, or occasionally a large bottom section. Mute artifacts help define the landscape. The relative local abundance of single and double crib barns, for example, distinguish the region from neighboring territories to the north, east, and west. (1980: 31)

Thin soil covered the limestone bedrock in most places—there forests dauntlessly arose. Only the bottomlands where streams and washes cut

Back to the Land

through the hills provided prosperous soil and thus the patchwork of small farms that were southern Indiana's trademark (Sanders 2002: 2).

These qualities separated southern Indiana from the vast corn-soy region that surrounded it to the north, east, and west, and linked the culture of the region instead to the upland South. But it was neither isolation nor hardship, Loomis emphatically concluded, that gave the region its propensity for traditional ways. Rather, the region provided an auspicious setting—the unusual shape and size of fields, for example—in which traditional methods were genuinely superior to progressive ways. From this, an atmosphere evolved in which rational choice and reward resonated with a shared regional aesthetic.

It was this traditional aesthetic, the "diverse, positive motivation of tradition" (Loomis 1980: 249) that served as the region's salient link to the 1970s back-to-the-land movement. In 1976, for example, *National Geographic* depicted the people as "Indiana's Self-Reliant Uplanders" and their region as a "laboratory for the natural ways of doing things" (Thom 1976: 348). Just as in Dudley Laufman's New England, southern Indiana became a popular site for experimental rural living. There, as in New England, "kids from the communes" were attracted to the dance. Whereas the general popularity of folk music and the presence of Indiana University were the more visible influences, the deep-rooted cultural pattern of self-reliant living in this "cultural island" may have been the most important.

The dance group's back-to-the-land ties place it within the historical context of the commune movement which, like the folksong revival, mirrored the political and cultural landscape of the 1960s. According to the history by Hugh Gardner (1978), the escalation of the Vietnam War in 1965 inspired a modest interest in the formation of countercultural communes, which had numbered only three before that date. With the media exposure of the 1967 Summer of Love and the political apocalypse of 1968, the numbers of new communes increased exponentially. A 1970 *New York Times* survey counted two thousand, which, in a very short period, accounted for more than all that had existed previously in U.S. history.

This historical moment also gave rise to the issue of social class, which had so much to do with the emergence of communes. For many,

Old-Time Music and Dance

the 1960s was a period of unprecedented material comfort, giving rise to a generation—the "children of prosperity," to use Gardner's term—with the leisure, education, and security that was "structurally conducive to revolt" (1978: 11). This atmosphere mostly affected economic security and access to higher education, whereas family lifestyle was still widely varied according to class background. If "dropping out of college" to get "back to the land" was an option Americans had in unprecedented numbers, it did not indicate a uniformly affluent upbringing. Still, it would seem ironic, as it did to Gardner, that communes overall should have been well suited to surviving periods of economic distress when they actually were more common during flush times. Communal land, in fact, required an initial capital outlay, which was often subsidized by well-to-do members or benefactors.

Along with the stresses of commune overpopulation, the economic downturn in the 1970s precipitated a dramatic incidence of commune failures. This is Gardner's chief interest—in the "communal commitment theory" that explains why some survived when others didn't. This will be my interest also, particularly in the more general concept of "intentional community," which encompasses less formal arrangements than the communes Gardner studied. For Gardner, the failure of commitment was indicated in the sale of the land and the dispersal of the residents. This materialist approach does not exactly address whether the ideals could have survived the structural failure, a possibility that the more general back-to-the-land movement may have provided. Nor does it address the desperation precipitated on young people by the Vietnam War, the draft, and the political disenfranchisement of those who opposed these. Gardner's conclusion that Americans have "trained incapacities for communal experience" (1978: 251) should be tempered with the long-standing dissatisfaction with the social ills in American society attributed to the lack of the very experiences that communes provide.

Theodore Roszak's celebrated account of the counterculture observes that the communitarian ideal had less to do with communes per se, however, than with an overall way of life that incorporates the continuity and comprehensiveness of sustained living arrangements (1969: 201–203). His point of departure in this observation was the critique launched by political activists directed at commune dwellers for their irresponsibility in shirking political action for utopian escape. Roszak's answer was that political action is "episodic commitment," which does not account for fundamental needs and sustained commitment. What, then, he asked, was the "life-sustaining receptacle that can nourish and protect good citizenship?"

> The answer is: you make up a community of those you love and respect, where there can be enduring friendships, children, and, by mutual aid, three meals a day scraped together by honorable and enjoyable labor. Nobody knows quite how it is to be done. There are not many reliable models. The old radicals are no help: they talked about socializing whole economies, or launching third parties, or strengthening the unions, but not about building communities. (1969: 203)

Roszak offered traditional utopias as possible but not certain models and said that whatever form they take, "these frenzied and often pathetic experiments in community will simply have to succeed" (204). It was an "urgent task . . . that the young who have greater expectations of life than their elders and who are more intolerably sensitive to corruptions should find an enduring mode of life that will safeguard those expectations and sensitivities" (203–204).

In contrast to organized communes, the "cultural island" model provided a more sustainable paradigm for community than did communal living. This model lacked neither commitment nor community and thrived during the 1970s and beyond. It was based on the proposition of shared ideas, which were well suited to the absence of communal property and political structure. It required little initial investment— either individually or as a group. The emphasis was on more modest acts of communion and an aversion to the kinds of problems that accompany material property. Foremost, it fostered an attitude of stewardship, rather than ownership, toward the community itself.

One well-documented model of this type of community is the Mateel area of northern California, vividly described in Jentri Anders's *Beyond Counterculture: The Community of Mateel* (1990). After the political collapse of 1969, disillusioned young people flooded northern California as refugees from technocracy. They settled in a wide variety of living arrangements but discovered, sometimes serendipitously, that many others like themselves had done the same. They set about to forge a

Old-Time Music and Dance

supportive social structure, engaging the local political system as best they could.

No doubt their particular social class origins followed them—perhaps as "children of prosperity"—but one reads with awe, not irony, their accounts of supremely austere "pioneering." If prosperity made them ill equipped for rustic life, they wholly compensated with commitment. They founded schools, organized food co-ops, held public offices, but mostly endured the hardships of living in resource-depleted, undeveloped areas. Ironically, they were most threatened in the end not with the stresses of economic recession but with the infusion of capital brought on by the introduction of marijuana as a cash crop.

Revived folk tradition was not always a part of these societies, but the antimodernist slant of communal and back-to-the-land theory made them apt companions. Folklore performance was explicitly associated with ritual communion and in its essence enabled the flight from technocracy. In communal theory, in turn, the advantages of pre-modern society were explicitly prescribed. As early as 1966, one commune adopted a practice called "voluntary primitivism" (Gardner 1978: 14–15), referring to the acceptance of a reduced standard of living as a deliberate withdrawal from modern life. Others followed Gordon Rattray Taylor's "paraprimitive solution" (Taylor 1973; also Anders 1990: 7, 37), which extolled the advantages of pre-industrial society.

In my experience, these works had no direct bearing on folk revival living in Bloomington or in other music and dance communities. Instead, the surest common resource was *The Whole Earth Catalog* (orig. 1968), the comprehensive listing of mail-order sources for all aspects of independent living. This book could be seen close at hand in counterculture households, including those in the dance group. But even this source followed the trends of the counterculture: its coverage of communes was phased out by the mid-1970s, just as editions were beginning to include considerably more folk revival resources.

The most important distinction among these approaches had to do with locality. Communes often sought isolation from their neighbors and were sometimes at odds to the extent that there were arrests and harassment by police. Some sought landscapes where they were unlikely to have contact with outsiders (Gardner 1978: 20). This was less the

Back to the Land

case for folk revival communities since proponents actually gravitated toward culturally charged localities, such as southern Indiana, seeking some degree of integration into traditional culture where it had a foothold. Often back-to-the-land folk revivalists found common cause with independent-minded locals, particularly in their stewardship of the earth and their high regard for tradition. And, as in Bloomington, many sought proximity to important civic institutions and even participated in civic life.

This is all merely to say that the confluence of folk revival and countercultural ideals had many auspicious sources. By 1973, folklore performance was charged with ideological energy from many points, not always identifiable. Still, one can identify fundamental distinctions. The communal approach was to rebuild society based partly on primitive models, with economy, interpersonal relations, political structure, and stewardship of the earth as key components. Rituals were devised to support the communal social order. In general, this approach differed from the folk revival, where the practice was to re-create ritual so that authentic society might emerge from it.

This was the setting from which the Bloomington dance grew. It had ties to the folk revival, to old-time music revival, to contra dance revival, to the counterculture, to communal society, and to southern Indiana. It was a setting where it was entirely plausible for Miles Krassen to have been fiddling outdoors in a public place, one where it was equally plausible for Dillon Bustin to have thought this significant. Bloomington was the kind of place such meetings should have occurred.

Yet, for important reasons, the dance was always said to have originated from its own circumstance: its influences were before it but not a part of it. This may well have been because during its period of greatest influence, the folk revival had articulated a contradictory message. It had come to most Americans through media artifacts such as recordings, concerts, films, television, and festivals. In these, folk music enthusiasts were called upon to celebrate community musical traditions yet were given few meaningful outlets to participate in roles other than as consumer. The early 1970s seemed to mark a significant transition: at folk festivals and bluegrass festivals, jam sessions in the parking lot or campground were beginning to challenge the stage shows in their relevance and intensity. There was even a burgeoning of community festivals, which might well include fiddle contests or folk music performances.

A dance, however, could articulate this shift toward total involvement better than any of these institutions. It could be produced entirely by its participants, so that everyone achieved the sense of involvement that was ordinarily reserved for stage performers. Structurally, there was no audience at all, no consumer role. For those accustomed to culture spoon-fed through the media, a dance could seem like no less than a miracle. And it was discovered as a miracle, crafted in bits and pieces from traditional models.

Thus a limited and a peculiar historical vision prevailed upon this experience, fueled on the one hand by the compelling need for collective self-discovery and cultural autonomy and on the other by the spiritual affiliation with the past. Slavish replication of the materials of music and dance was discouraged. Instead, the group reveled in the comprehensive atmosphere of traditional community. In the founding of the dance, a functional separation had been delineated in folksong revival institutions between those designed to celebrate authentic cultural objects and those designed to produce authenticating participation.

Nor was this an isolated transformation: everywhere, as historians of the late 1960s have recorded, political activism was being transformed into the politics of experience—communal living, self-help psychology, the environmental movement. Contra dance was a more-than-suitable form for this new ethos: it required a sustained community of modestly skilled practitioners; it made a poor commodity and was thus resistant to the attention of the media; it was labor intensive, mobile, and seemed inclined, almost as a political act, to incorporate any space to its needs; its texts professed no creed or dogma, though they alluded thoroughly to an unexpressed ethos entirely at odds with the mainstream; and, particularly in places like Indiana, dance was beholden to history but not to its artifacts. For all these reasons, the Wednesday Night Dance, at that apocryphal stump in 1972, had to be invented as a circumstance.

Back to the Land

5   THE GREEN HOUSE

Throughout the early years of the Bloomington dance group, two events—the providential meeting of Dillon and Miles and the authenticating presence of the dance—seemed always on the surface of consciousness. More obscure, however, was another set of facts that comprised the dance's more modest beginnings. The first dances were held in the summer of 1972 in a location always described as "the green house at the corner of Ninth and Washington"—in fact, the northwest corner, just four blocks from the Kirkwood civic-campus corridor. This fact was generally known and perhaps satisfied some of the desire to know the "truth" behind the more illustrious story. Dillon lived in the green house at the time the dance began and at one point invited Miles to move in. Ted Hall lived across the street. They and their friends decided that they wanted to get some dancing going. So they spread the word and even distributed notices inviting people to learn how to do "old-time American dancing."

Dillon, who had learned to call contras, was in charge of dancing, and Miles, who at the time preferred southern tunes, was in charge of music. The first dancers at the green house included Deedie Bell, Pat Cole, Ted Hall, Kathy Heath, Gay Heishman, Tom Heridia, Linda

Higginbotham, Barry Kern, John Levindofske, Andy Mahler, Martha Nathanson, Phil Wynn, and Sidney "Pip" Wynn. Some of these individuals were active in the dance for many years and are enshrined in its lore; others moved away and are all but forgotten. The first ensemble that played consisted of Miles (fiddle), Bob Lucas (banjo), and Jim Gage (guitar). The group called itself Buckdancer's Choice and actually got a few performing jobs, one as warm-up band for Earl Scruggs when he played at the Indiana University Auditorium. Later that year Bob became involved with the bluegrass band Gold Rush, and the group dispersed. No other band arose to replace Buckdancer's Choice, so music at the dance became associated, then by default and later by choice, with less formal "open stage" ensembles.

Linda Higginbotham, with always-keen social sensitivity, recalled an innocent yet euphoric atmosphere. The dance was held in the living room with the rug rolled back; many of the dancers lived in the neighborhood. Others would drive in from Stinesville and from the Needmore commune, both places where back-to-the-land settlements were congregated. Sometimes dances were held more than once a week. Most everyone was young, in their early twenties. A few high schoolers attended that summer; once Kathy Restle's parents came by to see that she wasn't involved in something unseemly. Although no one knew they were doing something that would someday be important, there was an intensity about the whole thing. People hardly knew one another, but through dance they seemed linked to an enduring community of their own making. For years to come this feeling would give the dance an elevated importance in the lives of the individual dancers.

In July of 1972, only a few months after the first meeting, the Bloomington *Courier Tribune* published an article and photo spread depicting youthful, innocent, and eager dancers. In "Forgotten Dances Revitalized," the article outlined the intentions of the group. There was considerable effort in historical research on the dances so as to ward off contemporary influences. But according to Dillon Bustin, the particular way history was engaged was not obvious: "You should think of it not as reproducing something from another time, but as rediscovering what was yours and has been lost." The writer described the dancing just as veterans remember it during that period—as "lusty and vigorous," with steps that were "quick and flashy." The dance, Dillon hoped, would reclaim its important social function: "You could encounter everyone you knew at the town hall, and every couple danced with everyone there." There was "more communication then because the dances were more of a community effort."

By the end of the summer, the dance had outgrown the living room of the green house and had to move. The new location was the basement of the Lutheran church adjacent to Dunn Meadow on 7th Street. The room was long and thin, with a bare concrete floor. More important, it was a quasi-public space and, unlike a private home, supplied a key infrastructural element for the dance's status as public event. In this setting, anyone might show up. The church was also a site of authority—both as lessor of the facility and as a cultural presence.

This was the first of many sites that would, in varying degrees, wield some authority over the dancers' use of its space. The Bloomington dance group, as well as most all of the contra dance groups across the country, gathered in rented spaces—often churches, school buildings, or public recreation buildings—and had had some experience of disagreement or even eviction in which their relative status was articulated and felt. If the group wanted to feel anti-authoritarian, if it wanted to experience its events as spontaneous, ephemeral, or marginalized, here was the ideal infrastructural setting. One can look to the profusion of group-owned square dance club buildings across the country to see the opposite effect. In Bloomington, the transformation from private to public space amplified the effect the performance space would have on the experience as spontaneity: to have rented a space at the outset would have been too explicit a "founding." Bloomington could look back to no such event.

Dillon recalled becoming less involved for a while during that winter. The move to the Lutheran church, in fact, had been engineered by Miles and Linda, and for a caller the group turned to Barry Kern. Dillon recalled seeing the posters advertising the dance with "Bear Cat Kern, caller." Barry had been exposed to dance before the contra group started and had called to recordings at least once. He had attended Dillon's calling workshops in the green house. But he was also aided by a particular book on which some accounts place great importance. As some told

Old–Time Music and Dance

the story, Miles, Linda, and Barry hastily assembled a group of dancers for rehearsal just a day before the Wednesday dance. Barry went to the Indiana University library to look for books on dancing and stumbled upon Lloyd Shaw's *Cowboy Dances* (1939). He borrowed the book and in a single day learned enough for his debut, the first dance at the Lutheran church.

Barry did not recall this exact sequence of events, attributing a good deal less to serendipity. It was from the Shaw book that he learned to improvise, however, combining square dance figures in innovative ways. He also noted that the book later became a reference for other Bloomington callers. From this and other sources, Barry introduced squares to the Wednesday Night Dance and was long identified with them. His high-pitched, rhythmic vocalizations, a perfect match for the energetic dance style popular among early Bloomington dancers, became his trademark. If any charisma had grown around Dillon as the group's proprietary caller, it was undermined by Barry's quick rise, by necessity, as an alternative. Much as with the musicians after the breakup of Buckdancer's Choice, a circumstance led the dancers to make their way on their own. And this was a circumstance of no small importance: the initiation and training of new callers and musicians flourished in Bloomington. As groups arose elsewhere, they were sometimes "owned" by certain bands or callers, and competitors were disallowed.

As the dance grew in stature, it began to exert its own influence as a folk revival institution. Consequently, it played a part in attracting musicians from elsewhere. That autumn, with encouragement from Miles, David Molk moved to Bloomington. Brian Hubbard and Tom Sparks were soon to follow, relocating from New Jersey. Gary Stanton, already a graduate student in folklore, began playing mandolin. And music store proprietor Dan Willens began playing guitar. A small "scene" had arisen, with a self-perpetuating atmosphere of competition and charisma, and with musical skill as its most precious asset.

Dan had moved to Bloomington in 1970 to teach guitar lessons. Soon after, he opened a second-floor music store and studio located on the busy southeast corner of Kirkwood and Walnut, adjacent to the county court house. Until the 1990s, the rental spaces above the downtown stores were cheap domestic or business rental properties accessible to the countercultural epicenter. Dan's involvement in the dance quickly became enthusiastic, and when the need to expand his business arose, he sought to incorporate dancing into his ambitions. The plan was to design a store to accommodate community music activities such as the Wednesday Night Dance. The location he chose (315 E. Kirkwood) was in the heart of the campus fringe area, on the busy town-gown corridor. Dillon recalls that the rent was quite high, enough of a financial risk to the group to call for an assessment of its commitment and identity.

But it was the remodeling of the interior that was the most compelling measure of community support. A friend of some of the dancers, David Shimbechler, knew of a barn in South Whitley near Elkhart, Indiana, whose owners wanted it demolished. So the dancers devised a plan to use the lumber for paneled walls. A group of some thirty volunteers convened, including Dan, Dillon, David, and Robbie Wyatt, and they drove the five hours to South Whitley. They tore down the barn, returned to Bloomington with the lumber they needed, and erected interior walls in the store.

The floor was laid from raw lumber from Owen County. Dillon was living there that year, and when the landowner's plans for a commune fell through, the yellow poplar that they had cut became available. They hired carpenters from the Needmore commune, who laid the floor in a rather uncommon pattern. But the wood had not dried sufficiently, and when Dillon returned that fall after a summer away, the floor had warped and twisted. It was impossible, as was the fashion then, to dance barefoot. Yet here was precisely the kind of hardship designed to summon the group to common struggle. What better touch could be added to this geographically prominent rented space, completely transformed by an extraordinary mobilization of communal labor, using recycled materials that had communal and rural origins!

As was common with acoustic-oriented music stores of this era, the walls of the Guitar Studio, as it was called, were covered with accessories and instruments. There were numerous plants in the store—passersby sometimes thought it a florist's shop. There was a small stage used for concerts, poetry readings, and the dance band. Once a week a coffeehouse was held, called the Fine Times at Our House Coffee House,

Poster for the Fine Times at Our House Coffee House, from the Guitar Studio period of the early 1970s. The use of the term "Good Times" in the title is thought to be an error. Courtesy of Dan Willens.

alluding to the recording of Indiana folk music titled *Fine Times at Our House* (Dunford and Rosenbaum 1964). And there was always a pot of hot herbal tea, a special blend that Dan devised for the store. This particular breed of music stores was an important vehicle in the dissemination of the participatory and self-authenticating aspects of folksong revival. They were entirely distinguishable from ordinary music stores

The Green House

by their ambiance, marked abundantly with the symbols of folksong ideology. They were actually more like schools or spiritual centers than stores and operated, as Dan put it, on "all charisma." Consequently, their entrepreneurial underpinning was often invisible or even insufficient to keep the business afloat.

At that time, and for only a brief period, the dance was called the Center for Traditional Music and Dance. Apparently the dance was held sometimes on Thursday night, though no one recalls it taking place on any evenings other than Wednesday. Admission to the dance was free, and the space was usually packed with wild, rough dancing. But Dan recalled that through the entire run of dancing at his store, there was never a single instance of damage to or theft of store merchandise.

For a time, the organization of the dance was more formally structured, with membership cards, dues, and letterhead stationery that included a barn swallow logo designed by Kathy Hirsh. Dillon was at the center of the organizing effort and recalls being urged by national institutions such as the Country Dance and Song Society to make Bloomington a chapter. His own dreams for the group, partly realized in this setting, were to have workshops and lectures on topics related to traditional music and dance. Bagpiper Lois Cuter, for instance, gave a workshop sponsored by the group.

During this period the dance group moved decisively from its status as an informal gathering of friends to a public event with at least some formal structure. Partly this was by necessity—the need for more space. It was also fueled by the ambitions of Dillon and Dan Willens. Certainly the stature of old-time music and contra dance as cultural artifacts, and the role of the group as its local custodians, also played a part. But this degree of formality and presentational motive in the dance was a brief departure from a lengthy history as an informal social ritual. The model of ritual community that was to emerge, based primarily on examples from southern old-time community music and dance, would become an important template for Bloomington social life.

6 THE OLD-TIME COMMUNITY

Bloomington's music scene was changing at that time also. Miles began playing Irish music and was less involved in the dance. The recordings released on Rounder Records in 1972 and 1973 of the Fuzzy Mountain String Band from Durham, North Carolina, were having an impact nationwide. In Bloomington, their influence was all the greater when, a few years later, band members Tom Carter and Blanton Owen enrolled in the Folklore Institute. They occasionally attended dance group events and played music with local musicians.

The Fuzzy Mountain recordings were numbers 10 and 35 in the catalog of a new Massachusetts-based company which marketed directly to the old-time music revival with recordings of the most popular bands. Rounder also had reissue and traditional releases, but, unlike County, it promoted young old-time bands from the beginning and in the same series as their traditional material. The company made explicit contributions to the revival in its celebration of the aural style of revival bands and in its depiction—in narrative liner notes and vivid cover photography—of old-time revival lifestyle.

Fuzzy Mountain took a different approach to old-time music revival than did the New Lost City Ramblers, at the time the best-known prototype for old-time performance. Where the Ramblers had looked primarily to vintage recordings for material, members of Fuzzy Mountain visited living traditional musicians in their region who in their youth were contemporaries of the classic string band performers. As the band coalesced out of informal jam sessions, a distinct focus emerged: "playing mostly personally collected old-time Appalachian tunes, and playing them 'right'—as the source played them" (Hicks 1995: 21). Tune collecting became an integral part of the band's accumulation of its repertoire, with practice sessions devoted to introducing the "newest gem" from a field tape or to perfecting the style from an older one. The liner notes to their recordings paid scrupulous tribute to the traditional source (and sometimes the source's source) of each tune, sometimes by recounting the circumstance of its learning: "we have . . . learned our tunes from the traditional fiddlers in person, through many visits to their homes and to the countless fiddlers conventions which are held from Easter to Thanksgiving throughout this part of the country."

If the effect of this was to nurture a respect for living traditional musicians, it also began to describe the contours of an old-time music revival community. As Fuzzy Mountain members put it, they were "part of a larger group of friends . . . who share a love of traditional dance music." Cover photos depicted them as young people with an unassuming back-to-the-land appearance. Their musical style was entirely unintimidating, featuring restrained tempos and modestly ornamented melodies typical of field recording or jam session performance. The sense of community they projected was amplified by the fact that the band never toured and seemed on the recordings to exude a studied disregard for the theatricality of performance. The recordings were noticeably informal, with different personnel for most every track; the first album was recorded live with mike inputs Y-ed down to two channels. The band also appeared to have only a loosely determined sense of membership—they seemed more a group of friends than a "band," in the conventional sense of the term. In fact, the group emerged first from a regular open jam session. Although they restricted participation in practice sessions after they began recording, there was a vivid atmosphere of community, with a coterie of listeners at the twice-weekly jam sessions and periodic holiday parties (Hicks 1995: 21).

Jam sessions were the quintessential act of old-time community. They were infinitely expandable, presupposed no standing social or political structure, and could be convened almost anywhere with little effort. Although musical individualism could be expressed in them, jam sessions were distinguished from other musical events by repetition, synchronization, and egalitarian participation. They adapted easily to physical and social spaces, both indoor and outdoor, and had no official beginning or end. Seated or standing postures were directed inward, toward a musical and spiritual center where no listener ever sat. If there were listeners, they were on the outside, seemingly superfluous to the performance. A single thirty-two-bar tune might go on ten or twenty minutes, with musicians drifting in and out, until someone toward the center raised a leg to indicate the last time through.

The most common jam sessions were organized parties in homes or impromptu gatherings on festival grounds. But they could also be assembled spontaneously—in parks, airports, motel rooms, stairwells—wherever two musicians had their instruments. Musicians carried their instruments everywhere, even where it was entirely inconvenient, and bulky, bumper-sticker-covered cases made it impossible not to recognize one another in a crowd. And if spontaneous jamming in an unlikely place was awkward, it was all the more a political statement, asserting the viability of an underlying world social order where rank strangers of any extraction could become intimately familiar on short notice. A musical instrument was a ticket to this world, and became the most valued possession among one's meager belongings. In public places, the simplicity, ease, and pleasure of this act thrust forcefully against the backdrop of international wars, inequitable distribution of world resources, and acquisitive capitalism.

In localities, jam sessions were more often gatherings of friends, whose familiarity was reflected in the core repertory they shared. Interludes between tunes were peppered with lively banter, with food and drink, with talk of all that had transpired since the last get-together. The pace of the event followed the contour of tunes played. If someone introduced a new tune for others to learn, it might be followed by an old warhorse that everyone could play. Normally there was only one session going at a time, although larger parties might accommodate

The Old-Time Community

more. There was lively conversation away from the music session, and often food was cooking in the kitchen. Local sessions were less explicitly political, though there was certainly a vague awareness that in other households residents were passively connected—by entertainment media, television, etc.—to a world over which they had little control.

Fuzzy Mountain did not articulate this, of course; it was more that their sound and demeanor enabled it. But, in fact, there was a kind of community ethos inherited from an earlier old-time revival band that emerged in Durham and Chapel Hill, North Carolina, in the mid-1960s—the Hollow Rock String Band, consisting of Alan Jabbour (fiddle), Tommy Thompson (banjo), and Bertram Levy (mandolin). Jabbour was the chief fieldworker of the group, having been introduced to Library of Congress field recordings in a ballad course at Duke (Bernhardt 1986). Inspired by hearing authentic ballad singers, Jabbour bought a tape recorder and began visiting traditional fiddlers. In 1964 he began an influential apprenticeship with fiddler Henry Reed of Glen Lyn, Virginia, whose haunting, uncommon tunes were definitive of the band's repertory.

The social ambiance of the group was the province of Tommy and Bobbie Thompson, who hosted informal bluegrass gatherings at their home even before the band formed. On the invitation of Bert Levy, Jabbour began attending these sessions and eventually introduced the tunes he was learning by visiting and recording country fiddlers. As the group's focus converged around Jabbour's field-recorded repertory, it became apparent that something very special was emerging from the gatherings. Word of these sessions spread, and musicians from elsewhere began visiting Chapel Hill and Durham to play with and record the group.

> During these visits, as well as at conventions, musicians often made tape recordings of the Hollow Rock repertory, providing for themselves a musical library to study and learn from back home. Copies of these tapes often found their way into the tape-sharing network becoming established at the time. Thus the music became available to a growing number of musicians as the Hollow Rock repertory quickly diffused from a living room in Glen Lyn, Virginia, to homes throughout the land. (Bernhardt 1986: 74)

Eventually Jabbour, Levy, and Thompson began holding separate rehearsals leading to the recording *Traditional Dance Tunes* (1968).

More so than the Fuzzy Mountain recordings, this recording and the one that followed it in 1972 bore the aural markings of a fixed ensemble. But it was still a provisional sound, drawn by the convergence of their own collective imagination and experience around tune texts not at all their own:

> Our task then was not to simulate what we heard but rather to create something of our own as a rendering of that tune. We were transforming tunes into a band rendition like nothing we had ever heard. (Jabbour, quoted in Bernhardt 1986: 77)

Still, the most important influence on their band sound was the acceptance by contemporary traditional musicians they encountered at festivals and old-time music gatherings.

> We didn't know what we were doing except that it was coalescing into something that excited us. But when they said to us, "Boy, you were playing that right. That's the good old-timey sound," you can't imagine how gratifying it was to us whippersnappers to hear some oldtimer say that. (Thompson, quoted in Bernhardt 1986: 77–78)

Asked about any possible influence by the New Lost City Ramblers, Jabbour explained that there was none, that he didn't hear the Ramblers until later. The Ramblers were adept at imitating the band sound from the 78s, whereas Hollow Rock began with a traditional fiddle melody and created an overall sound of their own making. "For us," said Bert Levy, "it was the tunes, not the band, that we celebrated. Passing on and preserving the life of the tunes was peremptory" (Bernhardt 1986: 78).

Hollow Rock's 1968 release was on Kanawha Records, a West Virginia old-time music company with only a few titles and a modest marketing operation. I remember learning of the album only after hearing Fuzzy Mountain, and I had to find the address and order directly from the company. Rounder, in contrast, achieved wide visibility with festival booth sales and retailing through alternative music stores. So, while Jabbour is considered a key influence in the burgeoning interest in living old-time music tradition, it was the Fuzzy Mountain aesthetic

The Old-Time Community

which cemented this aesthetic to a contemporary lifestyle for many people.

The impact of these unassuming Rounder recordings was astounding, with sales reaching old-time music enclaves worldwide. Musicians rapidly absorbed and passed on their easily accessible repertoire, which became the surest currency of the growing phenomenon of old-time jam sessions. Surely few other recordings, particularly of instrumental music, have so completely undermined the customary passive listening practices of recorded media. The effect of the Durham/Chapel Hill repertoire was vividly apparent because so many of the tunes or variants were unique to their particular source. This was especially true of Henry Reed, whose unusual repertoire became a kind of prototype for aspiring musicians to emulate. The most illustrative case was the simple, poignant, and widely disseminated "Over the Waterfall," which could always be identified with Reed, Jabbour, and the Durham/Chapel Hill old-time community. In 1986, Thompson recounted a scene that would be replayed many, many times:

> It was probably 1970 or '71 before I started hearing those tunes around. I remember one time walking down the street in Chapel Hill. There was some guy playing "Over the Waterfall." He had no idea where it was from. And David Bromberg put it on one of his albums, too. I just started hearing things like that and I knew that our album was making a difference in the world. (Bernhardt 1986: 81)

Thus a key impact of Jabbour, Hollow Rock, and Fuzzy Mountain was to foster the discernible repertory by which this particular music could be instantly distinguished—even walking down the street in Chapel Hill—from other country music forms. The "gems" of fieldwork, like those of prewar 78s, were not merely keys to antiquity but also keys to a compatible disposition and worldview among those who played them.

In Bloomington in 1972, these effects had been fully registered, so that hearing a fiddler play in public would have triggered the inventory of historical, emotional, and social intertextual references that enabled the meeting of Miles and Dillon. Whether it was "Over the Waterfall," "The Rights of Man Hornpipe," or "Red Haired Boy," a chance listener could readily guess the social and cultural dispositions of a musician. These pointed automatically to a common repertoire of tunes, and from

Jam session at the cabin of Bob and Debbie Herring, near Paoli, in southern Indiana, from the summer of 1975 or 1976. From left, Teri Klassen (guitar), Martha Nathanson (fiddle), Scott Andrick (mandolin), Bob Herring (fiddle), Randy Marmouzé (banjo). Photo courtesy of Teri Klassen.

there to the engaging atmosphere of parties, potlucks, jam sessions, festival trips, fieldwork recording expeditions, and tape exchanges, which were the social practices of the old-time community. These practices had been informally circulating during the 1960s, but it was Fuzzy Mountain that gave the old-time community aesthetic coherence and visibility. Their music was social music—because it was presented as such, because it was easily replicated, and because it was collected from living musicians who themselves were participants in traditional musical community.

Old-time community had ties to tradition but also to the counterculture, arising from the desire to find an alternative to conventional society. Its simple rituals provided the social nexus for participants who sought refuge from mainstream society in simple, low-impact living. It was extracted from tradition, but for the old-time revival it was a deliberate act. But it was not the act of community that was intentional:

The Old-Time Community

community flowed effortlessly from the social rituals as if an affirmation of their power.

So this was not yet "intentional community," nor did parties and potlucks have the character of social institutions. Clearly, dance provided key leverage in the emergence of community consciousness. In tradition, dances were typically community events. And the more substantial social mobilization involved in producing dances provided a palpable sense of community consciousness. In Bloomington, the move to a public space and the need to find a new band and caller both necessitated this kind of social mobilization.

But another factor was the rapid growth of the Bloomington music and dance community that grew from the dance. With dance, the initiatory experience was very accessible, providing a common plane of experience for veterans and newcomers alike. With only a little determination, it was relatively easy to participate in the dance. With music, the expanding repertoire of common tunes and the ethos of participation had a similar effect. A new cadre of local musicians started to play, including Steve Hinnefeld, Randy Marmouzé, John Keltner, and Robbie Wyatt. The dance was also attracting musicians from other regions. The combination of generational turnover and influx of outside musicians was beginning to result in something of a "scene" that extended beyond the friendship base of the first generation of dancers. It also led to a new aesthetic element, mostly as a result of three charismatic newcomers who understood and finessed the music in a way that lay beyond the grasp of the common aesthetic of the group: Brian "Hawk" Hubbard, Tom Sparks, and David Molk.

David had come to Bloomington from Oberlin College in Ohio. Oberlin, with its music conservatory and liberal arts college, was an important site in the early folk revival. Even in the 1950s, Oberlin had a resident performing group, the Folksmiths, who merited a feature article in *Sing Out!* ("Folksmiths" 1958; see also Rosenberg 1995a: 72, Cantwell 1996: 274). By the 1960s, Oberlin had an established transient old-time music community whose interest in the music was passed on through generations of students even to the present. David was among a dozen or so individuals who came to Bloomington over the years and affiliated with the dance group. Brian Hubbard had moved to

Bloomington from New Jersey with his high school friend Tom Sparks. Discovering old-time music in their teens, they had formed a band called the Dry and Dusty String Band, which at one time included fiddler Fats Kaplan. In Bloomington, David Molk joined them, and the instrumentation was usually Brian on fiddle, David on fiddle or banjo, and Tom on guitar.

All three were viewed by dancers as consummate musicians. Brian's elusive repertoire, tameless improvisation, and ability to grasp the musicianship of old recordings were all inimitable. While in the Midwest he studied the styles and repertoires of Dan Gellert and Garry Harrison. Importantly, both of these mentors were themselves young old-time music enthusiasts whose sources consisted primarily of regional field recordings (Garry accumulated a valuable collection of southern Illinois fiddling) and archival and commercial material (Dan was a diligent student of classic recordings). Tom provided solid guitar backup. He would go on to learn Irish fiddle from Tony DeMarco and others, participating in and winning contests in Chicago and Ireland. David seemed to be able to master any instrument and had a vast range of musical interests. With Peter Gold, he had produced a "Folk Music of the World" program in which they played instruments from over the world. At his store, Bloomington Music, he gave lessons on several instruments to those who would become the next generation of musicians at the dance.

The group played local engagements at The Gables, a restaurant that sometimes sponsored folk music, and in the Monroe County Public Library auditorium. They took part in the Indiana Fiddlers' Gathering near Lafayette, Indiana, and the New Harmony Festival of Traditional Music. And they played for the dance, both as a group and individually. At one point, it was said, some recordings were made by the group in a local studio. The recordings were never released, and a mystery remains regarding the location and status of the tapes. As musicians, the three were spontaneous and elusive; many say their best music was played informally at parties. No musicians, it seemed, were so consumed by the old-time idiom as these.

Consequently, stories circulated about their musical abilities, such as one that Mark Feddersen recalled. With David, Bob Herring, and Ka-

Strawberry McCloud, David Molk, and Randy Marmouzé at the New Harmony Festival of Traditional Music, 1977. Photo courtesy of Gary Stanton.

thy Connors, Mark was driving from Bloomington to a public school performance in Indianapolis. They were in his van, and they were late. Mark was driving rather fast, he remembers, and David was in the back playing a tune on fiddle and harmonica simultaneously. He was known for this skill and can be heard playing both on the recording *An Anthology: Old Style, Old Time Fiddling* (1977). Then David put down the fiddle and, still playing harmonica, began juggling, all while the van swerved around corners on the way to the job.

The distinct otherworldly qualities of their music were known even outside of Bloomington and had the important effect of binding the emerging communal generation of old-time musicians to the mystical world of the past. Chad Crumm, a contemporary old-time fiddler based in Philadelphia, remembered this chance encounter with David Molk as a turning point in his musical career:

> One day I was walking through Harvard Square and saw a guy playing fiddle in the street. It was one of those moments for me, and

Old-Time Music and Dance

I said, "this is closer to the answer for me." It was David Molk, long blond hair and purple pants—like something out of a medieval fairy-tale—he was playing harmonica and fiddle at the same time. It sounded like an organ grinder, and it blew my socks off. His bowing had the old-time sound that I was looking for.

I lured him into an alley to get him to slow down and show me what he was doing with his bowing. I asked if I could get a fiddle lesson from him, so the next day he came to my place and spent four hours with me working on my bow. We worked on "Forkey Deer." At that point my fiddle playing escalated—it just took off. I got my basic bow technique down. I mean . . . it's all in the bow. Next day Molk was gone. He's the one who really put me over the edge. (J. Cohen 1996–97: 23–24)

To play music alone in public for an unassembled audience, one can imagine, was an act of extraordinary vulnerability. It brings to mind the performers on the 78s, who attempted to "connect" with an audience they could not be certain would listen. It brings to mind the fragile social world of the early old-time revivalists, who, having eschewed conventional means of social discourse, sought spiritual connections with others through musical encounters. These encounters exceeded the aesthetics of presence—the experience of making music together, as in jam sessions—and instead invoked remote experiences to which the music alluded.

The Dry and Dusty musicians were important in that, more than others, they embodied this mystical connection with the past that was an important component of old-time music performance. They were meticulous students of technique, but the result was not mere imitation. Instead, they seemed animated by some originary spirit of the music. But in this case the originary power of the music was not explicitly deferred, as with the Fuzzy Mountain back-to-the-sources approach. There was no tangible artifact, nor was musicianship a mere technical matter. Instead, Dry and Dusty seemed a mystical or charismatic em-bodiment of the past. Little wonder, then, that there was thought to be a recording made and lost, its confining limits forever inaccessible to the here and now. More than anyone, these musicians were able to tran-scend the referential status of recordings, introducing a charismatic aes-thetic in a context where it was eagerly anticipated.

The Old-Time Community

Brian "Hawk" Hubbard fiddling at Sugar Hill, 1983. From left, Robbie Wyatt (banjo), Brian Hubbard (fiddle), Bob Herring (guitar). Photo courtesy of Tom Morrison.

A chief component of the allure of the Dry and Dusty aesthetic was its repertoire. The center of gravity of this repertoire was a body of unusual tunes—many difficult to play, most with distinctive bowing and uncommon structures. I recall visiting Brian Hubbard once when he had discovered the reissued recordings of the Stripling Brothers, whose tunes at the time seemed incomprehensible to me. These tunes did not enter the common repertoire the way the Fuzzy Mountain tunes did—they were just too difficult for social groups to play together at the time. But both the tunes and musicians who played them were important components of the evolving musical community, establishing an aesthetic presence not entirely yoked to the past but fused with the mystical threshold where the past was encountered.

The charismatic aesthetic penetrated the Bloomington scene, which bristled with excitement as a consequence. This was a remarkable place for old-time revival to have arrived at, a place where music alluded to vivid social experience. Community events were now infused with creative energies, which reverberated on the hidden membrane that separated past and present.

7  THE JUKEBOX

Veteran dancers consider the mid-1970s as a period of excitement and significance for the dance group. Musicians who passed through Bloomington were impressed with the dance, which was uncommon in folk revival communities outside of New England. There was a reliable stock of talented callers and musicians; dancers' skills had been sharply honed during several years of activity. During this period, the group found a new public venue that seemed to suit its needs perfectly. And musicians began forming important cultural ties with rural southern Indiana.

Dillon Bustin was a key influence in arousing interest in southern Indiana culture. Dillon and Kathy Restle, married in 1974, were performing frequently as a duet and were becoming increasingly attracted to the cultural richness and independent lifestyle common in the rural southern counties. As Dillon put it, "From 1974 to 1977 I rented a few derelict farms in Orange County, Indiana, trying my hand at subsistence husbandry and all the while collecting fiddle tunes, ballads, hymns, and square dance calls from old-timers in the region" (1990b: 7). Among his new acquaintances were native southern Indiana musicians Ken Smelser and Ronnie Moon.

For stimulating his interest in southern Indiana, Dillon was indebted to Linda Lee, who viewed the region as an intellectual, aesthetic, and political inspiration. Her Orange County homestead became a gathering place for traditional musicians, environmental workers, and intellectuals. For Dillon, this was a vision that articulated the connection between progressive politics and rural life.

On a trip south to look for land, Dillon and Kathy met Bob Herring. Bob was a young guitarist, and the music the three played together seemed to go well. The three decided to form a band using the name Rain Crow Countryside Band, taken from the southern Indiana term for the mourning dove. On most Wednesdays, the three would drive up to Bloomington to play in the dance band, where they soon began to enjoy the music and company of a fast learning fiddler—Frank Hall. Later, Frank would join the Rain Crows, just in time for the busy U.S. bicentennial season.

The intent of the band, echoing Dillon's interests, was to present Indiana folk music and its historical background. Much of their early repertoire consisted of material collected by Dillon and Kathy and presented as a part of "festivals, exhibits, and curricula for historical societies, museums, and schools" (Bustin 1990b: 8). Later, with Bob on hammered dulcimer, they adopted the name Indiana Rain Crows, and began incorporating songs composed by Dillon about his experiences in southern Indiana. Dillon would later record these songs on *Dillon Bustin's Almanac* (1983).

Dillon may have had the most conspicuous interest in southern Indiana, but the tangible connection was felt throughout the community. In fact, changes in the infrastructure of the dance made it far less adept than before as a vehicle for cultural promotion. In 1974 the Guitar Studio closed, and the dance moved back to the Lutheran church. In January of 1976 another dance group music store opened, this one by David Molk with Tom Sparks. Called Bloomington Music, it was located on the northeast corner of Kirkwood and Walnut, on the second floor above a well-known bookstore called the Book Corner. David remodeled the small room with the high, pressed-tin ceiling that was the store, but the long dingy hallway that led to the store seemed to set it in ineradicable obscurity. David taught lessons there, some to dance group members who were taking up old-time instruments. The store

The Rain Crow Countryside Band performing at a Young Audiences of Indiana concert at Thrall's Opera House, New Harmony, for an audience of schoolchildren, 1975 or 1976. From left, Frank Hall (spoons), Kathy Restle (fiddle), Bob Herring (harmonica), Dillon Bustin (singing). Photo by Nis Kildegaard.

stocked accessories and books, but its main feature was acoustic instruments of all kinds, many of them old. John Levindofske, who did instrument repair for the store, recalled a variety of instruments including a soprano sax that customers would frequently play.

The separation of the dance from the Guitar Studio may have been a significant structural juncture for the group. The storefront setting had given the dance an important promotional vehicle; with that gone, the dance was now a public event without any proprietary ties. With Dillon's interests absorbed in southern Indiana life, key elements of the organizational bureaucracy fell idle, and the dance reverted to the loose, self-motivating atmosphere with which it had begun. Barry Kern and Linda Higginbotham, who had been among the first "green house" group of participants, spent much of the year in Hawaii. When they returned, they indeed noticed a changed dance. Most significantly, they found the dance had moved yet again. The new location was one that would be called home for a considerable period—the Jukebox.

The Jukebox was a city-owned building maintained by the City of Bloomington Parks and Recreation Department. It was located a few blocks south of Kirkwood, somewhat isolated from Kirkwood's casual influences, and approximately midway between the courthouse and the campus. The building had been constructed as a Works Progress Administration project, built for public recreation and once adjoining a swimming pool. The room used for dancing was long and thin, with a wood floor and a small corner stage. Indeed, the room was so small that dances were often very crowded, enhancing the intensity that the dance was soon to experience.

The group had become more cohesive socially, spreading their shared social activities outside the dance. And in the absence of Barry and Dillon, two new callers had emerged, Andy Mahler and Laura Ley. Andy was a creative sort, composing most of the dances that he called. Laura was a voracious learner, poring over books such as Rickey Holden's *The Contra Dance Book* (1955) and writing down the dances she enjoyed. Both reflected on their calling as done out of a sense of duty. Andy's stint was somewhat short-lived, while Laura is recognized by many as the primary caller of the mid-1970s.

At the Jukebox, the dance seemed to come into its own as a self-motivating social form—to an extent that it scarcely resembled the promotional efforts associated with the Guitar Studio. Girded by an expanding friendship network, a typical dance would proceed with little premeditated effort. Musicians would show up one by one and jockey for the best seats on the stage. Callers rotated effortlessly throughout the evening without recourse to prior scheduling. In the summer months, dancers would mingle outside in the adjacent public park; musicians might disappear into the darkness to swap a tune away from the fray on the stage.

A lot happened on that small stage. Some believed there was an invisible musical hierarchy, with subtle yet effective mechanisms employed to control the stage and perhaps exclude unwanted participants. A fiddler might pick an obscure and difficult tune to frustrate beginners

Laura Ley calling at Lower Cascades Park, summer, late 1970s. From left, Bob Herring (fiddle), Bill Thatcher (bass), Teri Klassen (guitar), Randy Marmouzé (banjo), Laura Ley (calling). Photo courtesy of Laura Ley.

or might change keys frequently to drive away an unwanted banjo player. Today, the prevalence of "bands," with fixed personnel, the diminished importance of participation in music, the ubiquity of sound amplification, and the use of spacious dance halls all make it genuinely difficult to comprehend the extraordinary intensity of the Jukebox.

The music scene there was sometimes chaotic, often with as many as ten musicians with diverse styles and experiences crowded onto the little stage. Brian Hubbard was playing frequently then, as was Scott Andrick, Mark Feddersen, Steve Hinnefeld, Frank Hall, Bob Herring, Teri Klassen, Randy Marmouzé, Gary Stanton, Robbie Wyatt, and several others. Blanton Owen and Tom Carter participated occasionally during this period. Sometimes bluegrass banjo players would sit in.

The spontaneity and enthusiasm associated with the Jukebox was juxtaposed against the intense and deliberate interest of some dancers in southern Indiana culture. Throughout the 1970s, the dance group was a magnet for those who settled in rural southern Indiana. Moreover,

Miles Krassen with the band at the Jukebox, mid-1970s. From left: Frank Hall (fiddle), Miles Krassen (fiddle), Brian Lappin (banjo), Bob Herring (guitar), unknown, Scott Andrick (seated), Tom Sparks, Dave Laymon. Photo courtesy of Ted Hall.

affiliation with the campus was diminished, even to the point that there could be a kind of aloof, anti-intellectual ambiance at dance events. And there was not yet a network of other dance groups at this point— Bloomington was apparently up to something all of its own making. These factors helped foster the atmosphere of engagement with southern Indiana culture.

This atmosphere of engagement was a factor in the role played by an important musician who began attending the dances at the Jukebox— Strawberry McCloud. Born in 1907 in Bourbon County, Kentucky, Strawberry was older than most of the dancers—in fact, he was a contemporary and musical companion of the celebrated 1930s recording artist and fiddler Doc Roberts and had once toured with Clayton McMichen. He had retired from a career in construction and at one point had worked for Indiana University. When Strawberry began attending the Wednesday Night Dance, his connections with Clayton

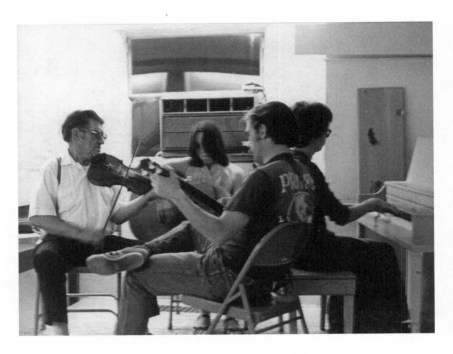

Strawberry McCloud with the band at the Jukebox, April 1977. From left, Straw-berry McCloud (fiddle), Teri Klassen (guitar), Ted Hall (banjo), and Donna Doughten (piano). Photo courtesy of Ted Hall.

McMichen and Doc Roberts made him somewhat of a celebrity in the group. And he seemed to enjoy that status, settling with little difficulty into the role of the master fiddler.

Strawberry's first contact with the group was Randy Marmouzé. Even before he began dancing, Randy was working on a construction project near Smithville across from Strawberry's house and heard about Strawberry from a carpenter on the crew. Randy began to visit him, as did David Bailey, who lived nearby. After the death of his wife, Strawberry moved to Bloomington, and it was then that he became a regular at the dance. He loved the dance—Randy recalled that he was always ready and waiting when Randy stopped by to take him to the dance. Strawberry frequently played with Randy and with Jeff Claus when he and Judy Hyman moved to town. He performed at the Indiana Fiddlers' Gathering and was recorded on Jeff Claus and Doug Crosswhite's

Anthology: Old Style, Old Time Fiddling (1977). In his later years, until his death in 1980, he shared his Grimes Lane house with dancer René Oschin.

Strawberry's status at the dance was important as a prototype, because he alone among the Bloomington dancers would have been considered a genuine folk performer by then-conventional standards of authenticity. There were certainly circumstantial factors that contributed to this perception: he was older; he even needed help getting to and from the dance. Moreover, the music he played was purely a part of his own world, a world in which no dancers had had a part, a world of the "sources" of the music, a world that belonged also to Doc Roberts, Clayton McMichen, and the "memory theater" of the 78s. He was a "rediscovery," whose identity at the dance in large part preceded him. These circumstances were imposing and undeniable.

But there was a contradicting circumstance that was equally imposing: Strawberry belonged with the dance. He was never the object of ethnographic scrutiny—his role in the dance group, from the beginning, was as a willing participant. In this, the social disposition of Randy Marmouzé, David Bailey, and René Oschin, who were his chief acquaintances at the dance, were key components. And while the glory years of the string bands were far behind, the dance musicians cared deeply about his music to an extent Strawberry had undoubtedly not experienced for some time, if at all. Now, in his final years, this was Strawberry's genuine musical world—for, genuinely, there was none other that existed. Week after week, the exigencies of this shared experience contradicted and eroded the sense of deferred authenticity by which Strawberry might otherwise have been understood. When Strawberry died, to whom but them—the musicians whom he loved and who loved him could legitimately ask—did he pass on his music?

In relation to the dance, he was as much the discoverer as the discovered. He was at home at the dance. There was no institutional chasm—as with so many folk performance venues, as with McMichen at Newport, as with the Fuzzy Mountain recording expeditions, even as with folk clubs or the Center for Traditional Music and Dance—that might contradict the sense of self he was accustomed to bringing to his music. This was a powerful process, duplicated many times over in the old-

The Jukebox

time revival, neglected in most accounts of authenticity, that led dancers and musicians to a new sense of self and other. It was enabled at the Wednesday Night Dance by a confluence of circumstances—the move to the Jukebox, the general interest in southern Indiana, the collapse of institutional structure at the Guitar Studio, and the gentle demeanor of those who were Strawberry's closest friends.

8 THE ORANGE SHEET

The free-spirited atmosphere of the Jukebox drew its strength from the social effects of old-time community music and dance. Through this traditional form, dancers enjoyed one another's co-presence in a manner unavailable to their mainstream contemporaries. Dancers came to the dance to connect not so much to the past, but rather to one another. Emerging naturally from and around this ritual event was a foundation of informal friendships and an expanding interconnected network of social forms with which to enjoy them. The dance became the dance group, a generative social engine through which new structurally compatible forms were created. These seemingly trivial forms were essential components of the emerging community.

In their outward form they were marked by ironic reversal, which undermined their status as community symbols. In this respect, the most prominent was the Orange Sheet, the dance group phone list that was enjoyed in its self-effacing status as an official accounting of the community. According to Ted Hall, it began as a simple, practical matter. Many of the dancers, because they were students or lived in group houses, were not listed in the telephone book. Thus the need arose for a telephone list of the dancers. Ted recalls that it was in 1973 when he obtained a free ream of orange paper from a recently out-of-business Louisville company. Over a few successive Wednesday Night Dances, he collected names, addresses, and numbers from all who wanted to submit them, and he printed the list without charge on the equipment of his employer. In successive years the list continued to be printed on orange paper—long after the initial supply was exhausted.

The Orange Sheet was for many years the only tangible evidence of "membership" in the dance. Yet here was its potency as a symbol: it was literally titled "The Orange Sheet," effacing its status as a membership list and reaffirming the existential priority of the dance itself over any other structure. It was simply a list of names with addresses and telephone numbers, collected at the dance from anyone who wanted to submit them, and listed alphabetically, with no evidence of underlying organizational authority or hierarchy.

Ted Hall was also instrumental in organizing the after-dance gathering. The dance traditionally ended each Wednesday at 10:30 P.M., but the energetic dancers were increasingly finding ways to extend the evening past that point. Ted recalls that people would often socialize after the dance, but it was he who suggested reconvening at a particular place. That place was Rapp's Pizza Train, a pizzeria on the southwest corner of Sixth and Washington, one block from Kirkwood and the central town-gown cultural corridor. Hank Berman, the owner, was happy to see the large group pour in each Wednesday without fail. He frequently brought out free pitchers of beer, and when the group later opened its first bank account, he donated a small sum. The side room of the restaurant was reserved each Wednesday for the dancers, and Hank welcomed the informal music that the group brought. Usually the tables would be rearranged into a long line, assuring, just as in the contra dance itself, that no one would be left out. For periods of time, members of the group, notably Michael Wagner, worked there. For nearly a decade, until it closed in the spring of 1982, Rapp's was as regular as the dance itself.

As more dancers took up old-time music, there were also more frequent informal music sessions. In the early years, of course, music at the dance was dominated by people who already knew how to play when they began attending. But as the dance grew, others who came as danc-

Old-Time Music and Dance

The after-dance gathering at Leslie's Italian Villa on Sixth Street, 1985. When Rapp's closed, Leslie's opened in the same location and became the venue for after-dance socializing. From left, Tom Stio, Bill Baus, Diane Drisch, Bruce Taggart, Kara Keeling, Lee Schmid; from right, Leslie Worth, Frank Hall, Spencer Mackall. Photo courtesy of Tom Morrison.

ers began to take up the common band instruments—fiddle, banjo, and guitar. What some called a "confidence discrepancy" arose among musicians of differing experience. So, beginning sometime in 1974, Ted Hall began holding practice sessions at his house (then 518 N. Washington, near the "green house") for what the group called "B-band" in reference to their relative inexperience. Ted recalls that the original group was exactly eight: Ted (banjo), Bruce Cassal (banjo), Gay Heishman (fiddle), Kathy Hirsh (fiddle), Teri Klassen (guitar), Dave Laymon (banjo), Laura Ley (fiddle), and Bill Meek (fiddle). The group was not at all exclusive, and before the decade ended numerous others would participate in B-band, including Donna Doughten, Kathy Duckett, Melissa Leavell, René Oschin, Anne Reese, Gary Stanton, and Bruce Taggart. B-band seemed a perfect articulation of the Fuzzy Mountain

An early B-band meeting at the home of James Chiplis. From left, Donna Doughten, Teri Klassen, Anne Reese, Ted Hall, John Levindofske, Bruce Cassal. Photo courtesy of Teri Klassen.

aesthetic, with old-time instrumentation, a loose sense of membership, modest tempos, sparse melodic ornamentation, and, foremost, a sense of friendship that ran as deep as their common musical interest.

During this period, another group was meeting occasionally to sing from the shape-note tune book *The Sacred Harp*. The tradition of group singing by shape notes was widely popular in the nineteenth century but settled into the southeastern U.S., where *The Sacred Harp*, first published in 1844, has been used ever since. Its discovery by Depression-era folklorists and regional writers established for it a place in the folksong canon, and thus also in the postwar folksong revival. But Bloomington's involvement with Sacred Harp singing pre-dated even these meetings. Around 1970, Andy Mahler and Deedie Bell spent time in New England participating in the renowned Bread and Puppet Theater. The performance in which they played, "Stations of the Cross," included several Sacred Harp songs—Andy recalls "Kedron,"

Old-Time Music and Dance

"Idumea," and "Wondrous Love." Andy and Deedie returned to Bloomington with enough interest to continue singing, and they met with Peter Gold and Cindy Ross occasionally for Sacred Harp and round-singing. Cindy later moved to New England and appeared with the Word of Mouth Chorus on the influential Nonesuch recording *Rivers of Delight* (1979). In the mid-1970s the Bloomington group met weekly at the 12th Street home of Barry Kern and Linda Higginbotham and included Barry, Linda, Deedie Bell, Chris Collins, Mark Feddersen, and Andy Mahler. They performed once at the Eagle Creek Folk Festival.

Also in 1974 some began playing volleyball. What must have begun as casual amusement turned for a while into obsession as the group met twice and during some periods as many as five times each week. Andy Mahler and John Keltner were among the organizers, and the location was for a number of years a vacant lot at the southeast corner of 12th and Fess and later the 17th Street Park across from Andy's house. Linda Higginbotham, Ted Hall, and Robbie Wyatt were also frequent players. The net was stored in an unused doghouse in Andy's front yard, so that anyone who knew this could set it up to play. Sometimes there were impromptu dances held in the picnic shelter.

Volleyball had no official connection to the dance, of course, but like other such activities, it was a social hub with a largely overlapping populace. To such an extent was this the case that information and influence flowed throughout both activities. One might have expected this to have a kind of decentering effect on the dance, providing a social sphere for competing values. The move out of the Guitar Studio and eventually to the Jukebox, where the structural influence of the venue was diminished, may well have amplified this decentering possibility. In the long run, this may well have happened.

But the more salient and immediate effect was actually the opposite. As dancers spent more and more time together, even in non-concentric social spheres, the dance experience as a whole began to have an all-consuming effect. The dance seemed to grow more powerful in its capacity to absorb and resolve the ever-expanding number of spheres of influence. It was always a good bet that new ritual activities would be familiar, or at least odd in some familiar way—that there would be a reverberation of accessible values throughout all of them. In fact, volley-

The Orange Sheet

Volleyball at 17th Street Park across from Andy Mahler's house. At the left is the shelter where potlucks and impromptu dances were held. From left, unknown, "Rocky" Buck, Paul Tyler, Bob Herring, Frank Hall, Ann Prochilo, Linda Higginbotham, Ann Barlow, Zoe Randall, "Satch" (Andy's roommate, near the bicycle). Photo courtesy of Laura Ley.

ball may well have been an apogee in the shift toward self-authentication. Like the dance, volleyball players took an external structure and over time accumulated stylistic nuances to develop an intensely autonomous social ritual that answered primarily to their own social tastes. Like the dance, they appropriated public spaces and employed sets that could expand to capacity as new players arrived. But with volleyball, the sources of authentication that originally fired the cultural engine of old-time music revival were at their farthest remove.

Volleyball as authentic? Indeed, it was this quality of the dance group—its capacity to authenticate trivialities—that so attracted me, both as a folklorist and a participant. Once dance devised itself as the substitute of the substitute, as the communal essence to which recorded old-time music alluded, it unleashed a generative colossus that presided over the minutiae of community life. Like prewar old-time music, it could incorporate modernity into antimodernist structures. In contrast, with conventional folksong revival there remained a vast ironic distance between contemporary life and folk tradition, a distance mediated by "poor substitute" devices such as recordings. Dance community, in contrast, was not a reenactment but rather a habitation of tradition. It conceived tradition as a kind of circular nostalgia, whereby community was a generative principle that incorporated itself as both subject and object of its own nostalgic yearnings. Now it was contemporary life that stood apart as tragically ironic, and even so unlikely an endeavor as volleyball, as a distinct stylistic object, could be swept away in the symbolic freshet that the dance community had become.

There is much to be said about this process as it happened in Bloomington, of course, but a few words on authenticity itself will be helpful in establishing this as the operative process. The hallmark of possessive authenticity, as Dean MacCannell and others noted, is the souvenir—a reproducible object whose significance is drawn not from its inherent qualities but from its attachment to some authentic site. Much—though not all—of folksong-revival performance involved external reference to deferred authentic circumstances, which in turn exerted a contradicting influence on the circumstance of re-creation.

In the formative years of the dance, however, the shift from deferential authenticity to self-authentication was entirely evident in the quality of its artifacts. As the dance group matured, its souvenirs—T-shirts, posters, recordings, and also travels to cultural sites—were increasingly concerned with its own events. And how quickly, when I began inquiring in 1986 among veteran dancers about the early years of the dance, did sites of significance spring to their minds—the stump in Dunn Meadow, the green house at Ninth and Washington, the Jukebox. Yet these artifacts were deployed not so much as objects of deferred experience as they were signals in a code of recognition. No one ever visited the old dance sites—they were completely erased as artifacts. But those who had danced at them shared a powerful sense of common experience not accessible to newcomers.

This pattern was revealed again in the final stages of this book, when I asked for help gathering photographs. The morris dance team, with

The Orange Sheet

In the winter months, a group gathered at the home of Bill Meek to watch televised Indiana University basketball games. From left, René Oschin, Teri Klassen, Molly Gregory, Bill Meek, Mary Sue Morrow, Ted Hall. Photo courtesy of Teri Klassen.

its capacity for vivid visual display, was a popular commemorative photo subject. Jam sessions were also common, captured in a wide variety of settings. But apparently the Wednesday Night Dance itself was rarely photographed. There were undoubtedly many reasons for this, which, however, its capacity as a commemorative object could not overcome.

The most impressive commemorative gesture was the snapshot of the group who met at Bill Meek's house to watch televised Indiana University basketball games. By so many accounts, Rich Nevins's among them, crafting social experience out of television viewing should have been a notable triumph, however ironic, over a technology designed to seduce its audience into captive passivity. And indeed it was: in the photo the group appears consumed with the wry satisfaction that became a staple of dance group experience.

The dance could articulate the overall lifestyle in part through a kind of code of shared self-awareness among dancers, manifested in part through the consecrating effect of participation in the dance, in part through the particular deployment of the body in dance. Old-time set dance, as its dancers will so often assert, imposes upon participants a formal structure seen in its essence to be egalitarian and participatory. Even dance composers, who might well adopt a proprietary posture toward their compositions, are instead compelled to enjoy and encourage the free circulation of their dances (Dart 1995: 84).

Through structure, dance experience transformed folk revival performance practice from staged, commercial display to participatory community event and severed the chain of desire that propelled possessive authenticity. In its place there emerged an event and a community that seemed to offer a kind of existential authenticity, deriving its symbolic power from its immediate structure and not from its remote origin. The sense of purpose initially derived from these artifacts and the collection of remembered community experiences were the organizing concepts that brought symbolic unity to the group. The dance, as the weekly event at which the dispersed participants came literally face-to-face, stood at the center of this complex mode of living in Bloomington and some other communities.

In one sense, the chief object of the dance was to achieve self-renewal. Often dance itself was the initial experience, but it integrated a host of other objects and structures into a kind of holistic lifestyle that reverberated with redundancy. This was, in part, what concerned the story of the group's serendipitous founding: from the meeting of Miles and Dillon, a new, hybrid cultural persona arose, something molded from old-time music and contra dance, but not exactly either. From North and South, but not exactly either. From the ephemeral here and now of the counterculture and from the cloudy, mystical past of "memory theater," but not exactly either. Still, it was not merely structure operating on passive participants that gave the dance its soul-quenching property. It took faith. One had to participate wholeheartedly in the dance, to become a citizen of the dance, to contribute to its special aura, to unite with its purpose and meaning, to remove oneself from the wasteland that the world outside had become.

The absence of any obvious authenticating device is what makes volleyball an interesting and not at all trivial matter as an extension of the Wednesday Night Dance. The volleyball players were very serious about their enterprise and could be impatient with casual players. But, at least at the outset, their seriousness was drawn not from competitive sport or the fitness movement, but from the same wellspring of values as the dance. Like the dance, their game was open to casual players but was ascribed with inviolable formal qualities that casual players sometimes dispense with. In its relentless intensity, volleyball amplified the values of the dance experience in general and confirmed the significance of the dance community.

And so volleyball, for some, took its place in the orbit of the Wednesday Night Dance. With no inherited affiliation to traditional culture, volleyball instead developed stylistic nuance and thus also cultural autonomy. But there were other satellites, varying in intensity and autonomy, and their number grew as the dance matured. Those which involved folk music and dance—such as clogging, morris dancing, *Sacred Harp* singing—arose also in the orbits of other dance groups. Later, most of these would develop their own social structures and cultural networks that even extended nationwide. But in these formative years, so much depended upon the gravitational field of the Wednesday Night Dance itself.

9

ANNE'S A BRIDE TONIGHT

These formal activities—from the after-dance gathering to the volleyball meetings—traced the outlines of the dance group socio-cultural orb. But there were other occasions where its social and cultural expanse resonated less explicitly: the less formal socializing—the parties—that spurred what Linda Higginbotham called the "golden age" of the Wednesday Night Dance. She recalled being surprised that a chance encounter with a few friends on a summer evening could evolve into a party without any planning at all. Serendipity, the unexpectedness of a meaningful encounter, was, of course, not mere chance at all. It emanated from the generative power of the dance group, the cultural genealogy that provided familiarity and place to events that might seem to happen on their own.

There were also overnight parties—at Bob Herring's Orange County house, at Linda Lee's, and at the Loftmans'. For many years a group of dancers would spend a summer week at the beach at Pawleys Island, South Carolina. And there were expeditions to folk festivals, some as far away as Virginia and Pennsylvania, where activities at the campsite were at least as important as those on the stage. These events developed their own aura of authenticity, affirming the generative power the dance had accumulated. It is not so much that these spontaneous gatherings happened—they were, in all appearance, quite ordinary. But there was a sense that they were not isolated gatherings, but each a reiteration of other gatherings and, foremost, of the dance itself.

The most important generative social encounter of the Bloomington dance was the myriad of romances among the dancers, which were identified as a marked linguistic category by the term "dance group romance." Contra and square dance, of course, exhibited its own dyadic jargon—of "partners," "couples," "corners," "opposites," "shadows," "trail buddies," "actives" (active couples), and "inactives" (inactive couples)—all alluding to an unspecified yet compelling significance of a briefly significant other. It was endemic to set dance—perhaps its chief purpose—to bring individuals into this brief yet meaningful dyadic co-presence. The significance of this encounter was further predicated by coordinative movement and touching, often with the added admonition to "give weight" (lean back and hold one another in a posture of mutual support) and "make eye contact."

Of the twenty or so common dance figures, the swing was generally thought to call for the most personal exposure. Not only was it sustained for a lengthy moment, but it was most often performed in "ballroom position" (a quasi-embrace with hands supporting one by the small of the back and the other by the shoulder). Contra dance choreography in the post-1970 revival was generally thought to favor interaction with dancers other than one's partner, echoing the desire for non-exclusivity and social openness. And it genuinely did. But Mary Dart was surprised to find that in contrast to the many choreographic changes that facilitated interaction with other dancers, the "partner swing" figure made a dramatic comeback in popularity around 1973 after several decades of decline (1995: 145).

All these effects could be perceived even more vividly as the special province of the contra revival when measured against the backdrop of the club square dance revival. There, according to custom and to written rules, a dancer's "partner" remained so for the whole evening. Moreover, giving "weight" and "eye contact" were not encouraged. Club square dancers who crossed into contra events could be delighted or alarmed by these differences.

Old-Time Music and Dance

In the dance community, "significant other," of course, was an explicit marking in its own right. The term's usage seemed designed to open a limitlessness otherwise circumscribed by the strictures of conventional romance or even of prevailing gender relations. Convention was always close at hand—for example, in the language of "husband," "wife," "girl-friend," or "boyfriend"—and its limits at the time could be severe. This economy of convention—the system of values by which conventional gender relations were conducted—was deeply embedded in mainstream social interaction, and especially in romance. So, with some delibera-tion, this limitless significance of the "significant other" was articulated both in the dance itself and at its remove in sustained relationships within the community where romances bloomed and faded and were ceaselessly observed and discussed.

At the dance itself, convention was ever-present in the vividly anach-ronistic argot of contra and square dance. This notorious "ladies and gents" jargon presupposed the most odious gender rigidity and male privilege—and beyond that a decidedly heterosexual structural config-uration. The discriminatory effects of this inherited language, however, could be readily isolated from the pure neutrality of the dance itself—otherwise dance would not have continued to attract those who lived so faithfully by gender neutrality as a cause. Efforts to resist this language had been inscribed into local practice from the beginning, as Dillon Bustin expressed in the 1972 *Courier Tribune* newspaper article:

> We've also tried to make the calls less sexist. In the past, the calls were always directed at the man—"Swing her, Take her down," etc. But now the calls say, "Swing him," etc. For various reasons, some-times men like to dance with other men, and women with other women, so the calls have had to change with the times. ("Forgotten Dances Revitalized")

Until the mid-1980s, patience with these unpleasant trappings had not run out, and so the greatest effort was given to containing them under an umbrella of contempt and denial.

Under this umbrella, in what seemed like infinite abundance, the dance itself generated, reiterated, alluded to, and over-determined the possibilities of sustained dyadic significance—dance romance. At any moment on any given Wednesday night, so much was at stake in a

Anne's a Bride Tonight

contra line. Imagine if you can the unbearable and vivid flood of emotions accompanying the specter of a recently estranged romantic partner approaching, for the first time, from up or down a contra line and the anticipation of that first non-romantic embrace. Or the ever-present possibility of new romance, of the play of gaze and touch elusively suggesting more than itself. This is partly why dance was at once so loved and feared—there was always a chance of absolute exposure to the possibility of the other of dance, of romance, of sex, of friendship, of betrayal, of rejection, of marriage—of all significance that exceeded the encounter in the dance, that could never be contained by it.

The powerful and wide-ranging emotions surrounding dance romance further infused the community with the life breath of authenticity. The dance as folksong revival, which initially took its values from the reenactment of traditional practice, was now a system—an economy—for managing the social relations of the community. And all of the supposedly salacious couple dances that replaced it—from the waltz to the twist—suddenly seemed quaint and restrictive compared to the breathtaking touch and gaze that endured along the length of a contra line.

But if romance provided an emotional underpinning for community, it also opened the community to the very economy of established convention that it sought to deny. To consider folk revival as "inauthentic" was always to recognize another cultural economy—the biographical past—that it could not enclose. As much as it might have seemed otherwise, dancers most often began their romances as strangers to one another. Romance, then, was precisely the site where the illusion of the enclosed economy of dance relations came in contact with the various economies that each dancer in some way sought, in the very act of self-fashioning, to subordinate, deny, or obscure.

Under such circumstances, falling in love could be an experience of discovery filled with risk and uncertainty. Of course it was. But it was other than mere youthful impetuosity, generational momentum, or transgression of class. Dance romance was all of these as a reiteration of the dance itself, whose very purpose involved resistance to the enveloping hegemony of mainstream convention. A dance romance was so marked in the hope that every dyadic moment alluded not merely to

Old-Time Music and Dance

itself but to the enduring nexus of values that was, uniquely for each person, the dance. Of course it was. Of course it was on one surface denial and defiance of convention and perhaps also upbringing, and on the other surface the tangible reality of utopian dance community, each side seeking to contain the other within the logic of the "of course," within its economy, as a deviant form.

Escaping the economy of conventional romance, however, was not so easy in the privacy of the dyad as it was in the dance itself. Romances could be rocky as they drew out unforeseen differences from outside the scope of the dance—perhaps from an artfully elided past. But no one was ever discouraged from trying. Dancers came, moreover, from a genuinely wide span of upbringings, often obscured from the surface of dance experience by its inscrutable unity of purpose. On the other hand, in part *because* they were dancers, many had become oddities in their own families, or more importantly they became contra dancers partly *because* they wanted to refashion themselves. In any case, dance romance went hand in hand with self-fashioning, as did the effortless euphoria of shared self-discovery with the brute will that sustained relationships eventually required.

This risk and uncertainty were enhanced by the widely available understanding that romantic relations were motivated by a call to pleasure and not to duty. But pleasure before duty only broadened the scope of romantic responsibility to include the vastness of the psyche. Thus considerable communicative work, self-examination, empathy, and even measured betrayal were undertaken to overcome inherited obstacles to romantic fulfillment—such as jealousy, possessiveness, insecurity, inhibition. If romance was faith and not obligation, then, some would reason, even tests of faith could bring greater fulfillment.

Postwar youth culture had laid the foundation for this. Rock music lyrics, such as those on the early Beatles recordings, had erected the inauthentic self as the chief barrier to romance and had infused music with the power of release and restoration. From there and elsewhere, there had evolved a subculture of communication, articulated in large part by an expanding language of introspection and empathy drawn in pieces from necessity, from the psychology of self-help, from Eastern philosophy, but also from the tangible authentic experience that could

Anne's a Bride Tonight

be observed in folksong. Perhaps Bob Dylan brought folksong to mean this—through the refracted light of Ginsberg and Rimbaud—and later was discarded as its messenger. Perhaps not discarded but self-effaced, as Greil Marcus suggested, by the rediscovery and embrace of the Harry Smith *Anthology* in Dylan's *Basement Tapes*. Perhaps, mostly, the call to romance came in vivid relief from the ballads, where Barbara Allen and Sweet William died from unrequited love, where Matty Groves lost his life after being discovered in bed with the king's wife, where a drunken husband is fooled into thinking his wife's lover is a cabbage head. Wherever it took its cue, dance romance was absorbed into dance as yet another ritual articulation of the double consciousness—of self as subject and object at once—to which folksong revival aspired. And in dance circles double consciousness meant higher consciousness, an inscrutable power wielded over the isolated individual, over the past, and over the culture of the mainstream.

To grasp the logic of folk revival romance, let us take a foray into a pair of texts with ties to the Bloomington folk revival, both deeply introspective, and one widely accepted as emblematic of authentic romance. The first text is Jana St. James's *Memories of Madison County* (1996), which bears explicit markings to folksong revival in Bloomington. In this presumably autobiographical narrative, St. James records a passionate love affair with then-married folksinger Robert James Waller in Bloomington in 1967. The underlying motivation of the book is her suggestion that the affair served as the psychological foundation for Waller's wildly popular *The Bridges of Madison County*, the second text in the pair I examine. The plausibility of St. James's narrative relies heavily upon an emerging moral logic that prevailed in Bloomington folksong revival culture at the time. These events pre-dated the dance, of course, occurring in the period just after the decline of the I.U. Folk Club when the explicit political moorings of the folksong revival were giving way to the politics of the personal.

St. James carefully situates the rationale of her affair within the moral world of the folksong revival, increasing its potency throughout the narrative as it comes in contact with her more prosaic social entities—dormitory friendships, sorority life, her family, and, in the end, the hippies with whom she shared, "commune-style," a south-side apartment. Waller ends the affair on the birth of his first child; although St. James is deeply hurt by this, she never discredits the logic that propelled the affair—the folksong empathy that held them together. During the affair, so compelling is the regard for authentic empathy that Waller's wife herself is unwittingly integrated into this world and occasionally benefits from it—so that in the end St. James makes it far less easy to determine, in a dangerous romantic escapade, even across the chasm of betrayal and deceit, who are the winners and who are the losers.

St. James offers this up explicitly as a counternarrative to *Bridges*, which buttresses a patently implausible sequence of events (so say Iowa farm moms who identify with Francesca) with verisimilitude drawn from the well-timed revelation of "facts" external to the core narrative (the *National Geographic* article, the discovery of the letters, etc.). Perhaps the clever handling of transgression and desire make Waller's a better book, but St. James is to be credited with the historical recovery of the moral world that *Bridges* must obscure to achieve its narrative purpose. Waller's *Bridges* lovers can yield to pure reckless abandon precisely because the characters transgress the limits of a community where their love cannot exist by any acceptable moral reasoning.

If the characters betray Francesca's marriage in Waller's *Bridges,* St. James translates this into Waller's own betrayal—not of his wife, but of the moral purpose by which he once lived. With every act, he becomes a grotesque contradiction of his own professed sincerity. Unable to acknowledge authoring his own life, Waller must author *Bridges* so that, just as Francesca leaves the letters for her children to find, he can leave a trace of tangible authentic passion for those who know only a world where it is forbidden.

St. James's testimony is compelling, then, in its calculated development of the moral logic of the affair. In contrast, the affair in *Bridges* is entirely transgressive. It can betray that particular marriage precisely because it never exceeds the rationale of marriage itself. It is an affair conducted entirely under the auspices of the foreboding all-or-nothing question of divorce—the "community" implicitly requires that Francesca choose between leaving her husband and children and even the community itself or ending the affair and sealing it in secrecy. Only years later, with the discovery of the letters, is the logic of the affair

Anne's a Bride Tonight

reopened by the daughter, and this unlocks the vault of her own passion that was previously uninheritable, sealed as inexplicable inhibition within the veil of family secrecy. *Memories,* on the other hand, never *seeks* to threaten or replace that particular marriage, but rather imposes violently upon the categorical imperative of the marital relation itself. Francesca is unhappy because her particular marital relation is unfulfilling; Waller is not at all discontent with his particular marriage but with the limits that appear ever more confining as he views them through the lens of folksong.

In *Bridges,* community isolates Francesca, cruelly drawing away at precisely the moment she needs it. Its absence extends even beyond the secret seal of the letters to a vague hope Francesca has for her children, who will find them. In *Memories,* community envelops Waller as the moral affirmation of folksong, which validates all authentic emotions. In folksong revival community, authentic emotion is the foundation of healthy relationships; in conventional romance, it is a danger to be avoided. This is precisely the impetus for *Memories*—to recover what *Bridges* must suppress and then hope for in vain. And it is precisely in the presumed span of time between the event of *Memories* and the publication of *Bridges* that the dance flourished, emerging from the apocryphal stump, from a single chance encounter, an affirmation of that transgressive discovery and desire which was the folksong revival.

How plausible, then, that in *Memories* the chief vehicle of the couple's authentic passion, the meaningful and exclusive occasion for their being together, was at first not sexuality but guitars. By this means they crossed to the backstage of folksong revival, where its secrets were held even if not fully possessed, where they were separated from the world around them, from the deafening silence of Waller's wife, by the membrane of the proscenium arch. Before such a scene, sandwiched historically between the event of *Memories* and the writing of *Bridges,* there had to be discovered a stump. A stump, at least, was a *place* (and if it wasn't actually the stump, it was some other *place*), and the new motif of the topology of self-authentication, the sacralization of space at which dance revival became so adept.

Within these sites emerged the interiority of authentic community, a refuge of sincerity where dance romance flourished as a thrilling defiance of a cynical world outside. These sites incorporated self-reference into the community in a way that the staged events of the coffeehouse era could not. Even in the Cambridge scene of *Baby, Let Me Follow You Down*, where romance and place were so important, one gets the feeling that both were impervious to the authenticating reach of folksong. The legacy of the stump meant that authentic empathy, egalitarian performance practice, and utopian community were at once the subject and object of performance and were dispersed throughout the community and reiterated in limitless possibility. Thus, in the time before the dance, even St. James and Waller found themselves isolated, their perfect empathy drawn from the utopian other of folksong. The dance sought to incorporate this utopian other into itself as folksong revival community.

As a consequence, dance romances were often public matters, sifted and reshaped as they passed through the morally charged channels of talk. And dance events—even as they articulated their own manner of exclusivity—were integrative, providing many avenues of authenticity otherwise confined by the proscenium arch. Playing guitar was important, but so also was playing euchre and volleyball. Had the events of *Memories* taken place a decade later, the three would each have had a coterie of sympathizers, with the jilted one getting the lion's share of support, likely breaking the silence of betrayal. It was not that such events were not painful or unfair, but rather that in the utopian community injury was not compounded by disgrace. Nor was it that betrayal was encouraged, but rather that, as with the opening of Francesca's letters, there was a hope for emotional rejuvenation. Certainly there was an opening of the isolated, intransigent dyad to the complexity of the community, where authentic empathy was highly regarded and could achieve a value above any isolated configuration where it was absent. This was lived folksong, a mode of existence where the salient themes of folksong were merged with the vivid experience of community.

With varying degrees of intent and awareness, romance was a moral and political act. Some undertook experimental living arrangements and could expect and receive tolerance and perhaps even encouragement from the group. David Crosby's song "Triad" might have served as a model for some. This is not to suggest that the opening to the community eliminated isolation, secrecy, and betrayal, but rather that the

Anne's a Bride Tonight

opening of romance always had this as a possible achievement. The incentive to transcend the cultural gulf that divided self and other came from the philosophy of the counterculture, but what folksong contributed was to make more vivid the cultural gulf that was to be crossed. Dancers could take such non-judgmental pleasure in one another's affairs—because narratives of romantic transcendence, of the triumph of authentic empathy, affirmed fundamental moral principles just as did the content of traditional ballads.

None of this is to say that conventional dyads were not common, nor that they went unappreciated. Indeed, the most salient consequences of the opening to the community were the grand dyadic celebrations marked so deliberately and extravagantly as "dance crowd weddings." Here was an institution sacred to church and family that was overlaid with the most potent dance revival symbols. With each wedding, there was always a dance afterward, and often the entire event was held outdoors in some rustic arbor. Weddings brought dance crowd values in palpable contact with the biographical past of the betrothed couple; thus they were the consummation of a cultural rapprochement for which the couple would have spent much time and effort preparing.

The site of the wedding, like the stump, should have had the effect of a topological opening, a rupture of the situational symbols by which conventional weddings wielded social authority. Tamara Loewenthal and Lee Schmid were married outdoors in the park adjacent to the Jukebox. Frank Hall and Mary Beth Roska were married, by Bloomington mayor Tomi Allison, in 17th Street Park, where volleyball had been held for so long. Dee Mortensen and Dean Lawler had their wedding on the unimproved property where they would later build a house—celebrants made a quarter-mile trek to the top of the ridge for the ceremony. Eloise Clark and I chose the state park where the dance weekend Swing into Spring was always held, and called it a "Nuptial Weekend." Others used country homes or backyards in town.

One could count on an expansive potluck meal, and if there was a cake or other catered food, someone in the group might well have made it. The ceremony was usually officiated by someone who was outside the group yet sympathetic to its purpose. Attire was rarely formal, certainly not for the guests; a bride might well have made her own dress.

Jam session at the wedding of Randy and Martha Marmouzé, 1977. From left: Bob Herring (guitar), Andy Mahler (harmonica), unknown, Judy Hyman (fiddle), Frank Hall, Randy Marmouzé (banjo), Mark Feddersen (mandolin). Photo courtesy of Anne Reese and Bruce Cassal.

Champagne was sometimes served, but so was homemade beer made by some dance group brewer. A couple might scarcely have given any thought to a honeymoon, but in its place, as ritual consummation, the morris dance team would dance around the couple just after the ceremony, making explicit reference to fertility and sexuality.

The first "dance crowd wedding" was probably the wedding of Dillon Bustin and Kathy Restle in 1974. Dan Willens catered the event, and flowers were contributed by group members. But some attribute more significance to the wedding of Bruce Cassal and Anne Reese later that year. The wedding party was held at a house on Smith Avenue between Lincoln and Grant. Dancing was done outdoors in a parking lot next to the house. As a gift to the couple, Dillon composed the dance "Anne's a Bride Tonight," introducing to contemporary contras a square-dance figure in which partners duck under their opposites' arch to meet a new

Anne's a Bride Tonight

The morris team performs at the wedding of Cliff Emery and Linda Handelsman, summer of 1983. From left: Claudio Buchwald (fiddle), Frank Hall, Teri Klassen, Andrea Morrison, Pat Gingrich, Linda Handelsman, and Cliff Emery. Photo courtesy of Teri Klassen.

opposite couple. This dance was later published in Ted Sannella's *Balance and Swing* and became part of the national core repertoire for a time. Weddings of others in the group would follow this potluck-and-dance model, serving, as weddings do, both as group affirmations and ceremonies of personal transition.

Of course, the nature of any particular individual's transition was hardly pre-determined: often, in fact, it had little to do with housing arrangements, finances, sex, or even childbearing. Dancers indeed lived in widely varying arrangements, and the question "Why get married?" (or "Why have a dance wedding?") had a multitude of answers. Often the rationale was pragmatic and personal; still, dancers could look outside their enclave and, seeing considerably more intolerance and less fulfillment, feel grateful for the range of choices their community provided. Possibly the cultural answer to that question had less to do with personal transition than with having sensed some kind of resolution

Old-Time Music and Dance

with the group regarding the multitude of relationships that involved the couple, their families and friends, and the dance group.

Indeed many weddings, while insignificant in the transition of the couple itself, constituted significant encounters between the dance group and the couple's families and non-dance friends. It was in respect to the two arenas of romantic economy that the intense effort and symbolic play of weddings was constituted. Thus although those weddings saturated with dance symbols were great affirmations for the group, so also were those with conventional trappings. Dance weddings seemed designed to announce a particular manner by which the couple had come to be recognized within the community and by which the couple had represented the group to those in their biographical pasts. Even those with the most conventional living arrangements and mainstream values earned the profound commitment of the group.

There was also a distinct irony surrounding weddings. In fact, to some degree a dance wedding was not genuinely a transition at all, but a public encounter with an established couple at a moment of comfort with the community. In this respect a dance wedding was an extravagant joke, a celebration of a promise of a commitment and manner of living which, by the group's own moral code, should already have existed as its prerequisite. Veteran dancers recall with such exquisite pleasure the moment in the van en route to a morris dance performance when Tom Stio and Amy Novick shocked the group with the announcement of their fifth wedding anniversary. They had kept their marriage secret for five years, while the group assumed they had been living together unmarried! This revelation, a perfect inversion of mainstream dogma, was the source of considerable amusement for some time. This joke was grounded squarely by the seamless camaraderie that dance group weddings seemed designed to celebrate so lavishly. What ultimately mattered was not that Tom and Amy had adopted one living arrangement or another, but that they had so elegantly flaunted the obligation to adopt any.

Anne's a Bride Tonight

10 OPENING UP

For weeks to follow, the story of Tom and Amy's surprising anniversary announcement made its way through the communicative pathways of the dance. It had become narrative, of course, and it was imbued with values that would seem to fuse the moral world of its teller with the real events of the story, however extraordinary. Such, in fact, was the nature of much dance group talk. At Rapp's after the dance, at parties, and at most any idle moment together, spirited talk was one of the invigorating pleasures of dance group life.

Narratives were most always realist genres—gossip, rumor, and personal narrative—whose narrative momentum was propelled by a moral dimension situated not in the telling but in the told, in the narrated life. Indeed, dancers took great interest and pleasure in one another's lives—in romance, success, health, adversity, adventure—particularly when they were recounted and given dramatic structure in talk. Dancers spent much of the week apart from one another, and talk served to bind the moments spent together. Particularly as other dance communities sprung up, dancers also traveled frequently, and talk would likewise bind them to their friends in other communities. The accumulation of stories, in turn, linked narrated events to broader experiential categories, establishing public relevance for individual biography.

On the dance floor, the accumulated excess of identity that had been ascribed in talk to a name was inscribed on the body of the community and of the individuals. In the contra line, with its intense yet contrived encounters, was there any way to avoid bringing biographical excess to bear on social bodies? Is "gauntlet" too strong a word for this? Is this not precisely how the dance counteracted loneliness and isolation, by incorporating the chronic excess of unembodied biography? This is how I experienced it: biographical talk interpreted raw experience and transformed it into terms that mattered, both of which were ultimately embodied on the dance floor as authentic identity and community. In this way also the ideals of the community were manifested dialogically—neither entirely as subjective experience nor as objective ideal, but at some point where the two converged.

There was also a therapeutic aspect of dance group talk. It is useful to recall that the period of the dance was sandwiched between the post-WWII and postmodern eras, both of which celebrated, for different reasons, individualism over community. Between these bookends arose the communicational paradigm in psychology, itself set between Freudian or behavioral individualism on the one hand and evolutionary psychology on the other. Thomas Szasz's "The Myth of Mental Illness" and Gregory Bateson's double-bind theory of schizophrenia had inspired the holistic psychology movement, which positioned the etiology of mental illness outside the individual. The political implications of these theories were well established, such as in the famous SDS (Students for a Democratic Society) Port Huron Statement of 1962, which pinpointed social alienation as endemic to the critical societal ills of the day (Roszak 1969: 57–59). Thus in the counterculture there was a prevailing belief that talk could heal both self and society, and dancers moved effortlessly and frequently into the roles of healer and subject. At the urging of another dancer, I became involved in Re-evaluation Counseling, a movement offering training in peer counseling, but this experience mirrored informal therapeutic talk that routinely transpired in the dance group. The most profound implication pertained to the

Opening Up

dance itself: if the preponderance of social ills lay in the unbridged gulf between self and other, then dance, as an act of social conjugation, could have profound therapeutic and political effects.

Indeed, many came to the dance with troubled pasts and found refuge in romance, friendship, and community. Having eschewed wealth, social status, and political power, many aspired to self-realization and found their most potent demons inside themselves. So therapeutic talk consisted often of finding common cause with others in the group. Indeed, it was an epiphany of relief to find others who struggled with obstacles to self-realization, sometimes as a consequence of submerged psychological wounds. It is difficult nowadays to grasp the rarity of this. In the 1990s, radio and television talk shows made these matters commonplace in public discourse, and the evangelical religious movement brought personal spirituality to a previously staid mainstream religious atmosphere. But in the 1970s a community such as the dance group was an oasis of consolation. And if, at the time, outsiders took the therapeutic consciousness to be unambitious, self-indulgent, or just weird, dancers took it as evidence of their holiness.

The setting of talk itself sometimes defined a vague topology, most often occurring in contexts tangibly adjacent to the Wednesday Night Dance. Of these, the regular after-dance scene at Rapp's was the most prominent. But there were also idle moments just before a dance, while sitting out entire dances, on the way to or from the dance, at parties, or wherever several dancers might be together. If a more dedicated circumstance was desired, dancers might "go for a walk" or set aside time to "catch up on news." There seemed to be a systematic spacing involved: talk (the "catching up") was embedded between the dance itself and the events that dancers would report as life (the "news").

Some talk did occur during dancing. But after contemporary dancers began composing dances, the contra form seemed to evolve toward what were called "busy" dances, which featured continuous activity and minimal idle time for everyone. Mary Dart's *Contra Dance Choreography* (1995) is a comprehensive study of this trend. In fact, when instructors at dance camps taught traditional longways dances from the colonial era—which featured considerable idle time for the inactive couple— they would sometimes suggest that the dances came from a period be-

Old-Time Music and Dance

fore Americans lost the "art of conversation." In 1971, long before the dance "Chorus Jig" had lost its popularity to the "busy" dance craze, Dudley Laufman took a moment to extol the pleasures of the down-the-outside-and-back figure, which provided ample time for flirting and improvisation (1971: 3). My observation was that during my time in Bloomington, dance structure never prevailed upon the desire to talk, however great its advantage.

The community of speech, however, most often formed *around* dance rather than *through* it, as if the pure democracy of dance was meant to counteract the stratifying effects that naturally arose from talk. This structural separation of talk and dance may have occurred because the dance itself was the point of entry into the community, where participants could be superficially integrated without always being fully known. Some at the dance languished for years, intentionally or not, outside or on the fringes of the community of speech. For this reason, the death of a dancer could bring painful attention to the unexpressed excess of biography, which was processed through mourning. I have mourned the death of Jean Farmer and Orace Johnson in this way, marveling at those facets of their lives which I never took the time to know or acknowledge, grieving across a distance that now can never be bridged. And there were suicides, opening a whole abyss of unknown biographical excess, which to this day leave me wondering, what if I had known?

Through talk about self and others, biography often became part of a kind of public record. Although some secrets were kept, much of what might otherwise be considered "personal" was open to anyone whose interest in the subject was thought benevolent or at least benign. This could serve to purposely muster support during personal crisis—one dancer reported choosing a particular other dancer to tell of a crisis in her life with the expectation that word would be spread effectively. A good talker, then, was by these standards someone who handled information in a way that was benevolent or benign for the most people. Such a person would likely have been in contact with many people, might travel frequently, and would reveal her or his own experiences in a way that invited trust in others. Although dancers could probably identify particular "good talkers," this quasi-aesthetic sense was most

Opening Up

often manifested inexplicitly. Similarly, dancers in crisis would usually not issue "press releases," as this one did, but instead were vaguely aware that the information network had advantages and disadvantages.

As the dance grew and the circle of friends expanded in the 1980s, biographical talk maintained its role as a means to integrate new dancers into the group. But this did not always come without cost. At times the degree of symbolic exposure involved was considerable, so that some dancers confided that they deliberately avoided it. Bloomington's extravagant personal dramas were even followed in other cities, and outsiders were sometimes repelled by the extent to which the personal became public. Even for those who thought it a largely positive experience, the term "opening up" came to designate the increasingly salient act of self-disclosure. On rare occasions, the presumed confessional urge was so great that fiction overtook fact—a story might spread that arose solely out of its plausibility—and its "truth" was restored only with the most certain amusement.

Old-Time Music and Dance

11  GARDENING AND DUMPSTERING

The moral community of the dance was not wholly constituted in narrative, of course. The discrete events recounted in stories were indeed connected, albeit loosely, by a unifying orientation toward real-life choices. It was not so explicit as an ideology nor so rigid as a lifestyle—this is probably why narrative, rather than doctrine, was so important in its operation. Around 1980, for example, the dance began printing T-shirts for its two annual dance weekends. Other than phrases like "old-time music and dance" and pastoral scenes depicting dancers and musicians, never was there inscribed any epithet suggesting group doctrine. At that time and place, it would have been considered in poor taste even to have proclaimed, "I love contra dance." Again, T-shirts were a code of awareness, not an announcement of affiliation.

Some would say this was because no doctrine existed, and in a way this was true. Merely to participate in the dance, however, demanded from most an abrupt shift of consciousness regarding, for example, the deportment of the body, the meaning of work, the way group decisions were made, or the relative value of time and commodities. Thus, in the absence of explicit doctrine, much that swelled to fill the symbolic void had a striking, if serendipitous, similarity.

For example, modernist conceptions of work and leisure posited them as stark antitheses in the mainstream, each counteracting negative qualities of the other. The dance, drawn from traditional models, was not recreation at all but an important community event. One attended not to "let off steam" or relax, but to see friends, to catch up on news, to see who was there, or even to fulfill a vague sense of obligation. There were always some who just dropped by to visit or came to stay but not dance; even someone prevented by injury from dancing might well not want to miss the dance. If former dancers had relocated to another city and returned to Bloomington for a visit, they would be expected to drop by and would likely find themselves the center of attention. If a new dancer seemed to know already how to dance, there was a buzz of excitement and curiosity. This was the way the dance felt, built on the social fabric of community.

These effects were only intensified by the unrelenting cyclical pattern of dance events. As far as could be remembered, the dance was held *every* Wednesday. Even in years when Christmas and New Year's Day fell on Wednesday, enough dancers could be found to keep the dance going. By the end of the 1970s, the Bloomington dance had accumulated its own stock of important calendar celebrations, and these were rapidly supplemented by annual events that Bloomington dancers attended in other nearby cities. In Bloomington, dancers could look forward in January to the Bean King Party, in February to Ted Hall's birthday, in April to Swing into Spring, in May to May Day, and in August to Sugar Hill dance weekend. In most cases (and much unlike celebratory events that evolved in other dance communities), these local annual celebrations were *less* rigidly structured—providing for more informal socializing—than the Wednesday Night Dance itself.

Some of these were genuine calendar celebrations, standing as the communal experience of seasonal transition. These transitions might be seasonal climate changes or community responses to societal shifts, such as workload fluctuations or the public school calendar. Sugar Hill, in fact, could rent scout camps because the date fell between the summer camping season and the fall campout season, at precisely the time scouting families were taking vacations. Taken together, these weekly and annual events constituted a comprehensive appropriation of the secular calendar and its rhythms. At times, the pace could be so rigorous and demanding that it affected dancers' physical rhythms such as sleep patterns. It entirely refocused social energies, lending momentum to the constellation of alternative values that circulated in the dance. The unifying theme of these values was never more specific than a conspiracy among dancers to arrange their lives so as to accommodate the most music and dance. If an employer was inflexible with a dancer's work schedule and would not accommodate an important weekend trip, the group was quick to share the dancer's indignation.

But beyond this there was an overarching theme of attempting to maintain a low-income, low-impact, healthy, and creative lifestyle. Wealth was not afforded status; if excessively conspicuous, it might even be stigmatized. If someone's job was not going well, this dancer might consult a copy of *What Color Is Your Parachute?* (1971) before seeking another job. With the dance group providing such robust psychological fulfillment and social support, much of one's life could be dedicated to social justice, spiritual or intellectual devotion, or artistic creativity.

The range of types of employment was wide, though there was an overall gravitation toward skilled and creative professions. There were a few schoolteachers, nurses, and librarians, and several who did home construction and remodeling. Affiliation with Indiana University was commonplace, as faculty, staff, or student. There were also mail carriers, veterinarians, landscapers, and massage therapists. Some worked in restaurants or retail businesses or did handyman type work, and sometimes this would supplement a creative venture that hadn't yet achieved success. There was a strong contingent of musicians and dancers who earned varying amounts of money performing, and some of these had ensembles with Young Audiences of Indiana. Some from the group started home businesses in niche market areas. Others worked from home as professional photographers and instrument builders.

Mainstream church affiliation was not widespread, but many people nonetheless had serious spiritual concerns. There was a visible cluster who attended the Unitarian Church, and a few others the Society of Friends. Personal spiritual practices were also common, drawing inspiration from workshops, spiritual institutes, and books. Theology and spiritualism were sometimes the basis for closer bonding among friends.

Overall, however, religious expression was considered a private matter and did not figure into group life.

Indeed, values were expressed far less through affiliation with any institution than through day-to-day activities that penetrated time and space throughout the community. Many had vegetable gardens, for example. In this there was a resonating engagement with the cycles of nature that was systematically obscured by packaged foods. Gardens had a tangible social component, since they were common as conversation topics and resources for potlucks. Occasionally in winter, a seed catalog might be brought to the dance, and several people would share a large order. Throughout the growing season, there was talk of the relative progress of everyone's garden—what had sprouted, how the tomatoes were doing, how to outwit predators, what to do with so many zucchini, and so on. A visit to someone's home most always included a moment spent admiring the garden. And this was an important moment: a garden was a part of the aesthetic region of domesticity, neither public space nor a part of the private inner sanctum. So admiring the garden was for a visitor a key transition from public to private, a transition not so easily available at the dance itself. A visitor might even be drawn by urgency to help with some task, fusing self and other in a cycle of common struggle. And all of this was enveloped within shared tangible acts, which pointed to underlying motivations that might or might not be the same.

Most dance group gardens were what Ormond Loomis called "kitchen gardens" (1980: 101), designed to supplement the diet during the growing season. In this, they could be identified unmistakably by the predominance of summer vegetables, including less common ones. Even those few who farmed full-time or earned income from their harvest took their cue from this aesthetic, which favored crops that produced continually during the season over single-harvest crops. For many practical, aesthetic, and ethical reasons, some of the most common traditional southern Indiana farmstead products—such as tobacco, sorghum, grasses, corn, and livestock—were rarely seen on the counter-cultural farms of dancers. Instead, the produce that was grown could be harvested weekly and sold at the Monroe County farmers market—then located in a parking lot south of Third Street and adjacent to the

Old-Time Music and Dance

Jukebox, and later in a lot a block from the Old Library. For some who lived at a distance from town, this might mean bypassing closer markets to come to Bloomington. Bloomington was a larger market, but undoubtedly another important attraction was the social gathering that emerged from the market, which sometimes included music.

For a few years, dumpstering—retrieving edible food from supermarket dumpsters—also became a creative activity. Both gardening and dumpstering addressed broader ecological issues, prevailing against an imposing backdrop of a culture of waste. Gardening imposed the rhythms of nature on individual activity, produced food of a higher nutritional quality than could be purchased, was economical, and used land efficiently. Dumpstering counteracted what was considered the abhorrent practice by supermarkets of throwing away good food for trivial reasons—unsightly but perfectly edible produce or entire boxes of packaged goods whose carton had only slight damage, for example—and then passing the expense on to the customer. Nowadays, the best stores routinely pass such products along to food banks.

While dumpstering may have had this political underpinning, it was sometimes overshadowed by innocent pleasure. Dumpstering was visibly eccentric, provided a pretense of danger, yet, like so much about the dance, could appear entirely utilitarian. In its heyday, dancers loved to talk about and bring dumpster dishes to potluck dinners. Although supermarket employees normally looked the other way, one dancer was once confronted and asked to leave. He suggested that the store representative call the police, a move that would have given the individual access to the newspapers to discuss the store's policies. The employee backed down, and the dancer took what he wanted and left. On another occasion, a stash of high-quality meat was found that had clearly been placed there by an employee for pick-up later. That gardening and dumpstering were related was confirmed by a pair of Bloomington songs written to the same melody: Dillon Bustin's "Gardening" (recorded on Bustin 1983) and Pat Gingrich's humorous but less memorable spoof, "Dumpstering."

Potluck dinners were themselves a staple of Bloomington life, as they were of dance life elsewhere. Caller Sandy Bradley of Seattle, the most widely traveled caller of the late 1970s, titled her recording of that era

Gardening and Dumpstering

Anne Reese, David Bailey, and Laura Ley seeding herbs for replanting. Photo courtesy of Anne Reese and Bruce Cassal.

Potluck and Dance Tonite! (1979). A Cleveland dance leader told Mary Dart that when her group organized an open potluck dinner with the hope of renewing the sense of community, the event had a dramatic effect in producing a "deeper understanding of what we were striving toward" (1995: 175). One could scarcely imagine a simpler, more perfect celebration of community than a huge table filled with home-cooked dishes, resonating with all of the values that food preparation entails. Potlucks could be easily organized and might precede any party or special dance or might serve as the focal event of an open "stragglers" dinner for those who were not spending the holidays with their families. Food preparation was a matter of delight for most households, so that at potlucks carryout dishes (e.g., store-bought fried chicken) might never be seen at all. There were always plenty of vegetarian dishes, often made from Spartan recipes like those from the *Diet for a Small Planet* (1971) generation of cookbooks, and always enough vegetarians to eat them. I remember learning to make the ever-popular oatmeal-raisin cookies, which over the years morphed into nameless varieties with the addition of whatever various whole grains, dried fruits, and nuts were on hand. Overall there was an enormous store of knowledge of food preparation, fostered by the fertile atmosphere of potlucks and grounded in the use of fresh raw ingredients.

The culture of food was also inspired by the local member-owned food co-op, Bloomingfoods, which opened a storefront business in 1976. Located in an alley a half block north of Kirkwood, the co-op provided a wealth of resources for food preparation, many of which were, at the time, unheard-of in mainstream circles. The store was open to the public, but many joined as co-op members in order to receive discounts and other privileges. "Working membership" provided a greater level of discount in exchange for a few hours' work each week. The co-op sold fresh produce, kitchen equipment, toiletries, and books and newsletters, but the centerpiece of the store was a lengthy row of "bulk bins" in which organic grains, pasta, dried fruit, nuts, and so forth were sold at bulk prices. Learning to use these ingredients was a core component in countercultural food preparation education.

There was a high regard for used or vintage clothing and a collective effort to find the best resale outlets in cities where dances were held. In Bloomington, a popular vintage clothing store was operated by dancers Mitch and Eileen Rice. Some musicians and dancers—particularly women—would pass on clothing they no longer wanted to other dancers or sell it on consignment through vintage stores. Vintage attire was frequently well made and in excellent condition but had merely passed out of fashion. Some people mail-ordered clothing from plain religious orders, knowing that it was designed for comfort and endurance. Men would sometimes accumulate a collection of breezy vintage cotton shirts for summer dancing. Until sometime in the mid-1980s when manufacturers resumed the general use of cotton and rayon, these and other natural-fiber items were not easy to find. Most retailers, responding to market preferences, stocked clothing made only with what I sometimes heard referred to as "bullet-proof polyester." Once again, the consequence of these practices was a mix of efficient use of resources, access to better quality, and frugality. But also, a homemade dress or vintage shirt was likely to be noticed and admired. Just as the body in social

Gardening and Dumpstering

dance articulated community relationships and structure, the body articulated its values through clothing and food.

For many, low-rent housing was both prestigious and efficient. Several dancers lived for years rent free or in return for work. For almost a decade, I rented a small log house with a garage and sizable yard for $95 per month, well below the going rate. A prized location might be passed on to another dancer, "keeping it in the group." I "inherited" my log house from Fuzzy Mountain fiddler and folklorist Tom Carter. House-sitting for other dancers during lengthy absences was not uncommon; occasionally an individual would stay in several such locations in sequence. Dancers also shared group houses with one another. Sometimes household institutions were conspicuously maintained, such as vegetarian cooking, no smoking, or a common liking for holding dance parties. Some group houses became associated with dancers over a period of time; the "Boys' Club," above a storefront on Sixth Street, was so named for the group of male friends who lived there. The celebrated "green house" was a co-housing arrangement of friends. If someone was new to town or moving, they could expect to get help at the dance by announcing, "I'm looking for a place to live, if anybody knows of anything," or by making the same request individually.

The most distinctive homes were rural. The most exotic was surely the tree house that Barry Kern and Linda Higginbotham built. Jim Johnson and Nancy McKinley operated an organic farm, called Possumwood Farm, where they grew vegetables, raised free-range chickens, and boiled maple syrup. The most prosperous cash crop was cucumbers, which they sold to a pickle manufacturer. Allen Paton was easily the most resilient farmer. Leaving behind a career in mental health, he established farms on a series of properties and was a regular vendor at the farmers market for many years. Many others designed, built, rented, or remodeled rural houses while pursuing various careers.

Most city dwellers chose frame houses in older neighborhoods south or west of the campus. There were several dance crowd "neighborhoods" where small clusters of renters and owners lived. With friends close at hand, small social gatherings could be assembled on short notice. Bungalow architecture was common, and in this, there is little doubt that social features figured as prominently as economical ones. Scott Sanders has painted an extravagant picture of the features of Bloomington bungalows that would intuitively have been attractive to dance crowd residents:

> Unlike the chilly castles rising now in our suburbs, standing far apart in bland expanses of chemically treated grass, these cottages and bungalows nestle close to one another and close to the street, inviting visitors. Don't the wide porches make you want to climb the front steps and sit for a while in a rocker or swing? The sidewalks are thronged with kids, and the air is thronged with birds. Listen, and you'll hear laughter and talk, the sound of a hammer striking nails or a shovel striking dirt, the run of scales on a cello or guitar, the rattling of a spoon in a bowl.
>
> . . . These neighborhoods date from before the triumph of the automobiles, when we still used our bodies to get around, and before the triumph of television, when we still made our own entertainment, and before air conditioning sealed up our houses like tombs. They speak of the city as a place where people gather not merely for the exchange of goods and services but for the pleasure of one another's company. (Sanders 2002: 10–11)

There was a cluster around 12th Street just east of Walnut, and another around Lincoln north of Hillside. When prices there were inflated after the mid-1980s, a neighborhood sprang up on the west side, a half-dozen blocks west of the square.

Dance group owners of these homes were often avid remodelers and drew from the pool of skilled carpenters for large projects. Upkeep projects such as roofing and plumbing were common, but so were modifications particularly suited to dance group needs. The most distinctive modification was "knocking out a wall," usually between the dining room and back bedroom, so as to provide a space long enough for dancing. Although only a few couples would fit, this space provided the foundation for the best parties, with informal music and dance that could stretch into the night without limit.

Travel was another opportunity for cooperative effort. Bloomington dancers often carpooled to popular out-of-town events, making the necessary arrangements at the dance. They also housed visitors to the Bloomington dance or dancers who were visiting for any reason, and they expected the same hospitality elsewhere. Although it was unusual,

I once received a cold call from a California couple who had looked up my name in the published Country Dance and Song Society roster: they were passing through the area and wanted a place to stay. Most often, some kind of prior relationship, common acquaintance, or sponsored event was a prerequisite condition for a housing request. At a large event, one anticipated sleeping on the floor, often crowded with other sleepers, and brought along a sleeping bag.

Prices at dance events were kept low. At the Wednesday Night Dance, anonymous donations were taken, sometimes averaging less than one dollar per dancer. Discussions of prices invariably included the desire not to exclude anyone who could not pay. Tom Morrison—the organizer of Swing into Spring, a weekend of dance that included breakfast and two nights' sleeping space at a rented state park facility—was chided facetiously when after seven years he raised his price from $5 to $7. Sugar Hill, Bloomington's other dance weekend, which provided four meals and sleeping space for a weekend, raised its prices from $15 to $20 in the early 1980s but made the increase optional so as not to impinge upon the needy. Those attending paid whatever in the $15–$20 range they felt they could afford; most paid $20. Such prices were probably the nation's lowest for dance events of their type, a fact that contributed to Bloomington's reputation as a dance community. Some dancers in these formative years even aspired to keep the accumulated treasury low so as not to ever have to decide what to do with it.

Low prices were sometimes related explicitly to commitment. In discussions of price setting, it was invariably assumed or brought up that work was donated by most everyone. A familiar Sugar Hill maxim went, "No one gets paid and everyone pays to get in." This was impossible, of course, regarding goods and services unavailable within the group. Consequently, the problem was only deferred to the qualifier "within the group," raising the question of who counts as a group member. A professional caterer who also attended occasional Wednesday Night Dances was once paid for some prepared food for Sugar Hill. Word of this lapse spread through the community, and there was discontent over even this minor deviation from practice. In planning sessions immediately thereafter, the story became a warning against future oversights of this type. Thus despite the group's self-image as open and democratic, it is not the case that the distasteful problem of enumeration was eliminated (e.g., by the absence of recognized membership). Instead, it was merely deferred to these social mini-dramas—at first circumscribed by a breech (catered salads) of some limited yet popular cause ("No one gets paid . . .") and then expanded by redressive action to apparently unilateral effects and values.

Yet what exactly was prohibited at this threshold? Not the dancer. Not the food. Not even the catering, which might be acceptable given other circumstances. What was proscribed, rather, was the creation of excess value in ritual exercises designed precisely around the indeterminateness of giving. And this prohibition of excess value was held above everything—sexuality, marriage, dance, aesthetics, intellectual property—and was the chief guarantor of authentic experience. It was the very palpability of the utopian order. It was important because excess value opened itself to the necessity of second-order activities (e.g., protecting, wasting, stealing), to the necessity of a political order to accomplish these tasks, and to the necessity of retributive justice—the very artifacts of modernity that the dance was designed to preempt. And if catered salads resurrected the problem of counting or enumeration of "members," it was still not a matter of counting in or counting out. It was merely counting, uninscribing the limits of the individual from which an excess could even be recognized.

Of all the practices that emerged from the vague communal ethos of the early years, admission and reimbursement policies were always the most divisive. There was always dissent; there were always realms of experience outside the referential expanse of catered salads and other such social texts. By the end of the 1980s, the communal ideal had lost much of its vitality over this issue alone.

This panoply of rituals of identity embodied the ideology of old-time music and dance without ever explicitly expressing any doctrine. Taken as a group, these rituals were so eccentric, so labor intensive, and so austere that they were able to circumscribe a coalition of like-minded participants without ever identifying the ideological underpinnings that were shared. They provided the means of shared, purposeful identity

Gardening and Dumpstering

coupled with a sense of boundless personal freedom. This was possible in large part because the guardians of the mainstream had much invested in genteel social conventions with which old-time music and dance were palpably at odds.

12 THE BEAN KING

On the surface these rituals of identity could seem austere or eccentric. But what made them entirely unoppressive was the way they were so relentlessly enveloped by celebration. There was indeed so much to celebrate, and most any celebration was quickly swept up as an affirmation of community. The most common occasion was birthdays. Of the major calendar celebrations that were begun before the 1980s, only two (Swing into Spring and May Day) did not originate in some way from birthdays.

There was something fundamental about birthdays as celebratory occasions in the dance group. Everyone had one, after all. Although some individual in the dance group was singled out for the honor, it was not always clear if the celebration was held *for* the person or *by* the person. If someone decided to hold a dance group birthday party and announced the event at the dance, they would be expected to have a potluck and a dance that lasted late into the night.

Many dancers lived in the small frame houses that so populate older sections of Bloomington. There dancing was usually in an unpartitioned two-room space, such as an unpartitioned living room and dining room, that would fit a single contra line of eight or so couples with the band

Dance at a party at Ted Hall's house. Ted had "knocked out a wall" so that a dance line could extend over the span of two rooms. There was a nine-couple limit for dance sets imposed by the reigning Bean King, Tom Morrison. From left: Molly Gregory, Ted Hall, unknown, Martha Marmouzé, Allen Lombardi, Bill Meek, Teri Klassen. Photo courtesy of Gary Stanton.

and caller at the end. Sometimes not a thought was given to gifts or a cake. In these respects, dance crowd birthdays seemed well designed to refashion the conventional relationship between individual and group that birthday celebrations routinely articulated.

The most important birthday parties became regular events, and some even outlived their association with the birthday that they were designed to celebrate. Ted Hall held a party each year on his birthday, which over time became an obligation to host a calendar celebration. Sugar Hill was first held around a cluster of August birthdays yet quickly lost its attachment to that circumstance. Another was the January 7, 1976, birthday of Bill "Pigweed" Ryan, which eventually became, famously, an explicit inversion of conventional birthday practice. The 7th was a Wednesday that year, so Andy Mahler baked a cake for Pigweed and brought it to Rapp's after the dance. But January 6, the day before the birthday, was the Epiphany. Recalling the New Orleans "king cake" tradition of hiding an object in a cake to arbitrarily select a king (a tradition related to the practice that inspired Sir James George Frazer's encyclopedic *Golden Bough*), Andy baked a bean in his cake. The cake was cut, all pieces were distributed, and Frank Hall discovered the bean in his piece of cake.

Apparently, an annual "Bean King" tradition evolved rather quickly from this initial event, for in 1977, the second year, Mark Feddersen composed a song which was sung in the moments before the cake was eaten that year and every year thereafter. The arbitrary Bean King, who was expected to host the party the next year, had dutifully replaced Pigweed Ryan as the reason for the party. And each year a new verse was added to the song, making some comment about the outgoing king's reign. The song soon grew lengthy and served as a kind of oral history for the group, recounting events from years long past whose retelling each January 6 became a source of much amusement. The text was highly elliptical, of course, providing vague references to events rich in significance for those who had experienced them. The most recent version, with forty quatrains (!), has been published on the dance group's web page (http://www.bloomington.in.us/botmdg/) and includes a four-verse "recitative" defending the song's length and the necessity, in explicit deference to tradition over expedience, of singing all forty verses at the party.

Every Bean Party had its own story, but for many years 1980 was considered very unusual. The previous year, Amy Novick had won her second successive crown, a highly unlikely feat that cast a mood of scrutiny on the 1980 event. So all were shocked when the cake was eaten and no one found the bean! Customarily, even a slight delay in claiming the bean aroused suspicion that someone had swallowed it to avoid detection. Others contended that the bean had disintegrated and offered instructions for maintaining its integrity during cooking.

The matter had to be settled, so a second party was held, this time at Dave and Gail Ehrich's home in rural Brown County. Amy baked another cake, making absolutely certain the bean was included, and *again* no bean was claimed! Confusion held sway for a while, and then the matter was settled with dispatch. A square dance was about to be called when Dave shouted from the kitchen that a draw from a deck of cards—the queen of spades—would decide the question. Mark was at the head of a square dance set, waiting for the dance to start. Paul Tyler was to call the next dance and, as was the practice, swapped places in the square with Mark in order to call from the first position. Paul drew the queen in the place Mark had just vacated. Mark's role as a near miss is one that someone experiences each year. The Bean King song recorded the event as follows, alluding also to Paul as a folklorist and to the party he held in his house, where he had recently scraped off old linoleum tile:

> King Paul was the Fourth, they call the "Old Maid,"
> Since he drew not a bean, but the Lady of Spades.
> While he's studied the Classics and collected folklore,
> At the end of his reign he was scraping the floor.

It should not be difficult to imagine the way momentum gathered around the Bean King ceremony. Throughout the year, so much of dance group celebration was tangibly egalitarian. Here was the singular erection of group authority, and it was entirely ironic. It was yet another randomizing device, catapulting some unsuspecting group member to enduring celebrity entirely by accident. Yet even "celebrity" was ironic: in the song, Mark Feddersen was truly adept at reducing a king's reign to "scraping the floor" or some other scenario of inverted status.

At the Bean Party, following the song, the pieces of cake were distributed and held until the call to eat. This was an anxious wait, an enduring moment contemplating all about food that was not food, bringing into sharp relief that which nourished the physical and the social body. The bean itself was social excess—attention, authority, celebrity, responsibility. Those in the group who were customarily ambitious were routinely suspected of secretly wanting to get the bean and were thought to be frustrated each year they failed. Those who shunned attention and responsibility and didn't want the bean were thought to expend needless worry. Once, an infant, Ewan Schmid, got the bean; another time it was a stranger—someone who came to the Bean Party without ever having attended a dance. All of this to think about before the solitary moment of tasting, of swallowing, and, for one, spitting out the bean, as pure distinction of self and other, of social excess and social nourishment.

The Bean Party, 1985, at the home of Tamara Loewenthal and Tom Sparks, during the song. Seated, from left, Ewan Schmid (reigning Bean King, with the crown), Mark Feddersen (singing from the printed lyrics), Amy Novick, Claudio Buchwald, Paul Tyler (on guitar), Frank Hall, Mary Beth Roska, Clancy Clements, Susan Hollis, Teri Klassen. Standing near doorway, Melanie Chalom, Tamara Loewenthal, Laura Ley, Emma Rice, Tom Stio, Ted Hall. Others unknown. Photo courtesy of Tom Morrison.

And before this moment, the distribution itself was a public act of counting, a decision by "everyone" made for "everyone" that determined exactly who "everyone" was. And discursively, "everyone" was there, for "no one" would have dared plan some rival event. Invariably, there were squabbles over when to cut the cake—early so the children could get a piece, or late when the "old-timers" arrived. There was considerable effort (though never dispute!) involved in cutting the cake into the exact number of pieces as the tally of guests at the party. Though some declined to eat, no one was denied a piece, no matter his or her circum-

The Bean King

The Bean Party, 1985, a moment later, after Cliff Emery finds the bean. In his left hand, he displays the bean for all to see. Photo courtesy of Tom Morrison.

stance. The only prerequisite, according to the song: "Your teeth must be strong, and your eyes very keen." Thus the risk was entirely palpable that, because of this extravagant impartiality, the reign might fall to some peripheral person: the chorus of the song, sung after each verse, proclaimed, "be ye man, maid, or child, you're the king of the bean." Here was the utopian community—staking its future on this eccentric ceremony of renewal of the collective. To belong, the most precious asset of the group, was now as simple as holding a piece of cake in one's hand, waiting for the instruction to eat.

Or was it? There was a biting aphorism one would hear occasionally, that to genuinely belong at the dance necessitated a process called "breaking into the group." Truly, the dance's structures were simple and egalitarian, but they also were elliptical. It was never certain what "breaking into the group" meant, but I think that it went along these

Old-Time Music and Dance

lines: to participate was easy, but to matter was difficult. On the dance floor, this might mean being asked to dance, or being asked to dance frequently, or, more likely, having other dancers respond to one's style and creativity. In conversation, it might mean being able to count upon others to care about what you were saying. For a musician, it might mean having others learn your tunes. Once, at a party during my early awkward years in the group, I remember asking if I could join a euchre game that had a recently vacated place. "Do you know how to play?" I remember being abruptly asked and then abruptly advised: "Euchre is a kind of difficult game."

The difficulty, as I would learn, was not so much the game itself as the interplay of camaraderie and competition that was always more satisfying in long-sustained friendships. Like so much else about the dance, euchre is actually not difficult. I remember quickly absorbing the subtleties, getting a lucky draw my first few hands, and enjoying an initial run of winning. But like the dance, euchre provided a sustained moment of co-significance with a partner. As with the dance, in the long run, winning just didn't matter. I thought it did, and I eventually lost interest and stopped playing.

Veteran dancers and old friends did understand this better than others and naturally were inclined to want to be together. But, for important reasons, this posture did not spill over into policy. If anything, this exclusionary backdrop was an important restraint on the influence on casually involved newcomers. Likewise, the group's deliberate and tangible openness kept some level of experience readily available to everyone. Indeed, the dance depended on co-presence, not merely because of its tolerant, egalitarian ideology but also as nourishment for the power of its unconventional, inverted symbols.

To avoid the necessity of overt exclusion, in fact, the flow of newcomers was controlled by a proscription against advertising. A cautionary tale periodically circulated among dancers about the time the Indianapolis newspaper ran a feature story on the Bloomington dance. The next week a horde of beginners came to the dance, and it took several months for them to be integrated into the group such that the dance once again "flowed smoothly." Most often the subject of advertising arose when recent converts, overcome with enthusiasm, would suggest

The Bean King

"getting the word out" in the newspapers. Right or wrong, it was difficult for new dancers to understand the rationale of this prohibition.

Later, when the dance weekends Sugar Hill and Swing into Spring grew to the capacity of their facilities, there was more discussion of exclusion. Elsewhere this problem has become widespread, and most every group that hosts a weekend dance has had to confront problems with overcrowded facilities. When the matter first arose at the Bloomington dance weekends, the suggestion to limit or eliminate advertising was explicitly measured against alternatives: controlling attendance by raising prices would favor those who had the most money, whereas installing a pre-registration system that awarded admission by date of application or by lottery would reward fastidiousness.

Neither of these alternatives encouraged qualities that the group held in very high esteem. A pre-registration system would have preempted the friendship channels already in place. What if someone was invited by a friend and then couldn't get in? What if someone decided spontaneously to drop by and visit with friends? Pre-registration would also have introduced bureaucracy into what was then an uncomplicated gathering of friends. In contrast, merely forgoing certain information networks was itself much in keeping with the prevailing ethos. In its consequences, it favored those whose spiritual strivings brought them eventually into the compass of the operating friendship network. Still, some who later learned of this practice after having difficulty finding the dance did resent the process, particularly the idea that it might have been advanced with premeditation.

Avoiding exclusion by excluding the excluded. Including everyone by excluding everyone else. Naturally, such an idea was patently absurd; equally naturally, this was precisely the logic that prevailed under the utopian banner. By the end of the 1980s, when postmodern democracy had eclipsed liberal populism as the prevailing societal ethos, most dances turned to pre-registration and lotteries—radical capitalization— as a solution to most any problem. Indeed, radical capitalization exceeded every prevailing standard of fairness and equality. It was an attractive solution to the growing problems of privacy and liability. It replaced the ideology of tolerance with tolerance of ideology. Because its fundamental ritual of in-corporation was the admission charge, it generated more income and led to ever more extravagant celebration. And it was easy. Capitalization seemed to leap as a reflex to the solution of any problem.

In a different form the problem of exclusion arose in the use of dance space at the dance weekends. It was sometimes suggested, to alleviate the over-filled dance halls at Sugar Hill or Swing into Spring, that a second dance be held, simultaneously, in a building a short walk away. But this suggestion was most always rejected: it would lead to competition and, besides, "everyone" wanted to be together in one place. A few even advanced overcrowding as a deterrent, noting that many dancers would avoid weekends where good dancing is stifled by a crowded floor. But unlike the strategy of avoiding publicity, it was never suggested that overcrowding had any affinity to dance crowd values. In its lucid distillation of this approach, one could do little better than to look to Tom Morrison's solution for Swing into Spring: over the years that overcrowding was an issue, Tom developed a sense of just how many flyers to distribute to fill the hall exactly to capacity.

These subtle measures evolved with the object of keeping an unqualified open access at the group's most visible points of entry, while at the same time maintaining a coherence of values by the most indirect means possible. In a sense, this articulated one of the most fundamental social premises of the Bloomington dance: that for well over a decade, the group was consumed by celebration and by the desire to have the dance "flow smoothly." This illusion of consensus was accomplished not by isolation and restraint from within, as with marginalized religious sects. That is, the dance did not entirely withdraw from society—its inverted symbols depended for their vitality on proximity to the mainstream. Nor was its coherence protected by regimentation and exclusion, as with secret societies and status groups. In sum, the dance never sought to keep people in or out. Rather, it maintained its symbolic integrity by relentlessly saturating the immediate field of significance with inverted symbols that were widely and mutually accessible.

This is what produced the seemingly odd circumstance that comparatively rigid forms like contra and square dance would be enjoyed as anarchistic experience. Like the distribution of the bean cake, the dance contrived discrete and profoundly simple roles for its participants and

The Bean King

left largely to serendipity the determination of how these roles would be populated. In those formative years, this equation of freedom and serendipity propelled the social engine of the dance as a self-motivating institution.

13 THE INDIANA CONTRA DANCERS' LAMENT

Of all the sites where exclusion, consensus, transgression, and identity were negotiated, style held a special place because of its accessibility and potency. Particularly after the nationwide dance network took shape in the 1980s, dancers became more aware of the way dance style and performance practice articulated relations within the community. From this, there emerged a catalog of dance floor transgressions. Many of these were reported by dance leaders to Mary Dart and detailed in her book on contra dance and community (1995: 163–98).

There was, for example, the notorious "center set syndrome," an exquisite ritual of exclusion so named by East Coast dancers, whereby "good" dancers would scramble to find one another as partners and rush to the head of the center set (Dart 1995: 168; see also Dalsemar 1988). Concentrated in the center set, they could hope to enjoy various subtleties, such as the brief tug of the arm just before pulling into a swing. Or the knowledge of one's established personal preferences—to swing with a walking step, a buzz step, or the obscure Bloomington skip step that might identify them as veterans. Or the idea of "giving weight" to make circular motions smooth and fast, a notion that eluded rank beginners but that could be learned with only a little coaching. Or even improvisatory swing dance moves when idle at the end of a set. Yet the social stratification toward which this urge pointed could only undermine the risk and danger of the arbitrary dyadic encounter—not to mention the egalitarian promise of community—that was fundamental to old-time music and dance. No wonder, then, that it was thought a transgression.

More often Bloomington embraced a code of charity toward its new dancers, so much so that the periodic hue and cry was raised less against the ineptness of beginners than against the intolerance of veterans. If there was snobbery, in fact, it was more often directed at callers or musicians who were trying to get the group to cooperate with some newfangled or difficult idea. If a caller was insensitive or too insistent, a set of four dancers, even one including beginners, might change the dance spontaneously by one from the set calling their own more appeal-ing figures on the fly. This was entirely acceptable as an "orthodox stunt," as Tolman and Page had put it, designed to repel the too-decorous effects of a "chiding prompter" (1937: 19–21). All of this might have been perplexing to a beginning dancer: that it was a good thing to know something of the code of style, but as good to know that this was not really what mattered.

In spite of genuine and sometimes urgent concern for good style, there was never a breakthrough into explicit policy. There were never auditions or required levels of experience, and most everyone was aware of the effects of such practices on club square dancing. In Bloomington, it was even a troubling matter to call an "advanced" dance. If the overall "quality of dancing" became a problem for the group, Bill Meek might volunteer to teach his "Improve Your Contra" workshop, and it would be advertised with particular dancers secretly in mind. Old-time dance, after all, had originally been embraced deferentially—as tradition, as received wisdom, yet as something intangible apart from communal practice. Without recourse to higher authority, unresolvable stylistic quirks were ultimately inscribed onto their originator and tolerated. Enclaves of like-minded dancers emerged around matters of style, and those with unconventional or antisocial styles became caricatures of themselves. Because they had developed protective personalities, many persisted in their behavior, were accepted and even socialized, and be-came community leaders for having learned both sensitivity and

Old–Time Music and Dance

strength from their experiences. All of this from the inconceivability of counting anyone out, from the imponderable obligation to weather all storms together.

Consequently, more due to habit than deliberate effort, dancing in Bloomington grew to be very, very good. It was also idiosyncratic, perhaps as a consequence of incorporating stylistic innovation. This was a quality with which some, like Chicagoan Mark Gunther, had been impressed. Bloomington dancers, he said, "had a wonderful way of moving. Their posture and their style of movement was both individual and regional, and was probably mostly derived from very traditional New England sources. It was a kind of stride. I used to think of it as the Bloomington stride" (Kent 1997: 12).

In the early years of the revival, no stylistic transgressions were discussed so exhaustively as those condensed in the nagging problem of the twirl. In Bloomington, the twirl so exclusively incorporated style controversy that it almost seems to have been invented precisely to stand for the undercurrent of other troubles that lay in wait. The problem was that the twirl—where a woman turns under a man's arm, sometimes several times so that she spins—was not officially a dance figure. (The "California twirl" is a figure in squares, however, and may have been the origin of the twirl as an improvised move.) Rather, it was an entrenched, widely recognized, and easily learned stylistic option that could be attached to several called figures without, some would say, disrupting the dance. I remember it initially, in the 1970s, as a ritual of mild subversion that two dancers could spontaneously contrive. But it did indeed become popular, for its subversive qualities, for the sense of stylistic accomplishment, and for the mutual pleasure, possibly romantic, of having smoothly cooperated to manage it. Problems arose, however, when possibility became expectation: in a single dance, the question "to twirl or not to twirl" might arise a hundred times. The move was so simple, but it did require an abrupt measure of initiative and cooperation.

Compounding the twirl's unpredictability was the fact that its gender neutrality was not near so certain as in other figures—more than any other movement, the twirl featured decisively different movements for each dancer. Indeed it seemed to accommodate rather than neutralize

The Indiana Contra Dancers' Lament

gender. If the dancer in the man's position was taller, then his partner could more easily turn under his raised arm. If the dancer in the woman's position wore a skirt, it would whirl wildly as she spun. Where much else about dance structure was suited to a subculture striving to make gender not matter, the twirl provided a decisive lapse into essentialist metaphysics. Ultimately other figures were identified as harboring innate gender bias (see Dart 1995: 184–92), but in Bloomington's formative years, so much attention was focused on the twirl.

More broadly, it did not escape notice that while music and dance communities generally aspired to utopian feminism, they could not have chosen a more gender-stratified social apparatus for their social experiment. One can scarcely imagine the vast ironic distance that opened when radically liberated dancers, many of whom devoted much energy to evading traditional gender roles in everyday life, stepped into positions explicitly labeled as "ladies" or "gents." Yet this was precisely what happened, and it was the genius of traditional dance revival to have adopted a rigidly stratified structure that could be undermined so exquisitely by subversive ritual performance. Ordinarily the scripted figures of set dance made it easy to undermine the tyranny of the gendered body. The twirl, on the other hand, demanded unscripted cooperation.

If it worked well, the twirl was a masterpiece of finesse. In a split second, a tug or push of the hand would suggest the move, and a responding tug might indicate resistance, cooperation, or escalation. Escalation could, in turn, be redoubled, and redoubled again, always with the risk of failure. What must have proved most satisfying was for both dancers to have briefly given up control, to have transcended their intentions, to have achieved some new and dangerous sense of self and other, to have been given over to movement that exceeded the sovereign self yet that was itself sovereign as dance. And this achievement was so desperately fragile: with little effort, one dancer's reality could prevail upon the other's, and as David Kaynor so aptly put it, "preempt the experience" (Dart 1995: 188).

This was scarcely a mechanical matter, and its unpredictability as a stylistic option is precisely what made it so potent as a site of negotiation. The successful twirl depended on all predispositions that were brought to the dance. Status, skill, even momentary attitude and state of health—any of these could undermine the twirl. Yet nothing really circumscribed the twirl. These predispositions were not limits but, rather, the very boundaries that the twirl was designed to transcend in the moment of surrender. And in the groove of cooperative spontaneity, indeed, there were no limits. The twirl's potency derived from the abdication of conventional boundaries between self and other at precisely the moment—the unscripted moment of the twirl—when these boundaries were most necessary. Pure difference, the difference of the other, without the conventionally ascribed (e.g., gender) markers. "Supposing you were someone else?" wrote Dudley Laufman from the precipice of transgression, yet only through the complicity of presumption could one know or even experience the limits of the "who?" of the other.

For these reasons, however, the twirl all too easily *became* mechanical. If limits appeared, already having been exceeded, they might well have to be accounted for. This accounting was to character or style but often also to transcendent gender: the man initiated and the woman responded, and the roles of "twirling" and "being twirled" were said to *come from* gender. Without much effort at all, the twirl grew to become associated with the very conventional role expectations that many dancers originally sought to escape. With good reason, women complained—as women—of "having their arms ripped off." Transgression of cooperative spontaneity was transformed into gendered transgression.

Beginners' instruction in the twirl customarily involved only the rudiments: most often, the textbook instruction "the man turns the woman under his arm" was used. At first this instruction was looked upon with unproblematic deference to tradition. But dancers were increasingly inclined to want to disencumber the instructional language from its gender burdens, so the phrase was changed periodically to "the woman turns under the man's arm." The implication, and the desire, were to avert any suggestion that dance was the manifestation of male privilege. The intended movement was to be accomplished cooperatively, as if it wasn't to be determined in advance which was the more assertive role, as if it didn't matter which gender had which role.

My assessment of this period is that the twirl—because it was unscripted and interactive—mapped key elements of the defining social ethos of the dance. It was the moment in dance where most was at risk,

The Indiana Contra Dancers' Lament

where the utopian experiment was completely exposed. At the peak of its significance, by virtue of the unifying desire for unpreempted experience, the twirl was the centerpiece of the moment of dance. A moment wholly dependent on the fragile admonition of natural morality, which dancers hoped and believed would prevail in a free and open society. A moment where the ego was liberated from the burdens of alienated social reality, from all the social categories by which regulated behavior emanated, and fused with its divine origin. A moment grossly over-determined yet absolutely unpresumed, a moment with immense risk yet without loss. A moment that extended all of subjectivity—the vulnerability and openness of the self extracted from its protective orbit of substance.

During the early years of the dance, the gap between mainstream gender conventions and the social ethos of the dance was vast, so that the dance did seem more of a refuge from all that was before it. I remember dancing as if a neutral self were trapped inside a gendered body, as if dance were a way to let it out. And if this was merely a personal utopia, it was also one that I learned from the dance and from other dancers, most of whom seemed to believe that we all had uncovered some deep-buried truth that could only be known through the experience we all shared.

Only after the capitalization of dance revival, which no one seemed to think was itself a gendered movement, did dance emerge from naiveté to reveal unmanageable faults. By "capitalization" I mean the myriad of sociopolitical devices—representative democracy, boards of directors, membership status, liability insurance, non-profit tax status, standard admission charges, organizational affiliations, elected officers—whose categorical absence was once essential to music and dance experience. These devices constituted a gendered polity that deferred risk and responsibility throughout a hierarchical body politic, that introduced exchange into the economy of pleasure, and that neutralized identity such that gender manifested difference as a kind of font of original sin. Without the prerequisite of utopian aspiration, one could not be sure what were the other's motives, and every articulation of difference was exposed to the burden of gender and to the always-imminent danger of gendered transgression.

Genuine transgression, in fact, was once thought absurd. Even the botched twirl associated with "having one's arm ripped off" was ultimately a matter of infelicity—though perhaps, if it persisted, assigned to a grotesque masculinity derived from lack of gender enlightenment. So, for having done it, there was call for complaint, but no possibility of retribution or remedy. Indeed, dancers thought prone to such aggressiveness could endure for years. As with other stylistic transgressions, they were caricatured, thus amplifying the offense and assigning motive. Naturally, stylistic caricature became an expressive genre, designed to maintain both the utopian ethos and its imperfections. As narrative, caricature traversed an arch of genres that moved the transgression from offense to acceptance, appearing first as complaint or confession, later as humorous acceptance.

The amusing consequences of stylistic infelicities all converged in a famous example affixed to Bloomington. After the mid-1970s, when dancers began traveling to other groups and events, they began noticing immediately that the execution of the "balance" figure in Bloomington and related Midwest dance communities was startlingly idiosyncratic. Elsewhere, with rare exception, the figure was a step-right-and-kick-left. Dillon Bustin taught the figure in Bloomington as step-left-and-kick-right, and that is how it came to be done. Some attributed this oddity to a simple mental error on Dillon's part. Others, recognizing his somewhat mischievous attitude toward the matter, said he did it on purpose. Still others noted that it was also the style in some parts of Massachusetts, and they believed that Dillon learned it that way.

Whatever its source, it became prevalent in the Midwest and came to be singled out as an island of Midwest idiosyncrasy in a sea of nation-wide conformity. When two dancers performed the figure in the two different styles, they kicked in the same direction toward one another, not across one another, as was normally the case. Although actual contact was rare, even the most subtle movement of this nature was easily noticeable as a rupture of the delicate coordination of personal space.

Inevitably, the extraordinary fantasy of a collision and its social fallout preyed upon creative minds. It was in this spirit that Indianapolis's Eddie Grogan composed, in the form of a traditional folk ballad, the exquisite "Indiana Contra Dancer's Lament" (Grogan 1984). In it

The Indiana Contra Dancers' Lament

Sweet Willie from Indiana travels to New Hampshire and is smitten there with love for Fair Nancy the contra dancer. During their first dance together, he naively executes the Hoosier balance and kicks her in the shin. So wounded is she, physically and psychically, that she rejects him. Willie returns home heartbroken, bearing the grim admonition:

> Oh, come all you dancers from Indiana
> Come and take warning of which I do sing
> If ever you're dancing outside Indiana
> Step right and kick left when you balance and swing.

This is an absurd and hilarious narrative. Its incongruous effects rely heavily upon the grossly overdetermined left balance. Yet mutual pleasure in dance could indeed be undermined by overdetermination. Dancers did make pilgrimages to southern New Hampshire. Dancers did hope sometimes beyond hope that their moment together would go well. Dancers did engage their partners with romantic expectation. And all of these could converge to burden a moment so that a trifling gaffe could erupt into transgression. One can laugh unabashedly at Sweet Willie, knowing the innocent cause of his error—but one might laugh less were he to have been genuinely uncouth or aggressive.

In fact, overdetermination had to do with everything. Aesthetic pleasure, flirtation, transgression, absurd incongruity, moral community— all of these derived their intensity from the overdetermination, the ambiguity, and the extraordinary risk of the moment of dance. But this moment was also, as dance, a moment not linked intrinsically to any promise outside itself. The absurd incongruity of the "Indiana Contra Dancer's Lament" is its status as a lament: encroaching somber tones, enhanced by the artfully plodding ballad structure and the brooding minor melody, stand abruptly alien to the outrageous and unlamentable pleasure of dance as a sovereign moment. Its sovereign pleasure was not indebted to Willie's expectations or to any future moment they anticipated. One could take genuine mirthful pleasure in Willie's absurd desire because, unlike in conventional society, it was circumscribed by dance and by the utopian limits he clearly understands. Willie, after all, accepts rejection and returns home, as all along he is expected to do.

His motives are extraordinary but not intractable, as all along they are expected to be. And all that took him to New Hampshire has now brought him back home, humble but not humiliated, still alive with absurd desire that is absurdly insignificant in the sovereign purity of the moment of dance.

The Indiana Contra Dancers' Lament

14  THE GANG OF FOUR

When I arrived in Bloomington in 1976, I had already been dancing for several years and had been involved in several organizations that promoted folksong performance. But in Bloomington I sensed an astonishing difference in the concerns of the group and in the understanding of the group as a social and political entity. I would later learn that this was a crucial year when identity and structure became more of a conscious issue in the group.

Mostly during that year, during the Jukebox era, there was a series of meetings at which issues of group structure were openly discussed. There was one meeting at Donna Doughten's house and at least two at the Fourth-and-Jefferson home of Stan Sitko and Toby Bonwit. Stan and Toby, with Barry Kern, had built a large porch suitable for warm-weather dancing; thus their house became a common meeting place during the years that they lived there. Until just before they moved out, however, there was still no door to the porch, and dancers grew accustomed to climbing through the window to get from the kitchen to the porch to dance. Another meeting was held at Frank Hall's "Boys' Club" apartment on Sixth Street. Frank had moved quickly to the social and cultural center of the group, absorbing a variety of song- and dance-related skills. Consequently, his apartment also became the site of frequent activity. Something of the flavor of dance crowd meetings should be inferred from all of this: that they were not regularly held but arranged ad hoc around issues of importance, and that meeting sites were chosen for their proximity to, not their distance from, the celebratory social life of the group.

The issues raised then, and yet unsettled, were musicianship, finances, and leadership. Music at the dance, some claimed, was occasionally out of control and difficult to dance to. Money was only marginally important at the time but became an issue after the group treasury was established. But underlying these issues were differing ideas about the basic social structure of the group. Since the first time Dillon Bustin left Bloomington and a grassroots movement swelled to fill the void, an anarchistic mood had prevailed at the dance. Some group members, fitting nicely within the larger counterculture ideology, felt that leaders were not to be trusted, and that structure was stifling to creativity, festivity, and friendship. Even until the late 1980s, there was resistance to affiliating with the Country Dance and Song Society (CDSS) or even to applying for non-profit tax status precisely because both of these required the identification of group officers. And so many musicians then clung to the nourishing, jam session informality of the stage practices. On the other hand, lack of leadership and structure compromised a number of obvious benefits. Musicians and callers were not paid, thus, some would say, limiting their desire to excel, their professionalism, and their just reward. This was a burden on the dancers, felt particularly when the music was not good. Furthermore, as Dillon had argued before, the group missed the benefits of large organizations such as CDSS.

These were fundamental structural issues. The folk revival had inherited the principle tenet that musical performance was organic—arising spontaneously, as Cecil Sharp put it, from its social and cultural context. Having encountered the impoverished experience of imitation, old-time music and dance revival had in time resolved instead to create organic society in the image of community tradition. By the time these structural issues began their lengthy tenure in the consciousness of Bloomington dancers, the underlying premise had become entirely existen-

The Gang of Four

tial. The concern was not at all with re-creating authentic folk music, but rather with how to provide for authentic experience. The concern was with the desire to avoid partitioning of experience into consumer and performer, to assure access to and status at the dance for those with limited resources, and to preserve the inverted status of folk performance.

Only a few structural changes were installed as a result of those meetings—and certainly nothing to upset the prevailing informality of the weekly dance itself. Anticipating the need for money, the group opened a bank account. It was decided that a voluntary collection would be taken at each dance, but no admission would be charged. This plan was implemented, and the first dance collection was $14.15 on July 28, 1976.

This meager sum was not the first bank deposit, however. The year 1976 was the U.S. bicentennial, and throughout the nation folk musicians and dancers were being employed to perform at celebrations. Several dancers booked performing jobs for the Bloomington group, and a number of more experienced dancers, musicians, and callers took part. The original $200 deposit came from one such performance, not identified specifically in the records. Dancers recall performances for the Monroe County Democrats; a trip to La Crosse, Wisconsin, largely organized by Laura Ley; a trip to a location near Lake Michigan booked by Scott Andrick; and another in Columbus, Indiana. The performing group was also part of the Independence Day celebration on the Monroe County Courthouse Square.

At the time, it was far more conceivable than now to envision the entire community, both music and dance, as a performing ensemble. Indeed, this was the organic entity as the dancers then envisioned it. As stage performance, this concept surely was suggested by traditional dance performances at early folk festivals and more directly by the influential performances led by Dudley Laufman at the National Folk Festivals of the early 1970s. By the mid-1980s, when the issue of pay for musicians and callers was seriously debated, Ted Hall's perennial and half-serious complaint, "I think we should pay the dancers," demonstrated all too well that the notion of dance as a legitimate component of organic performance was losing ground.

As money accumulated, the issue arose of how to spend it, and this was the predominant theme of the meeting at the Boys' Club. The group decided to elect a permanent governing body, called the Gang of Four, who would "look into things." By secret ballot, Donna Doughten, Frank Hall, Ted Hall, and Laura Ley were elected to the esteemed group. Toby Bonwit, finishing fifth in the voting, was first alternate.

The inverted reference to the governing body of the brutal Maoist regime was not accidental. Ted recalled that the group "decided that nothing should be done" but was retained to "keep an eye on things." When in 1979 there appeared the lone issue of a group newsletter, it wryly announced that Toby Bonwit would replace Donna Doughten, charged with "conspicuous absence," on the Gang of Four. Rumors even circulated that Gang of Four meetings had turned into euchre games. Euchre, the "official" card game of the dance group, requires four players.

In all of this, the lingering felicity of the humor of inverted authority was testimony to the vitality of the utopian exercise and likewise to the fragile convergence of social experience with political concerns. Indeed, there were so many dance group social gatherings that there seemed little need for representative democracy—parties vastly outnumbered meetings, and political change followed the ebb and flow of talk at these gatherings. If the disdain for representative democracy was not expressed outright, it was at least a subtle subtext to the folk qualities of the dance experience. Dance group experience seemed living proof that the separation of polity from society was only artificial, borne from the isolation of the modern individual from his and her community (by television, rigid gender roles, suburban living, isolation of the family, etc.) and from the shameless neglect modernity had exacted on folk community.

Clearly then, at some level, the Gang of Four was not to be taken seriously. For years, they conducted no official business, and anything important was decided by general referendum. Mere mention of their name might produce a wry smile, and beneath it perhaps a deep satisfaction that the dance group and by extension the world might actually operate purely on the good will of its citizens. By the early 1980s, when the subject of the Gang of Four would arise in conversation, sometimes

The Gang of Four

not a single person present could, as a test of the authenticity of their involvement, name all four members! Yet the Gang of Four also performed an important symbolic function. They stood as elders or caretakers, and the specter of their authority probably kept many distracting matters from occupying the attention of the dance.

The only official Gang of Four dealing I was aware of was in 1981 when Sugar Hill first moved to the scout camp. At the time, Sugar Hill had no bank account of its own and needed seed money to prepare for the event—presumably to be repaid by collections. The endorsement of the event by the group was never in question: it was the dance group that was promoting it. But when it came to spending the money, Ted Hall was uneasy writing a check without Gang of Four approval. He made a few phone calls, transferred the funds to someone's personal account, and that was that.

On other occasions, the inverted authority of the Gang of Four was transformed into powerful inaccessibility. If someone came up with a notion to spend a lot of money or change the dance in some fundamental way, the answer was always that it would have to be a Gang of Four decision—possibly and implicitly meaning that no decision at all would be made. In this way, the palpable atmosphere of anarchy and utopian consensus that dancers so loved could be maintained outside the specter of visible self-authority.

The role of the Gang of Four as anti-leaders was also possible because two of the four developed effective and complementing charismatic authority during the late 1970s. Of these, it was Ted Hall who took on many infrastructural burdens and became something of a paradigm of public service. Ted saw the need for a phone list and conceived the Orange Sheet. He organized the B-band meetings for beginning musicians. Later, Ted maintained the books for the dance crowd bank account, and when the group later purchased a sound system, it was Ted who housed it and brought it each week to the dance. Through most of the 1980s, Ted took charge of the building key and opened and closed the building each week, requiring that he be at each dance from start to finish. Ted's subtle yet visible charity was archetypal as a manner of involvement in the group.

Yet Ted's music and calling were generally informal and practical in

Old-Time Music and Dance

intent and scope. Perhaps consequently, his unrelated counterpart, Frank Hall, who would become an accomplished professional dancer and musician, became a kind of standard-bearer for dance musicians and callers. The Rain Crow Countryside Band was the first of many professional ventures, leading Frank to become one of the group's most traveled emissaries. As time went on, Frank came increasingly to embrace a role as advocate for musicians and callers as well as for the Bloomington arts community. There was never any suggestion that those two individuals "represented" constituencies or ideas, but the lengthy service and participation of the two enabled the persistence and visibility of important ideas in the group.

The professional entities with which Frank was associated brought with them many innovative ideas that would come into proximity with dance group life. Frank joined the Rain Crows at the beginning of 1976—among their bookings were festivals such as Kentucky Music Weekend in Louisville and the Indiana Fiddlers' Gathering. They also played to historical societies, who appreciated the historical significance of the music. For the most part, the Rain Crows operated at a distance from the dance group—there the band had only an incidental effect on the musical community. Toward the end of that year, however, Bob Herring recalled that both he and Frank were becoming increasingly attracted to southern fiddle music. This would ultimately play an important role in the emergence of a new sense of musicianship in the group.

15  EASY STREET

During the early 1970s, the jam session was the defining act of old-time music revival. For beginning musicians, it could be a formative event, an epiphany that could carry a new musician into the vivid presence of old-time music's most deeply held values. At a festival, a few people playing together could quickly swell to a hundred as musicians—who might well be strangers to one another—brought out their instruments, tuned to a prevailing pitch, and played along on some common tune. Artifacts of this period—Miles Krassen's instruction books and recordings such as those by the Fuzzy Mountain String Band—announced and defined the ethos and technology of musical community. In some circles, Fuzzy Mountain was even distinguished as a "repertoire band," a term noting their emphasis on their stock of common tunes rather than on the band as a performing entity.

Soon after these influences had taken hold, a new and distinctive sound swept over the old-time revival like a fever: the energetic and charismatic style of the Highwoods Stringband. Unlike Fuzzy Mountain, Highwoods made its mark through extensive concert and festival touring. Word quickly spread through the revival of their stirring performances, and followers were drawn irresistibly to their unique musical

Jam session at a potluck preceding a Highwoods Stringband concert, 17th Street Park, 1977. Seated, from left, Bob Potts of Highwoods (fiddle), Tom Carter, Blanton Owen, David Molk (fiddle), unknown. Photo by the author.

style and with it their picturesque and romantic lifestyle. Highwoods concerts were simply a feast of new ideas for the revival, infusing brilliant showmanship and musicianship with the deepest sentiments of old-time revival and youth culture. Bloomington dancers recalled several visits to Indiana, the first to Madison in 1973. Steve Hinnefeld was part of a carload of dancers who made the two-hour drive to their concert. In 1974 they performed at the Indiana University Fine Arts Auditorium, in 1975 at the Monroe County Library, and in 1978 at Hunter School. The Hunter School venue was a dance event, promoted with special flyers, which would not have been the case for most traveling bands who played for the Bloomington dance.

Although they later relocated to the Finger Lakes region of New York, Highwoods members attribute much of the ethos of their band to a period some of them spent in the mid-1960s in Berkeley, California (Gerrard 1992: 27). This was a formative site for the counterculture, centered on an important campus fringe area of the University of California, where traditional music was being rediscovered as a repository of alternative values. Old-time music, it was determined, had an uncanny power for achieving ecstatic states of mind (no doubt likened to the effects of hallucinatory drugs) during intense jam sessions. But band members then had little money and performed on the street as buskers alongside circus acts, magicians, other musicians, and all sorts of street vendors who laid their wares out on blankets. This lent to music performance an urgent need for a different sort of intensity: to compete, they had to entertain. According to band member Mac Benford:

> The band grew out of a bunch of people who were playing old-time music on the streets in Berkeley and San-Francisco. We were playing to the tourists who knew squat about old-time music and what its real roots were, but there was something about the music that they liked, just simple as that. To hear it was uplifting somehow, so we had to emphasize things like its humor, its energy, sometimes its strangeness—those more universal qualities that it has. The ecstasy that we achieved became our trademark, the thing that we could use to make an impact. It came out of the music and spread around to everybody. We were able to emphasize the spiritual energy of the music, which made it possible for us to affect equally audiences who had grown up with old-time music and those who had never heard it before. (Gerrard 1992: 29)

But Highwoods members did not exactly invent this attitude. By the time they began performing, old-time record reissue companies were releasing the vaudeville-like skits of highly regarded traditional performers such as Gid Tanner and the Skillet Lickers and Fiddlin' John Carson with Moonshine Kate. These skits featured old-time bands as quasi-families of reckless moonshiners who adopted a trickster-like defiance of Prohibition and secular morality in general. Behind the fiction of the skits was the circus-like, competitive atmosphere of 1920s Atlanta—similar in some ways to 1960s Berkeley—from which these and other old-time entertainment strategies arose (see Wiggins 1987). In this context, old-time music was not merely rural music, but in fact embodied the first stirrings of urbanized rural nostalgia.

And one further reference: for some followers, the Highwoods performing aura was no doubt grafted onto the widely publicized imagery of rock-'n'-roll bands. One prominent milestone in the perception of the concept of the "band" in youth culture was the trickster-like depiction of the Beatles in *A Hard Day's Night* (1965). My recollection of 1960s youth culture is that forming a band was a desire, particularly among male friends, that exceeded merely making music together. It was also an undertaking that required considerable social engineering. Yet, incredibly, the focus was always on the music, the end which always justified the means. Little thought was given, even in the most diligent scholarly treatment of the period, to the mysterious origins of the social construction of the "band." Consciously or not, almost invisibly, in fact, Highwoods mirrored much of the band social apparatus that was circulating in popular culture. Their roguish posture incorporated dense references to their inverted social status, and their performances thereby embodied a key link between popular music, counterculture values, and the authentic repertoire of country music's "golden age."

Surprisingly, as Highwoods members came to learn, this approach was genuinely attractive not merely to young people but also to older rural musicians and fans who had followed string bands during their heyday. Beginning in 1971, Highwoods began traveling to contests and festivals in the southern U.S., which Mac Benford described as "100% polyester bluegrass except for us." In stark contrast to the tight, tense, competitive sound of bluegrass and contest fiddling, Highwoods exuded defiant looseness—in tattered blue jeans, in the signature "Highwoods bounce" of their stage presentation, and in the self-absorbed manner in which they succumbed to the intensity of the music (Greenstein 1979: 38). Even the unpremeditated unison of their twin fiddle arrangements— a device originated long ago by the Skillet Lickers and imitated by other bands—was now something new and unusual (Wolfe 1997: 85, 89). And if their "full band" instrumentation alluded to that of bluegrass ensembles, they also eschewed other stock features of bluegrass performance practice, such as taking solo instrumental breaks. Audiences in the conservative South had every cause to be repelled by them, but as Mac put it:

> Our music . . . obviously took them back to times and places in their own pasts, and they were good about expressing their gratitude. It was

their conviction that we were keeping something they valued alive that convinced us we were an authentic part of the tradition. (Gerrard 1992: 30; emphasis in original)

This gave the band a "sense of mission" that they were a vital and unique link between past and future, appointed heirs to a lost performing tradition and, hopefully, the progenitors of its recovery. It also gave them entry into the "family" of southern traditional musicians that included Tommy Jarrell, Kyle Creed, Roscoe Holcomb, and many others.

Clearly, Highwoods was an extraordinary and complex symbolic enterprise. Honed by brutally competitive street performing, they were able to develop subtle cues that alluded to and resolved worlds of significance that might otherwise have been wholly incompatible. In a fundamental way, Highwoods was theater disguised as real life. Onstage and off, Highwoods members played their roles so intently that it seemed they had been consumed by them. One can only imagine the impact they must have had on beginning musicians by arriving in their van, playing a concert, playing late into the night at a party, and driving off the next day for more of the same. Undoubtedly it was a difficult life, but audiences rarely, if ever, saw the difficulties. The appearance Highwoods projected and the attitude with which they approached their music indicated that above all they were having a great deal of fun (Vittek 1988). And if they could do it, so could everyone else. Again, Mac: "The impression people got from us was that it was *our* music and it could be *their* music. I think it made the music seem more accessible, and it made the people who got into it feel that they had a legitimate right to it—that it was theirs as much as any place it had come from" (Gerrard 1992: 30; emphasis in original).

So convincing were Highwoods performances that their followers increasingly refused to abide by the constraints of conventional audience and fan behavior. Perhaps bolstered by the overall drift to participatory performance practices, audiences took the theatrical world of the Highwoods encounter as the utopian ideal of their own old-time community. This, according to Mac, was a mixed blessing for the band: "Just as much as they wanted to come to the concert they *really* wanted to come play afterwards at a party or something. The more our sound got out there the more people took up the music rather than became fans or supporters" (Gerrard 1992: 31). For the band, it was a tragic irony that they could articulate the old-time ideal so well at precisely the time it came into the grasp of so many people.

By the mid-1970s, the Highwoods aura had reached Bloomington and was surely influential in tempting Bob Herring and Frank Hall to start a band of their own. They experimented with a number of combinations. Scott Andrick played guitar once under the name the Stone Cut Quarry Boys, a name that alluded to the limestone quarries nearby. At one point Miles Krassen was considered, and Randy recalls playing once with Steve Hinnefeld. But the ensemble that emerged included Frank and Bob on fiddles, Mark Feddersen on bass, Teri Klassen on guitar, and Randy Marmouzé on banjo. The name, taken from a poster advertising savings bonds, was the Easy Street String Band.

Mark gives credit for early encouragement to Grey Larsen. Grey had met Bob at a festival and had suggested that he come and perform at Arnold's Bar and Grille, a folk music gathering place in Cincinnati, where Grey then lived. As plans for the band began to fall together, the invitation to come to Cincinnati provided a catalyst. As it turned out, they played their first job as Easy Street in December of 1976 and performed at Arnold's the following summer.

Easy Street emerged in a succession of Bloomington bands that began with Dry and Dusty and then passed, particularly via Frank's experience, through the Rain Crows. Where Dry and Dusty had provided a local model for performance, it was the Rain Crows who established the possibility of economic success. Dillon recalls that, with bookings in Indiana schools, parks, and venues throughout the Midwest, he earned $20,000 with the Rain Crows during one year. This experience raised the level of expectation for everyone and passed into the ethos of Easy Street.

Easy Street was also the first Bloomington band to emerge from the social and cultural foundation of the dance group—by all accounts uneventfully enough to warrant further commentary. A band is ordinarily a second-order social formation, with pointers, sometimes complex and obscure, to its host social entities and its originating circumstances. Its symbolic power can be derived by transgression or resistance from this host entity, such as a community or family, whose originating influences are sometimes erased or obscured. This is problematic enough in popular musical styles, but folk musicians ordinarily have also to contend with an explicit ideology of organic community that the music, by definition, represents. Regional bluegrass bands, for example, experience enough discomfort with the discursive properties of the band status that they saturate performances with references to their originating circumstance—such as home and family—and to their structural qualities as a transformation of family (Bealle 1993).

The prominent band models in the music and dance world articulated different relationships with community. In contra dance circles, an important prototype community band was the Canterbury Country Dance Orchestra, with an indeterminate number of musicians, depending on the venue. One of their recordings, *The Canterbury Country Orchestra Meets the F&W String Band* (1972) was made after sending out an invitation, with a tune list, to all those who had played in the bands at various times. In old-time circles, the Fuzzy Mountain String Band portrayed themselves famously as a musical community, alluding to an indeterminate expanse of musical and non-musical roles. Indeterminacy was important but, in fact, had limits: the band was officially established when a segment of an informal weekly jam session "decided to have a 'closed' practice session" (Hicks 1995: 20). This model, with and without exclusion, was easily borrowed and localized, resulting in the widespread dissemination of the Fuzzy Mountain tune repertoire around informal community events such as parties and jam sessions.

With Highwoods, the absence of community was deeply ironic. The band's efficient professional persona was downplayed in favor of the defiant looseness of the celebratory utopia to which audiences always felt they belonged. Audiences reveled in the utopian anti-society of their extended performances, but the band itself was tied more to the hard life "on the road," to the hope of a stable income from playing music, and to its sense of mission as designated custodians of a forsaken canon of American music (see Benford 1989: 23).

So, fundamentally, a band is at once a manifestation and a transgression of community, and to have drawn from the fictional ideals circulating in the revival should have been problematic for local groups. But Easy Street finessed this transition smoothly, as I observed it, by estab-

Old-Time Music and Dance

lishing close proximity to the dance without making demands on its essential structures. The primary point of contact was the band's Thursday night engagement at Rapp's, in the same room where the group gathered informally after dancing each Wednesday. This was a public performance designed ostensibly for an accidental audience, but more often than not friends and fans prevailed. Onstage, there and elsewhere, Easy Street alluded heavily to the Highwoods performance aesthetic— with identical instrumentation, identical gender distribution, and a similar carefree spirit.

Also like Highwoods, they traveled frequently. Weekday performances for Young Audiences of Indiana took them to Indiana schools throughout the state. They played festivals at the Indiana Fiddlers' Gathering and Kentucky Music Weekend in Louisville, Kentucky. They played for one of the early Elkins, West Virginia, dance weeks. Randy recalls particularly the Clarksville (Tennessee) Fiddlers' Championship, where they competed and placed first for three years running. Others recall the trip to the White Springs Folk Festival in Florida. Laura Ley and Martha Marmouzé went along, so the van was packed with seven people, the musical instruments, the sound system, all their belongings, and a canoe.

Group expeditions such as this did result in a kind of ongoing entourage—an enclave with a common style of interaction and a shared archive of experiences. But in many respects the entourage experience was not an exclusive one. This was particularly true at festivals, where there was an established history of group trips before the band was formed. In a sense, the band emerged around the entourage and not vice versa, almost as if designed to reproduce for the group the heightened reality of the Highwoods encounter. Whereas for Highwoods this was an unforeseen consequence, for Easy Street it was an anticipated result.

In this, Easy Street might have approximated the quintessential traditional community band: to amplify communal experience without appropriating the community as fans. Indeed, the structure of ongoing dance group activities was largely unaffected by all of this: band members played in the dance band and in open jam sessions at parties and festivals. But never was there an effort to impose exclusivity on group events: rarely, for example, did they play for the Wednesday Night

Representing Young Audiences of Indiana, Easy Street performs at the Penrod Festival in Indianapolis. From left, musicians are Teri Klassen (guitar), Brad Leftwich (banjo, sitting in for Randy Marmouzé), Bob Herring (fiddle), Mark Feddersen (bass), and Frank Hall (fiddle). Photo courtesy of Teri Klassen.

Dance in the Easy Street configuration. There was also in other respects a happy reciprocity with the dance: for a small fee, Easy Street rented the dance group sound system for performances and shared their van with the morris dance team for trips.

Like Highwoods, Easy Street's tenure was brief and intense. Even by the early 1980s, they were traveling less frequently; in 1983 the band ended its affiliation with Young Audiences of Indiana and thereby gave up its largest and most reliable source of income. In 1980, the group released a record, *Money in Both Pockets* (Prairie Schooner PSI-104, recently reissued on CD). On this, arguably the surest artifact of their separation from the community, they took care to acknowledge their roots:

> We lean toward the "southern sound," but our music is also influenced by the dancing we've been doing here for the last eight years as a part of the Bloomington Old Time Music and Dance Group. We're indebted to the old time musicians who have made Bloomington their

home for awhile (often because of the university), or for good, because of the community.

Easy Street nurtured their organic relations with the dance and in doing so articulated the emerging post-Highwoods aesthetic. Whereas Highwoods crafted contemporary utopian allusions out of a distant musical world, Easy Street drew from what was close at hand. As the first genuinely transcendent musical form to arise from the Bloomington dance, what they did contribute was to localize the Highwoods aesthetic, providing a visible emblem of the larger old-time community.

16 DANCE CAMPS

During the latter years of the 1970s, particularly on the East Coast, where populated cities are in close proximity, there was beginning to emerge a cosmopolitan network of contra dance groups. This was partly constituted in local dances, but also in large annual dance events to which the most avid dancers, musicians, and callers frequently traveled. Because of its geographic distance from these events and its independent origins, Bloomington and other same-generation Midwest dances were isolated from this emerging network. By the end of the decade, however, cultural commerce with the distant movement had become established. As a pivotal event, some point to a particular 1975 trip to Pinewoods that included Dillon Bustin, Frank Hall, Ted Hall, and Laura Ley.

Pinewoods is a camp near Plymouth, Massachusetts, operated in the summer by the Country Dance and Song Society (CDSS), which holds week-long schools there in folksong and dance. Although such "dance weeks" or "dance camps" became widespread later during the 1980s, they were few in number before then. For most of the 1970s, Pinewoods, the Berea Christmas Country Dance School (Berea, Kentucky), and the John C. Campbell Folk School (Brasstown, North Carolina) were the main outlets for disseminating revived traditions associated with English and American folk dance. The spectrum of traditions they taught and helped canonize was taken largely from English folksong collector Cecil Sharp's range of interests and from the curriculum of the English Folk Dance and Song Society—in fact, EFDSS emissaries played a part in founding these American institutions. Ironically, it was EFDSS director Douglas Kennedy who urged the American branch to "loosen their focus and to acknowledge their service to the American as well as English tradition more, and to become independent of EFDS" (Wilfert 1989: 18; English Folk Dance Society was the original name). Renamed the Country Dance Society (and later the Country Dance and Song Society), the newly independent organization began incorporating American material into the curriculum, inviting teachers from the Pine Mountain Settlement School (Kentucky), Berea College, and the Campbell Folk School.

It is important to note that neither Pinewoods nor CDSS had any significant formative influence on the Bloomington dance group—as they did on so many other groups. Indeed, the stark absence of pre-1970s dance communities suggests the limited influence, despite promotional efforts lasting much of the twentieth century, of cultural organizations such as CDSS. In Bloomington, even Dillon Bustin's efforts at national affiliation were held in check by local opposition. Locally, it seems, the independent origin and character of the group were already well established on other terms. But dance camps would come to be seen as an increasingly valuable resource for and influence on Bloomington in all but organizational matters.

The first contact with Bloomington was in 1973, when Dillon and David Molk attended Pinewoods and provided encouragement for the 1975 trip. This latter group was larger, and its participants were then at the center of dance group social experience. Laura, then in her prime as a caller, recalls bringing back a number of new dances. But the most significant influence was the series of subsequent trips during this crucial period of the dance. The next year, in 1976, Mark Feddersen, Frank Hall, Ted Hall, and Teri Klassen attended the Berea Christmas School. I was there also, but I had only recently arrived in Bloomington. In 1977 Laura Ley, Martha Marmouzé, Frank Hall, and Ted Hall were back at Pinewoods. In the summer of 1978 Toby Bonwit, Ted Hall, Teri Klassen, and Stan Sitko went to Brasstown. In the 1980s many from the group served on the performer staffs of various camps; Frank Hall was coordinator of the 1986 Pinewoods American Week.

The week-long summer camp format for country-dance instruction was introduced very early at Pinewoods, dating at least to 1913 and to the earliest programs by Cecil Sharp and others. The first summer session was held in Chocorua, New Hampshire, at the camp of Harvard dramatics professor George P. Baker, and featured English country, morris, and sword dancing taught by A. Claude Wright. Later camps used facilities normally devoted to summer theater, scouting, and agriculture. In 1933, country-dancers took over the scout campground owned by dancer Lily Conant near Plymouth, Massachusetts, and there began the run of summer programs at the place they called Pinewoods (Wilfert 1989: 1–3). The Campbell Folk School in Brasstown, North Carolina, established a "short course" with a recreational focus in June of 1930, distinguished from the winter session of several months' duration. The first Berea Christmas Country Dance School was held in 1938, designed to supplement the Brasstown short course (Christmas Country Dance School 1988: 4; Culbertson 1986: 79, 98). It is worth noting that these formative events long pre-dated the folksong camps that operated mainly in the 1940s and 1950s in the Catskills, considered a component of leftist folksingers' "cultural warfare" (see, e.g., Cantwell 1996: 272–75). There is no indication that these folksong camps had any influence on post-1960s dance camps even though many dance camp participants were indebted to leftist folksong ideology by other means.

Summer camps are deeply embedded in American culture, having begun during the late-nineteenth century as an antimodernist initiative accompanying the rise of industrial cities (Eells 1986). Histories of camping take pains to note that in contrast with so many American institutions, summer camping is American in origin, without Old World roots. The earliest camps were situated so as to be accessible to urban areas in New England and the Midwest, and some were explicitly promoted as back-to-nature escapes from urban social problems and disease. Later, camps were adopted by social reform organizations such as the YMCA, adding explicit pedagogy to an experience that was thought originally to naturally incline campers toward well-being. Particularly in the post-WWII era, special-interest groups unaffiliated with the organized camping movement increasingly began organizing theme-based camp experiences (Erikson and Day 2003). These programs draw upon the aspect of camps that has endured from the beginning as a fundamental feature: the weeklong format as a ritual experience.

A dancer at a dance camp was among a hundred or so like-minded others separated from home, job, family, and friends and relocated most often to a remote rural site. Housing was in dormitories or cabins, where a dancer was likely to spend long hours together with other dancers, ranging from novices to the most committed of the nation's dance veterans. Ordinarily there was a program staff of fifteen or so musicians and callers who were sometimes housed with students. Classes were offered throughout the day, and dances were held in the evenings. For most, this was an exhausting pace, so that a common struggle against fatigue arose early in the week.

As the week wore on, a quasi-society began to develop as students found others with similar interests. Dance camp romances blossomed easily, unfettered by the burdens of everyday life. By midweek, there was often some kind of formal or informal ritual transformation—perhaps an expedition somewhere or a late-night encounter of interpersonal bonding, perhaps a party or social gathering in one of the cabins or in the home of a local dancer, perhaps a skit night where overly serious or flamboyant personalities were portrayed in comic inversion. If a popular teacher was becoming overbearing, students might conspire to "gator" the instructor at the evening dance: during a moment when the teacher was engrossed in serious instruction, an instigator would yell "gator," and the entire room of dancers would fall to their backs and wriggle their arms and legs in the air. For some this may have been a borrowing from the popular film *Animal House* (1978). Whereas in the film it was a ritual of expulsion and detachment, in the dance it was a means of restoration. On the whole, the momentum for these midweek uprisings was often the breakdown of student-staff social barriers or even the resolution of school-local cultural tensions. In any case, as is the pattern with other types of summer camps, this spontaneous mid-week ritual transformation served as an important shift in the proprietary locus of the experience.

Nor was this always beyond the purview of official discourse: camps nurtured the emerging collective consciousness. Jay Ungar's "Root Camp," begun in the 1980s, was probably exceptional at the time in its quasi-official rites of the emerging collective. His celebrated "Ashokan Farewell," for example, was composed as a waltz tune to accompany a parade commemorating the bittersweet separation and dispersal at week's end. But even at the older institutions, there was a backdrop of subtle indulgence that was fundamental to their purpose. At Pinewoods, for example, extracurricular parties were long fundamental to the experience, according to historian Ed Wilfert:

> Where there are morris dancers, surely there must be beer or ale, but the records are few about liquor parties in camp. When Ken Knowles was in Lads 9 in 1940, he gave such a party, with twenty-five campers in attendance. The practice of stuffing little cabins with partying dancers evidently goes back a way, but generally partying all night was not the norm. As for skinny dipping at night—didn't Mrs. Storrow begin that years and years ago? Some Pinewoods traditions are hard to document. (1989: 24)

It is of possible significance that Danish folk school pedagogy was fundamental to the camps, particularly Brasstown. According to its principles, students were encouraged to actively resolve the juxtaposed historical world of the dance, the immediate world of the collective, and the real-world community back home. These "schools for life" did not promote partying, of course. Nonetheless, professional educators should envy the level of pedagogical engagement that was maintained throughout the week in postwar dance camps. Informal socializing in various capacities was an important element of the deep engagement with the materials the camps offered.

What was truly remarkable, indeed, was not the internalization or experience of camp social life but the extraordinary momentum gathered to apply technical instruction in dance, music, and calling to the formation of local dance communities back home. For this, formal instruction was scarcely as effective as the informal indoctrination novices

Old–Time Music and Dance

received from other dancers, where the cultural value of music and dance was experienced firsthand and passed on from dancer to dancer. Until well into the 1980s, for example, there was rarely any curricular attention given to dance communities (as opposed to the dances themselves)—and this came much at the insistence of students. But informal influence was profound: by week's end, the idyllic collective at the camp had become the archetype of existential yearnings that dancers took home. Intense friendships and romances quickly developed, and with them arose common understandings about dance as the underpinning of a fulfilling social paradigm. This provided the core value in the development of a national folk dance and song network, one which featured considerable travel, long-distance romances and friendships, and long-anticipated annual events that brought friends together in intense celebration.

The absence of formal instruction in community development was not necessarily due to neglect on the part of the camps, but more to the prevailing conception of the relationship of dance to community. In the early 1970s, the EFDSS reprinted a series of "Community Dances Manuals" (EFDSS 1949–67) that at the time were the most popular instruction manuals for use in recreation in American and English dance revival. They contained dance instructions and printed music, according to Douglas Kennedy, "sufficient . . . to guide the dancers through the first tentative steps" (EFDSS 1973: 1). Accompanying recordings (with calls) and a sturdy binder for the manuals were sold separately. Much like the pedagogy of old-time music revival at the time (such as Miles Krassen's banjo primer), these materials were purposely spare in detail. They implored instructors to tolerate liberal interpretation of the notations and apologized for the incapacity of notation and instruction—another "poor substitute," one might say—to convey the inscrutable fluidity of living community. "We who are not fortunate enough to live in such communities," said Douglas Kennedy, "are glad to borrow the dances that they have evolved" (EFDSS 1968: 1).

Importantly, this notion led American country dance ethnographers to grapple with the notion of community in various ways. For example, Jon Sundell recounted his visit to four east Tennessee communities. The straightforward and repetitive music and dance did not always conform to conventional notions of tradition—there was no reluctance to use amplified musical instruments, for example. But there was considerable continuity in maintaining an event and setting that "enables people to enjoy themselves to the fullest" (1981: 53). Similarly, Bob Dalsemar discussed dance in five different communities in his *West Virginia Square Dances* (1982). Dalsemar detailed the sequence of events that composed each dance event, including such matters as when breaks were taken, what refreshments were served, who was paid and who was not, where the bands and callers came from, what admission was charged, who from the community attended, and what opinions people had about the dance as a whole. In the foreword, CDSS president Jim Morrison called the book a "new type of dance book altogether," contrasting it with the prevailing fashion of recreational dance instruction manuals that did not even recognize dance as a community event.

Country dance ethnography was derived from the notion of traditional community as the basis for folk revival. Coincidentally or not, this period paralleled the "contextual" movement in folklore theory, which stressed the social and cultural context, and not merely the text, of folklore as an emergent performance. Dance scholars who adopted this model were led instinctively to connect dance to community in much the same manner as in country dance ethnography. For example, Burt Feintuch interviewed square dancers in south-central Kentucky to reconstruct the tradition of house dances as community recreation. His conclusion was that in the frequency and importance of dance events, dancers "acted out a representation of their sense of their own community" (1981: 49). And Thomas A. Burns and Doris Mack (1978) observed a Grange Hall dance event in a small community in western Pennsylvania, connecting the symbolism in the dance to the rural farming community of those who attended. The common theme of all of these studies was the relationship between dance structure and the ongoing relations shared by participants.

These conceptions of traditional dance set informal socializing squarely within the realm of pedagogical interests. They permeated the revival and the dance camp experience, so that even with little or no explicit curricular reference, the emotional and conceptual ties to the utopian home community were immediate and profound. I vividly remember attending Winter Dance Week at Brasstown in 1981. Thirteen Bloomington dancers went that year, easily the largest local contingent of a total enrollment of just over eighty. The staff took care to house as many of us as possible in one building and offered no protest when we obliged by giving a party on Wednesday night. For one of the evening programs, we devised a skit, "A Hoosier Home Companion," based on the popular PBS radio program *A Prairie Home Companion*. Gary Stanton, then host of the folk music program *Music Down Home* (on WFIU, the Bloomington affiliate for National Public Radio), played the lead. The skit included an obligatory left-balance disaster as in Eddie Grogan's song and a rendition of the Indiana University basketball fight song that I arranged in shape notes.

It was not common for so many from one community to attend a camp. But what was typical was the way an unplanned midweek ceremony was devised, outside the agenda of the school, around a segment of the group who had known or discovered common interests. At the same time, I remember coming home from this week and others energized and excited about my own dance group. These camps were a profound validation for all our aspirations at home. They provided instruction in the technology of music and dance, but the campers were led by example to set above this the pleasures they took in one another. Our observations of dance in traditional communities as well as the reports that dance ethnographers gave us confirmed that this was much the way traditional dancers conceived of their dances also.

17 THE SOVEREIGN SELF

Dance camps and the institutions that produced them had their roots in turn-of-the-century English antimodernism and later the movement in America, called by critics a "culture industry," which sought to restore folk practices and artifacts in traditional or contemporary settings. The Country Dance and Song Society was founded as an American branch of the English Folk Dance and Song Society during Cecil Sharp's lecture-performance tours of 1914–17. The Campbell Folk School based its recreational curriculum largely on the model of Danish folk schools and on Sharp's music and dance interests.

A pivotal component of my own introduction to folklore study and folklore revival was a sequence of tutorial studies with Beatrice "Bicky" McLain at the University of Alabama. McLain had lengthy affiliations with international folklore study and also with the triumvirate of camps and thus was a key figure in mediating the two worlds. Her chief theoretical influences were Cecil Sharp, James Frazer, and Svend Grundtvig, and through them she implanted in her students a vivid connection between folklore survival and revival. She had some interest in political folksong and in folk revival performance, particularly in instances where they drew directly from traditional form and substance. At Christmas

Country Dance School, she led evening parlor singing for many years, where she articulated the connection between the camp experience and the world of traditional culture. Her perspective was emblematic of, if not influential in, the formative ideas of the camps.

Through the influence of these institutions, the postwar music and dance revival received much of the mantle of their theoretical foundation. Many participants in music and dance communities were unfamiliar with this background, but there were most always pivotal community members steeped in folklore theory to varying degrees. This influence was much greater when there was a more direct connection between the programmatic designs of the camps and the founding of folk music and dance performance communities. In the 1980s, the expansion of camps and communities diminished the influence of the programmatic ambitions of years past.

Nonetheless, common origins and common purpose link music and dance with the term "culture industry" and with practices such as folk art galleries, tourism, and regional cuisine, which provide an insulated, passive encounter with a cultural other. In the 1980s, troubling questions were raised about the origin of the motives for these efforts and about the conceptual framework of folk culture that made them possible. In an approach that came to be known as the "politics of culture," critical scholars sought out stated and unstated relationships between the pedagogical momentum of the culture industry and the peoples whose culture the folk schools and other institutions presumed to celebrate (see esp. Whisnant 1984). Often they looked to the origins of this movement, in which notions of cultural and racial purity had subtle ties to a reified and sometimes preconceived version of Anglo-American culture.

More broadly, they challenged one of the essential premises of folklore—the sovereignty of cultural self and other—with the notion that the cultural other was a construction, a projection of desire emerging from pre-existing structural inequities. In folksong revival, this premise had been enabled by the vast cultural gulf of WWII and by the resolute otherness of the "memory theater" viewed across that gulf. Affiliations with marginalized groups were believed not only to validate marginalized culture but also to undermine prejudices of race, class, and region

The Sovereign Self

that were harbored in the dominant class. This cultural exchange—purifying the dominant culture while uplifting marginalized groups—was the basis for a largely uncritical faith in the virtue of folk music and dance.

If the camps did not explicitly articulate cultural criticism, however, neither did they forbid it. Furthermore, with the participation of dance communities, postwar camps introduced a new environment in which community, locality, and pedagogy were dynamically associated. My interest here is in the way music and dance communities, originating independently of the camps, engaged this dialog with moral purpose. In particular, three themes—race, performance practice, and locality—aroused interest in music and dance communities, sometimes among those most touched by the reach of camp culture. And if this interest was not widespread, which it was not, it was engaged as if it was of general importance.

One notable subject was industrial magnate Henry Ford, whose extravagant music and dance programs were rife with disturbing contradictions. With Ford, so much of his "politics of culture" was explicit and personal: an unqualified faith in aggressive capitalism, vivid prejudices of religion and ethnicity as explanations of American achievement, nostalgia for cultural forms his own industries displaced, and his vision of a reconstructible past as compensation for that cultural loss, with his own boyhood home as the symbolic centerpiece.

Prominent within his reconstructible past stood old-time fiddling and early American dance. Ford sponsored immense fiddle contests, arranging network radio broadcasts and national publicity for the winners. A 1927 contest, organized in various parts of the country, featured 1,865 fiddlers. He organized dance instruction and wrote his own instruction manual, *Good Morning!* (1925), the first to systematically promote colonial dance as national experience. Overall, Ford's efforts to revive music and dance were extensive, and they were undertaken explicitly to counter the effects of the "evil" jazz movement and thereby also African American presence in mainstream culture. Moreover, even while based on authentic vernacular American traditions, Ford infused his revivals throughout with a gentile aristocratic code of etiquette (see Twork 1982). These revelations were disturbing to old-time revivalists

Old-Time Music and Dance

not merely in the fact that Ford provided a poor cultural ancestor. More than this, Ford's intractable historical legacy undermined the belief in folksong as a repository of virtue. In his hands, some familiar-looking cultural forms inspired the very prejudices from which revivalists sought escape.

In 1991, old-time musician and dancer Pete Sutherland, a Bloomington resident during much of the 1980s, wrote an insightful article for *Old-Time Herald,* alerting readers to the contradictions of Ford's role in old-time music revival. Through his examination of Ford, Sutherland was led to suspect subliminal prejudices in the revival, originating either in the music itself or in the behavior of those who revive it. He asked, "But as the majority of us active in the current revival came to the music from outside the culture, it seems to me that we ought to ask, what is it we are attracted to? Just what is it that we really believe we are helping to revive?" (1991: 36). To this dilemma he provided several suggestions, looking first to the distinctive style of southern old-time music in contrast to New England–style Scots-Irish music. The key source of this distinctive sound was not conservative "resistance to outside influences" but rather its systematic openness to the influences of diverse non-European cultures, notably African. He warned that in elevating "classic old-time music" to archetypal status as so many do, in idealizing the music and its traditional players, one embraces the same limited worldview that the music itself so boldly overcame.

The discovery of Ford as a Doppelganger to contemporary old-time revival is not exactly accidental, of course. Ford's cultural activities were widely publicized as news at the time they occurred, and his old-time revival was received uncritically by most who followed it. Even progressive-minded promoters such as Ralph Page approved, although a decade later he endorsed "improvising a bit of jazz" in old-time music, he was thoroughly contemptuous of dance decorum, and he thought Ford's perennial champion fiddler Mellie Dunham a rather ridiculous celebrity (see Tolman and Page 1937: 9). Newspapers of Ford's era stoked a heated rivalry between Dunham and southern fiddlers, who derided Dunham as "Henry's pet" (Wolfe 1997: 38–41; Cauthen 1989: 34). Thus while Ford's attention no doubt gave fiddling a boost, it is scarcely the case that it rescued old-time music from the jaws of progress. Richard Blaustein has suggested that Ford's experiences of the general decline of traditional life were widely duplicated in the populace (1994: 204; see also Cauthen 1989: 33). But old-time music, ever adaptable and inquisitive, was not yet among its casualties.

Most of Ford's programs, in fact, were contemporaneous with the golden age of commercial old-time recordings. Like the performers on the 78s, Ford's fiddlers were driven by personal ambition to transgress locality. Uncle Jimmy Thompson of Tennessee, who won Ford's championship in Detroit, also sought out recording, radio, and contest engagements in order to "throw my music out all over the Amerikee" (Wolfe 1997: 30–49, esp. 35). Mellie Dunham was honored to be able to "tickle the ears of the mighty," as one 1926 photo caption put it. But not all fiddlers acquiesced to Ford's conditions. Some Alabama fiddlers, out of range of many of Ford's Eastern and Midwestern contests, sought Ford's financial backing for a Fiddler's Auditorium in Ft. Payne; another sought to sell Ford a valuable violin (Cauthen 1989: 34). If Ford saw antique tradition in old-time fiddling, it could well be said that old-time fiddling saw exactly the opposite—progress and opportunity—in Ford.

When the post-WWII economic and cultural boom at last sapped traditional fiddling of its vitality, it was the fiddle contest that stood as the chief revival venue for traditional old-time musicians. Without the kind of harsh intolerance associated with Ford, this contest-based revival followed the population of traditional insiders into the fiddling association movement. There the cultural context that had surrounded it—the tragic irony of the Jazz Age and later the unpleasant austerity of the Great Depression—was happily discarded.

Unlike fiddling associations, however, the postwar "outsider" folksong revival was driven to expediency by a national crisis of values and so instead was deeply concerned with context. Who, postwar enthusiasts were compelled to ask themselves, would have thought their movement a handmaiden to modernization or prejudice? Most were horrified at the labor and environmental practices of extractive industries, unsympathetic with racial and ethnic prejudice, and impatient with any bourgeois gentility that crept into dance or music performance practice.

Yet, the once-vast cultural chasm of the "memory theater," which had shielded listeners from the murky moral world of the 78s or the cruel inequities of the Jazz Age in which they were produced, was now collapsing. Authenticity and moral realism, insider and outsider, traditional and revival—all once-reliable notions—were becoming increasingly vague and complex, exposing the kinds of contradictions that Sutherland described. It is hardly surprising that the revival produced a native cultural critique carved out of its own idealism, sharing with intellectual cultural criticism a deep concern over the consequences and moral disposition of cultural revival movements. Many, like Sutherland, constructed a kind of cognitive map of music and dance culture, establishing symbolic distance from sites, individuals, or historical threads that were prone to prejudice or intolerance.

Foremost for some was the need to resolve lingering effects of racial discourse that had shaped old-time music at various points in its history. African stylistic contributions to old-time music were certainly obvious: one need only have compared southern old-time tunes to their British Isles counterparts to see the dramatic effects of the Anglo-African style synthesis that emerged from New World contact. Some embraced the southern sound precisely because of its African stylistic manifestations. Yet old-time music revival, even as it emerged around a discourse that linked the ideology of civil rights and folksong revival, was equally obviously European American in contemporary practice. Long before Henry Ford, long before folk schools, there had been a racial divide that aligned old-time music with southern white culture.

The entire discursive compass of this racial divide could well be condensed into old-time music's signature instrument: the banjo. On the one hand, its uniquely African roots were by then clearly documented; on the other, according to quasi-myth, the five-string banjo had been "invented" by the Irish American minstrel Joel Walker Sweeny. Behind this emblematic account was a historical controversy: did the banjo enter Anglo-American tradition through minstrelsy, as many assumed? If so, did the instrument and its music incorporate minstrelsy's distasteful associations with racial caricature?

To answer this perplexing question, there arose a grassroots research movement among old-time music scholars devoted to the role of African American and European American contacts in the development of the banjo. Historians such as George Gibson have addressed this issue, looking for evidence of banjo contact at times and places unlikely to have been influenced by minstrelsy (Gibson 2001). The greatest interest has been in isolated frontier areas such as Appalachia, where geographic, economic, and cultural conditions brought different races and social classes into proximity. There has also been a reassessment of minstrelsy, focusing on its non-racial aspects. Dale Cockrell (1997), for example, has recounted the early period before racial caricature became prominent; there the banjo functioned as a vehicle for disorder, drawing upon its noise-making capacity. Rather than review these writings, I focus on one in particular, Cecelia Conway's *African Banjo Echoes in Appalachia: A Study of Folk Traditions* (1995), which is exceptional in its breadth and accessibility.

Conway's first concern was with nineteenth-century minstrelsy, where the banjo, as a chief component of the theatrical parody of slave culture, had increasingly embodied the stock semiotic devices that would come to define popular musical culture and reappear repeatedly in staged string band performance: authenticity, imitation, parody, sentimentalization of folk materials, and burlesque humor (1995: chap. 2, esp. 114–15). But her examination of historical materials led her also to a different destination. African American banjo styles were difficult and not easily adapted to Celtic American music. So, answering to the specific demands of banjo musicianship, there developed a subculture of inquisitive apprenticeship from which the complex syncretic style of southern old-time banjo playing developed (chap. 2, esp. 104–109, 117–18). If, as some theories suggest, minstrelsy was for white America the emotional prerequisite to the abolition of slavery, it was in the subculture of apprenticeship where the deepest psychological equity and tolerance were felt and where the most genuine cultural interchange was accomplished (esp. 117 and 332 n107). The dichotomy within minstrelsy of racial parody versus musical apprenticeship was for Conway the key historical juncture from which popular culture and folk tradition took their cultural and moral departure.

But not even genuine apprenticeship could be extricated from the racial compass of minstrelsy. Conway's more ambitious quest was to determine if, in certain areas, the point of contact was not minstrelsy at

Old–Time Music and Dance

all, but some other medium not defined so explicitly by the dominant racial discourse. To this end, she outlined the long and often fruitless struggle to adapt the banjo to Anglo-American ensemble performance. Not until the mid-nineteenth century, and then only rarely, is there documentation of banjos and fiddles playing together (80–81). Eventually the banjo ensemble emerged as a prominent component of minstrelsy, but in this it overshadowed the strain of musical culture that quietly developed beyond minstrelsy's grasp: the tradition of solo banjo playing in areas of the eastern mountains, within reach of the African American population in the Piedmont—yet where minstrelsy had little direct contact (102–104, 131–59). This observation is supported by the fact that in these areas, banjo players learned and continued to favor downstroking (e.g., clawhammer) despite widespread popularity of two-finger picking among minstrel players who came to prominence between 1865 and 1880 (133–35, 157–58).

It was among these isolated traditional musical groups, which had "historically been highly influential, inquisitive, and open to musical exchange," where the Celtic American and African American musical traditions were most profoundly and most easily brought to bear upon each other (158). In these settings, cultural, economic, and topographical factors provided an auspicious environment for grassroots racial tolerance sufficient to prevail over the entrenched prejudice that penetrated the dominant culture, particularly in the South. This predisposition to inquisitive apprenticeship guided the search by Celtic American musicians "for new, often African-American material, whether they acquired such material by direct contact, recordings, or radio" (153).

Did these conclusions have any bearing on the substance of old-time music revival? Among minstrel apprentices and mountain learners alike, it was a predisposition to face-to-face tutelage—inscribed upon each, both as prerequisite to and consequence of their being genuine folk musicians—that "sensitized them to folk materials and helped them become performers" (88). Underlying their particular historic circumstance was an "important truth about traditional musicians," that "good musicians tend to be musically receptive to new musical influences" (152). Citing Alan Jabbour, Conway identified the locales where apprenticeship produced the deepest racial synthesis (137–59) and where culture groups "with strong musical traditions may be expected to exert an influence out of proportion to their numerical strength" (137, quoted from Jabbour 1971: 1). She equated this subculture of apprenticeship with a genealogical "folk process" by which one can "absorb tradition," and she noted that "we may observe the continuing process among revivalists today" (87). She names several bands (e.g., the New Lost City Ramblers, the Fuzzy Mountain String Band, the Highwoods Stringband) and individuals as "examples of revival apprenticeship in old-time music" and adds that the apprenticeship process has been "institutionalized" by the National Endowment for the Arts and many state arts councils. And the string band, first posited as an exemplar of minstrelsy's impurity of motive, could now be proclaimed as "an ensemble that honors democratic interaction between the white fiddle and the African-American banjo tradition" (155).

Without suggesting that this is central to her overall concerns, one can nonetheless examine how Conway's reasoning engages a dilemma of gathering breadth, enabling the practice of folksong revival in a particular way. After having so carefully accounted for the unique conditions of apprenticeship in the nineteenth century (Celtic tradition, the proximity of the Piedmont, geographical insulation from minstrelsy, circumstantial co-presence in mining and railroad work, etc.), Conway leaves one only to guess what were the conditions, clearly different, for this "continuing process." Perhaps it is obvious: like the mountain apprentices, postwar revivalists embraced their mentors as saturated symbols of otherness, yet willingly susceptible to synthesis and rapprochement by a process uniquely available to them as folk musicians.

In these critiques, old-time music was enveloped by the historical allegory of American culture. Its practice was an archetypal experience that positioned its practitioners within a definitive American historical narrative. It posited cultural sovereignty not as an essential fact of American society but as a provisional device for cultural encounter. In this, the banjo revealed itself as an originary mediator for race, embodying the gamut of archetypal encounters among people whose engagement as self and other has been one of the defining themes of American culture.

These investigations—of Henry Ford, the banjo, and minstrelsy—addressed historical themes of race and ethnicity embedded in old-time music. There also were other arenas of interest related to the politics of culture, such as the social structure of performance practices within folksong revival itself. Here the concern was with structural characteristics of performance and the way they mapped social class structure and local accessibility. Certain types of performance structures, it was held, could facilitate or resist the privileged structures of the dominant culture.

In this, two key performance issues seemed to consistently map the divide between traditional folk culture and dominant cultural practice. On the one hand, traditional forms were accessible and continuous, so that they did not foster exclusionary practices within communities. On the other, they provided for spontaneous social interaction, and thus did not lend themselves to stratifying codes of etiquette. The overall concern was with the capacity for folksong revival to unintentionally absorb the privileged structures of the dominant culture, co-opting the very qualities folksong was thought to embody and designed to celebrate.

Thus one subject of interest was the pedagogical strategies employed in dance instruction. In 1982, Dillon Bustin pinpointed a crucial split in English antimodernism and folksong revival. He was particularly intrigued by a strain of antimodernism represented by Evelyn Sharp, Cecil's outspoken socialist and suffragist sister, and Mary Neal, a folk dance teacher considered a rival of Cecil Sharp. In Sharp and Neal, Bustin identified a contingency within dance revival that deplored the widespread and meticulous stylistic imitations that stripped revival forms of their social efficacy (Bustin 1982b). The emphasis here was not the engagement of the other, but rather the enactment of folk community.

More recently, Phil Jamison (1989, 2004) has expressed ongoing concern for the structural differences of contras and squares. His thesis, which I discuss in more detail later, is that squares better facilitate the sustained social relations of traditional community. Contras, with their expandable formation, their lengthier duration, and their relentless activity, are ideally suited to the impersonality of contemporary mass culture. He has identified the outline of a historical narrative of competition for acceptance, in which contras prevail by their facility for engaging popular sentiment.

For Ruth Katz, the issue was the structural properties of the waltz in the development of class stratification in European society (1973). The waltz was valuable as a means of class mobility after the French Revolution, Katz argued, only where its "unwritten rules could be learned through observation and participation" (368). In contrast, it was the "realism of particulars" that led to the establishment of dance professions and the reemergence of class stratification in European popular dance. The implication of these three cases was that attempts at community dance, no matter their source or content, could be undermined by performance practices. If the intent of dance pedagogy was to foster community, these concerns should be of considerable importance.

Interest in the social efficacy of forms was reflected by evolving practices in institutions indebted to English dance revival. At Pinewoods, "particulars" once reigned supreme during the EFDSS-affiliation years, when end-of-session examinations were given and certificates of completion awarded. Then, in 1939, CDSS established a separate teachers' course, which absorbed some of the pedagogical detail of the general sessions (Wilfert 1989: 29). It is also notable that in 1938, Richard K. Conant founded a session called "Pinewood Institute," which was a conference weekend for social workers with recreational dances held in the evening. The institute was discontinued in 1968 because of increasing demands for the use of the camp for dancing. At the Campbell Folk School, by the mid-1970s, the short course, once a means to disseminate materials and doctrine to recreation leaders, evolved over time into a recreational event, shifting the focus away from the "particulars" of the curriculum and toward reproducible social practice (Culbertson 1986: 80).

These critiques of pedagogy were amplified by observations and reports of the utter simplicity of traditional rural community dance. Bob Dalsemar noted that in the West Virginia dances he observed, the repertoire of figures was small, "usually less than twenty as compared with a hundred or more in modern club square dancing." Traditional dancers, sometimes offering the advice "better caught than taught," clung to continuity and familiarity on the basis that learning was easier if the figures were familiar and simple (1982: 4–5). Likewise, Jon Sundell reckoned the dances he visited would be "easy and repetitious" to an uninvolved outsider, but for the community, with its complexity of social relations, they provided "an event that is exciting and extremely sociable" (1981: 63–64).

Postwar old-time dance revivalists are generally aware of undesirable social effects of dance forms, as examples throughout this book illustrate. But sometimes other issues prevailed over social and historical concerns. In the 1980s, Richard Powers made the rounds at camps introducing an assemblage of dance styles under the rubric "vintage dance." For the most part, these were mid-nineteenth- to early-twentieth-century couple dances, presented with attention to the "particulars" of their original form. The most noticeable effect on camp curricula was to introduce popular urban couple dances, including those which historians had long assailed as having eclipsed set dance forms like contras and squares. There were similar historical parameters for George Marshall's jitterbug classes, which were sometimes offered in the Midwest when his band Wild Asparagus made a tour stop.

On many levels these urban couple dance forms confounded the principles on which community dance revival had originally been advanced. But on other levels they had great appeal: they were socially engaging, they were generously rewarding as aesthetic performance, and, like contras and squares, they had been pushed out of the mainstream by more popular forms. And even for those who didn't really like them, they appealed to the eclectic, inquisitive, and tolerant spirit that was fundamental to community dance. Rarely, if ever, did they intrude upon contra and square dance events, but were available in separate venues that attracted a separate following. They nonetheless brought urbane tastes into communities where a rough-hewn aesthetic had long prevailed, and they surely diminished the esteem of antiquarian social theory as the foundation for music and dance community.

Of all the pedagogical influences on the social character of performance, nothing was more influential than the dramatic spread of locally organized camps and weekends after 1980. Across the country, new camps were being founded in rented sites, and the old ones were in-

The Sovereign Self

creasingly being staffed by younger musicians and dancers with ties to groups such as Bloomington. Where traditional dance was once the province of the cultural other, dance groups had now become traditional dance. There was little need to consult historical sources since most communities had talented callers and musicians with an engaging and informative presentational repertoire. Thus the impact of the expansion of camps was to disperse the sources of influential ideas and also to adapt the curricula around social tastes of musicians and dancers, who by then were coming from an ever-widening span of local communities.

And at local dances, concerns over the social dimensions of the revival were increasingly directed toward local performance practice issues. Consequently, the conception of the camp curriculum as a prescriptive pedagogical formula gave way to a dialogue that embraced social concerns of home communities, stylistic trends fashionable within the revival, burgeoning talents of revival performers, and unmediated (e.g., by the camps) alliances between revival and traditional performers. Some believe this resulted in a cosmopolitan aesthetic, responsive to the will of a populace that increasingly had the appearance of a homogeneous camp culture. But this was a consequence of pedagogy that made dance more accessible and less stratifying than before.

The unpleasant effects of homogeneity were the subject of the third arena of concern, the relationship of music and dance revival with locality. As examples throughout this book illustrate, a prominent theme in dance communities was the embedding of affiliations with locality—relations with local traditional performers, local political action, and other ongoing relations with the local community. In this the dance group was a social type of integrative intentional community that in principle served, in Roszak's terms, as part of a "life-sustaining receptacle that can nourish and protect good citizenship." Embedded within this posture was a critique of the very notion of locality.

In the context of the camps, however, locality was among the most serious concerns of cultural critics. Consider, for example, local and camp differences in perspectives on music education. This was the subject of an analysis of the music curriculum at Brasstown by Anne Culbertson, a Bloomington dancer during the 1980s. She made only brief mention of the school's emergence as the subject of cultural critique, acknowledging the unpleasant contradictions in its early reform efforts and noting its less-than-unanimous local acceptance (1986: 132–33). Measured against prevailing trends in music education, however, the Folk School was seen as a benchmark in its capacity to promote sustainable musical culture. This was due, in part, to the fact that the Folk School was more—not less—accountable to the community than public schools, which had to "answer to parents, school boards, and state legislatures" (142). The implication of this was that if the Folk School was viewed by locals as unconventional, this may have been less because it differed from local folk culture and more because it differed from official public culture that penetrated localities through bureaucracies.

At the Christmas Country Dance School, the engagement with local culture took a similar course. A prominent theme in cultural critique regarded the neglect of local cultural forms in favor of imported material. At Berea, however, instructors aspired to teach local forms but were dissuaded from doing so because of religious proscriptions against dancing. But they were able to introduce English and Danish dance precisely because of its dissimilarity to local secular recreation. Founder Frank Smith was unequivocal in his assessment of the cause of this dilemma: the chilling effect of Calvinism, which he considered an unacknowledged outside influence, on the will of people to be able to enjoy traditional community dance (Christmas Country Dance School 1988: 4, 13). Like school bureaucracy, Calvinism erased its origins, its status as other, as it became embedded as a localized dominant influence.

And consider the reverse effect, when popular will eclipsed programmatic design as the operative motive in the design of camp curricula. In this transition, the 1970s were a crucial period when the Berea-Brasstown-Pinewoods camp triumvirate had a formative influence on new dance groups. At Berea, contras were first offered in 1969, taught by Ted Sannella, long before contra dance revival took root across the nation. During the years I attended in the early 1970s, the contra class was taught by Fred Breunig, who presented the material as fundamentally a product of New England tradition. After 1980, the expansion of ambitious and talented contra callers and composers from all points diminished the association of contras with rural New England. It was precisely with this more cosmopolitan spirit that they penetrated local

The Sovereign Self

culture so extensively in so many places. When presented as alien forms, as pertinent to cultural other—much as English and Danish forms had been introduced, with little success—there was a prophylactic effect on assimilation, an opportunity for choice and for cultural rapprochement.

It was in this same manner that dance communities brought to their context of place the capacity to illuminate and undermine the essentialist drift that criticism had taken in the name of locality. The question that ultimately arose was not what was local, but what was legitimate. This issue was most acute in "cultural islands," where concentrations of small-scale alternative rural life were palpable components of the cultural environment. If some were inhospitable to this, as Douglas Day noted of western North Carolina (1995: 188), should this be taken as unproblematic evidence that it contradicted "local" interests? It is one matter for ambitious culture institutions to absorb public resources based on grandiose claims of regional cultural reform and then use these resources to divest local culture of its genuine significance. It is quite another for individuals and institutions with alternative values to find refuge in remote enclaves, even if they seek to affiliate with some, but not all, established local traditions.

At moments when authenticity was at issue, music and dance proponents would inexhaustibly offer up local affiliations as evidence that their efforts were genuine—and that because folk institutions *don't* absorb resources, they nurture bonds between people whose tendency toward economic and cultural resources is not to exploit them. This was the enduring Janus-face of folksong revival, a belief in the transcendent quality of forms—such as in the regenerative powers of traditional music and dance—but also in the immanent reality of local practice.

The expansion of dance communities as interdependent loci of cultural authority, each unique in the way global concerns engaged the exigencies of locality, has metamorphosed from the concentric cultural reform that once was the hallmark of folksong revival. Most events nowadays—and there are so very many—are established in localities by residents largely for their own amusement. Moreover, interdependency among dance communities comes not from any organizational linkage but from the ever-abundant personal contact of individual dancers. Camps and weekends have rapidly multiplied also, so that by the end of

Old-Time Music and Dance

the 1980s, in old-time music and dance revival, little remained of what once might have been called a culture industry.

This is only to say that the movement now has more the character of a billow of popular sentiment than a plotted scheme. It is no less imposing, no less self-assured, and perhaps no less menacing simply because its unifying ideology is submerged in favor of a kind of synthetic social practice.

Some complain of the ubiquitous "dance gypsy" phenomenon, a cosmopolitan consciousness that has accumulated—as a consequence of postmodern technology, ease of travel, and affluence—not at the juncture of locality and official culture but in the global village that interrupts the confluence of locality and place. As a broad expanse of stylistic consensus, this movement has drawn strength from the limits on "particulars," but at the same time it has lost the attachments to locality and history that were hallmarks of dance revival in the 1970s and early 1980s. It is a world without other, of self without limit.

18 BLOOMINGTON QUARRY MORRIS

At the dance, those who were traveling to week-long dance camps were being exposed to a variety of dance styles other than contras and squares. One of these was morris dance. This traditional English ritual dance, observed, recorded, and taught by Cecil Sharp, had been at the center of the early English folksong and dance revival. According to Sharp's theories, folk cultural forms such as morris dance were invested with pre-industrial meaning and thereby could counteract or challenge the social effects of modernity. Sharp taught morris dancing to Americans, including Appalachians, during his American collecting trips, and consequently morris was adopted by the American Country Dance and Song Society and also by settlement schools and other cultural institutions in their instructional curricula.

This was the primary route taken by morris from English tradition to American folksong revival. But postwar folksong historians have identified other instances that call into question the pre-eminence of Sharp's antiquarian teachings on morris in America (see, e.g., Cockrell 1997: 47–53; Krause 1991, 1992). And even in recreational programs, for example, morris was not always antiquarian: in 1910 when Mary Neal came to New York to teach, her populist views on morris were covered in the *New York Times*. And there is evidence of some traditional community morris recorded in American literature and art. Although these instances suggest the precedent for a broad range of possibilities of American morris experience, it was largely Sharp's quasi-anthropological discourse that fueled morris revival at the time Midwestern teams were forming. Even so, 1980s dancers quickly found ways to subvert antiquarian doctrine, invoking from it explicit references to sexuality, boisterous behavior, celebration of community, and ritual inversion. Indeed, the historical and intellectual recovery of the populist morris revival came *after* the development of local populist techniques.

Bloomington's earliest significant exposure to morris was probably the 1975 Pinewoods trip that included Frank, Laura, Ted, and Dillon. In February of 1976, then–CDSS president Jim Morrison came to Bloomington and taught a morris workshop. The workshop was held at Bloomington Music—Paul Ford remembered dancing in the long, dark hallway. It is possible that later practices were held, but no one remembered them, and no team was yet formed. That December, Frank, Mark, Teri, and Ted were exposed to morris again at the Berea Christmas Country Dance School, and when they returned in January, practice sessions were convened with the idea of forming a Bloomington team. The Fieldtown tradition—morris dances are grouped stylistically by "tradition" or town of origin—was chosen as the team's first style. "Balance the Straw" and "Lads-a-Bunchum" were among the first dances learned.

The team practiced throughout that spring and gave its first performance at the wedding of Randy Marmouzé and Martha Steele, July 16, 1977. By then the team had uniforms of sorts—blue cambric shirts and jeans. A hobbyhorse had been made for the team—Mark Schneider wore it and played a major role in its construction. The dancers at that performance were Toby Bonwit, Mark Feddersen, Frank Hall, Teri Klassen, Laura Ley, Martha Marmouzé, Amy Novick, and Anne Reese. Melissa Leavell and I provided musical accompaniment on fiddles.

Probably the association of morris dancing with weddings was borrowed from other morris revival communities, which were few in number at the time. In any case, morris became a fixture at Bloomington dance group weddings, and its trademark association with fertility and sexuality was established as fundamental to the Bloomington morris experience. It was in such a manner that English antiquarian doctrine was naturalized as community tradition. The noise of the sticks and bells were said to "wake up nature," and the high leaping of the dancers, through sympathetic magic, to make crops grow tall. Morris was thought to stimulate the fertility of newlyweds, but it was also used to bless vegetable gardens and was given credit for the coming of spring each year. Performed before the public, a speech was usually given promising good luck and fertility—those in the audience not interested in fertility were warned to stand a safe distance away. Here was the ironic consciousness of folksong revival in full flower. This was all done in fun—no one really believed in sympathetic magic in this way. But even through irony, the morris performance, like the dance group itself, could accumulate around dancers a kind of sexual mystique that set them apart from a passionless public.

The team's first earned income came for performing at the New Harmony Festival of Traditional Music in May of 1978. Soon to follow were bookings at the Oliver Winery Festival just north of Bloomington, St. Mary of the Woods Renaissance Faire in Terre Haute, and the Fourth Street Festival of the Arts and Crafts in Bloomington. In each of these outdoor settings, morris was presented as a quasi-spontaneous performance in the manner of street theater. The team would initially gather away from the performance area and perform "morris on," a traveling step that took them through the crowds by a deliberately circuitous route, gathering the audience along the way. Even where a stage was available, the morris team insisted upon open areas where crowds could be gathered spontaneously. Morris thrived in such settings because it was colorful, visually potent, and entertaining, and perhaps also, the dancers might have said, because it added a kind of ritual authenticity to an otherwise commercial and formal event.

Frank Hall developed an engaging monologue for performances of the Bloomington team. He would appeal for money with promises of good luck and fertility. Then he would describe the symbolism of the costumes. The sticks and bells were to wake up nature. The fish—the team symbol—represented the fish atop the Monroe County Courthouse. White, he would say facetiously, represented the team's virginal

Bloomington Quarry Morris performs at the New Harmony Festival of Traditional Music, 1978. The group sports its laid-back uniforms—cambric shirts without baldricks. From left, Mark Feddersen (on three-hole pennywhistle), Mark Schneider (in fool's costume), Teri Klassen, Anne Reese, Frank Hall, Laura Ley, Toby Bonwit, Emily Humphries-Baer. Photo by Nis Kildegaard.

character, and blue was for "Blue-mington." Melissa Leavell and I, and later Linda Handelsman and many others, were most often the musicians. Sometimes Paul Tyler would sing "The Nutting Girl"—a song which featured nature images that thinly disguised sexual abandon—before the group performed the dance to that tune. During this period, Kevin Enright was the most effective in the hobbyhorse role; he would work the crowd, collecting money and giving occasional rides to children. In his infancy, Ewan Schmid was touted as the morris baby and was sometimes presented as evidence of the fertility powers of the dance.

The drama of morris gave the dance group a delightful mechanism for presenting itself to the community. But it was also dance, and this would become an increasingly important aspect to Frank Hall and other team members. While contra and square dance is largely a matter of floor patterns, morris involved challenging, vigorous stepping coordinated with handkerchief or stick movement. When the Bloomington team began traveling to perform with other teams, it became apparent to many that its members were less ambitious than others. Only reluctantly, in fact, did the team give up its homely cambric and denim for crisp white suits with colorful blue baldricks.

Whatever their source, the demands of precision movement were fundamental to the morris experience. New team members could not be quickly integrated as in contras and squares. Normally, there was a recruiting season in the early spring, during which initiates were prepared for the busy performing period that extended through the summer. Practice sessions were not recreational events, but deliberate, repetitive efforts to master difficult movements. Performances took careful planning involving transportation, logistics, and organization to assure an adequate complement of experienced dancers.

Most often it was Frank Hall who kept pace and grasped the aesthetic demands of morris more quickly than others. Much as with the dance as a whole, Frank took up the cause of style and execution, pitting himself against a sometimes reluctant opposition who felt their camaraderie and leisure were under siege. Although he was not alone in these sentiments, most would credit him with the lion's share of concern for style in these formative years.

Until 1981, Frank assumed, informally and without discussion, the roles of "squire," responsible for team organizational matters, and "foreman," the team's authority on dance style and repertoire. But that year the team attended the first Midwest Morris Ale in Madison, Wisconsin, and there held an election to establish officers. Amy Novick was chosen as squire and remained so through 1984 when, as was her ambition, the team hosted the Midwest Ale in Bloomington. The team chose McCormick's Creek State Park, where Swing into Spring was held, as the site of the ale, and it attracted around twenty teams, some from as far away as Denver, Colorado.

An ale is a kind of morris dance convention and was established in the Midwest to be held each year over Memorial Day weekend. It was modeled after the Marlboro Ale (Vermont) and at first attracted a dozen or so Midwest teams, including the more experienced teams from Minneapolis and Madison. The first site was Madison, and thereafter it was to rotate among various Midwest host communities. A dozen or so Bloomington dancers attended the 1981 ale, and despite new uniforms and a new, improved hobbyhorse, it was entirely evident there and in successive years (Madison 1982, Ann Arbor 1983) that the northern teams took morris a great deal more seriously than Bloomington. Bloomington's self-identity as unambitious and "laid back" served as the backdrop for the team's bold move to host the 1984 ale.

By this date, Bloomington dancers had considerable experience organizing weekend events. Jane Henderson, who had cooked in fine restaurants for many years, took charge of meals. In previous ales, teams carpooled on all-day "tours" to performances throughout the surrounding area. In all there might be three tours with three teams traveling together, each tour stopping to perform three or four times throughout the day. Then all the teams reconvened in the late afternoon at the camp for a large performance together. Touring was risky: unforeseen logistical problems or lack of a crowd could bring a disappointing conclusion to a long drive. But with the advantage of spontaneity and the sheer strength of numbers that several teams together could provide, there was usually an exciting performance and a responsive crowd. Sometimes considerable strain was placed on the disposition of public space, particularly given that at many sites few people had any idea what morris dancing was. Some details had to be worked out in advance, such as whether it was legal to collect money, where exactly the dancing would take place, and how a crowd could be attracted on short notice.

Amy's chief mark on the ale tradition was to rent school buses, which would otherwise be idle on Saturday, so that groups of teams could ride together and not have to drive or navigate. This was a wonderful innovation because it provided a good atmosphere for sustained social interaction and even for informal English singing, which was a popular informal activity at ales. Buses continued to be used at succeeding ales.

Bloomington Quarry Morris still thrives with much the same principles with which it originated. In years immediately succeeding the Bloomington ale Martha Marmouzé (1984) and Amy Letson (1986) were elected as squires. Earlier, in 1979, morris dancer Mark Rosenthal moved to Bloomington and quickly established himself in the role of morris fool. He also introduced the team to rapper, a related form of English ritual dance. Rapper is an intricate sword dance performed with flexible rapper swords. It requires a good deal more skill than morris; in fact, some rapper dances have acrobatic figures such as flips. For this reason, it is more difficult for a community to sustain a rapper team. It employs a fixed set of five dancers, and the team that Mark coached consisted of Frank Hall, Pat Gingrich, Bill Meek, Tom Stio, and Paul Tyler. Mark soon left Bloomington, but the team remained together. They seldom gave performances, and when in 1982 the Shuffle Creek Dancers added rapper to their performance repertoire, the community rapper team was dissolved.

In both rapper and morris, the demands of precision movement brought newfound awareness of the politics of style. Originally, as a natural appendage of the dance group, morris and rapper were well served by community aesthetic principals that featured a natural pace of learning. The encounter with precision aesthetics, however, called into question this original aesthetic. It also presaged a drift away from organic continuity and toward representation as the link between presentational form and social ritual. This relationship between morris/rapper and organic community was always a part of folk school curricula, and it was in this spirit that morris was incorporated into dance group life. But it was not fundamental to social life in the way that contras and squares were. Where the social effects of contras and squares could be broadly integrative, morris and rapper were largely transitional, relying on established relationships of well-integrated participants. Moreover, events such as the Midwest Ale provided a different social and aesthetic realm—a trans-regional guild that superseded local community and provided an attractive complement to local experience.

19  MAY DAY

With the popularity of Easy Street, with trips by Bloomington dancers to dance camps, and with more frequent travels to festivals, the Bloomington group was beginning to become known among dance groups nationwide. During the late 1970s, the level of interaction with other old-time communities increased discernibly. Musicians and callers passing through the area were inclined to stop and visit, and some influential musicians moved to Bloomington during this time. This phenomenon was occurring in other places also, but the impact in Bloomington, as a small and isolated community, was to lend credence to the group's sense of purposeful community. Once some friends visiting me chanced upon North Carolina fiddler Bruce Green in a grocery store, reporting their serendipitous encounter as evidence of the attraction of old-time musicians to Bloomington, as evidence that Bloomington was a kind of "old-time Mecca."

Consequently, the small circle of friends who were once the dance group was slowly expanding, accepting travelers and newcomers into its center. Among those who would quickly make an impact were Jeff Claus and Judy Hyman. Jeff and Judy moved to Bloomington in the summer of 1976, just after they had met some of the Bloomington musicians at the Brandywine (Pennsylvania) festival. They were noticeably confident musicians. They knew their way around at festivals and played with authority. Judy played a hard-driving fiddle style and Jeff a vigorous and steady guitar. They had clear opinions about old-time music—notably that tunes should be played with little or no variation. Jeff's guitar style would be a major influence for Teri Klassen. Jeff became close to Strawberry McCloud and played with him frequently. Both were regulars at festivals and were known for their stamina at late-night sessions.

Judy came to Bloomington to study violin and for some time after their arrival played little old-time music. Jeff soon enrolled in an M.A. program in Instructional Systems Technology at Indiana University. In 1977, for one of his courses, he produced, with Doug Crosswhite of Tennvale Records, a classic LP recording of old-time music revival. Titled *An Anthology: Old Style, Old Time Fiddling*, the work included the fiddling of musicians then rarely recorded, such as Dan Gellert, David Molk, Brian Hubbard, Bruce Molsky, James Leva, Harold Hausenfleck, and Strawberry McCloud. The selections by Bloomington musicians constitute the best overall representation of old-time music in Bloomington during this early period.

The importance of this recording was its anthologizing of old-time revival musicians as ethnographic objects. In this respect it suggested the format of Ray Alden's influential two-volume recording *The Young Fogies* (1985), which outlined a vague chronology of the development of old-time music revival beginning with the New Lost City Ramblers and ending with the Tomkins County Horse Flies. Like *Young Fogies,* Jeff's *Anthology* was genuine in its ethnographic spirit. It was issued by Doug Crosswhite's recording company, Tennvale Records, a small company dedicated to productions of old-time fiddling, mostly by traditional fiddlers from the Tennessee River valley region where the company was based. The recording included a balanced sample of musicians with consummate skills and presented them in a way that deliberately drew attention to variations in style. This came, it should be noted, at a time when many young musicians were learning fiddle and might not yet be said to possess style independent of their mentors. After several years in Bloomington, Jeff and Judy left for the Ithaca, New York, area.

They later formed the Tomkins County Horse Flies and played a leading role in the sparse avant-garde old-time music style that came for a while to be known as "bug music."

Arriving soon after, in 1977, were Bill Thatcher and Teresa Broadwell, with Bill to study ethnomusicology at Indiana University. Teresa played fiddle; Bill played banjo, guitar, and bass. Although they were involved with the dance, their tastes were more eclectic and Teresa's fiddle style more progressive than most. Bob Lucas invited them to form a trio, and with the name the Bob Lucas Trio, they performed largely vocal arrangements of Bob's compositions and old-time songs. This group dispersed after a short while, and Bill and Teresa joined Bill and Kathy Sturbaum to form the New Moon Swing Band. New Moon featured tight classic jazz vocal arrangements with violin, guitar, and bass. They made one of the early recordings on the Bloomington-based Redbud label.

Of the old-time musicians who arrived during this period, however, only Brad Leftwich stayed in Bloomington and had a lasting impact. Already a proficient old-time musician, Brad had been a part of the thriving Lexington, Virginia, old-time music community in the mid-1970s and had played with the Plank Road String Band on both their recordings. But most significant was his relationship with celebrated North Carolina fiddler Tommy Jarrell: of many who visited Jarrell, Brad was his most serious and most accomplished student. Throughout Brad's career, Tommy Jarrell's influence has remained salient and profound.

Brad came to Bloomington to study anthropology at Indiana University and for a while played music infrequently. He became close to members of Easy Street and sat in with them for some of their last bookings. In 1981, a personal and musical relationship with Linda Higginbotham became serious. With Brad on fiddle and Linda on banjo, they formed a performing band with a series of different guitarists. In the mid-1980s Brad took a job at Indiana University and dropped plans to play music full-time. For some time after that, no Bloomington old-time music band aspired to earn a living through music. Still, after other Bloomington old-time musicians became less active, Brad and Linda continued to record and perform the conventional old-time sound with which Bloomington was long associated. Under the name Leftwich and Higginbotham, they made several recordings, including *Buffalo Gals* (Redbud Records 1011, 1984) and *No One to Bring Home Tonight* (County Records, 1985), which was the first recording in the County 700 series to feature younger musicians from outside traditional old-time music areas. In Bloomington, Brad began offering lessons to aspiring fiddlers and became a key link in the progression of old-time music to new generations of Bloomington musicians. During the 1980s, Brad and Linda's ambition and integrity were constant and grew to become the bedrock on which a host of ensembles, and perhaps much of the stature and vibrancy of the Bloomington old-time community, came to rest.

On the whole, Bloomington in the late 1970s was characterized by the influx of musicians who had considerable experience in other old-time music communities. This was possible because a network of music and dance communities nationwide was beginning to exert influence on the revival. Travel was more frequent, and dancers carried ideas and expectations from community to community. The "golden age" of innocent and spontaneous self-discovery in Bloomington was beginning to give way as Bloomington took its place in the array of other communities nationwide.

I should note here that this was also my period of arrival, in 1976, as I describe later in detail. My years in Bloomington corresponded to the growth of the historical self-concept of the group as the network of other dance communities grew up around it. Although I was predisposed to think along those lines, I am also certain that the many steps that led to this book grew out of a general feeling of historical value that emerged among Bloomington dancers during that period.

For the Wednesday Night Dance itself, the most influential of the late 1970s arrivals were probably Paul Tyler and Pat Gingrich. They moved to Bloomington late in 1978; the next year, Paul enrolled in the Folklore Institute. They had moved from Detroit where they, especially Paul, had helped organize dancing. They had participated in Detroit's strong international folk dance community, and Paul performed at a local coffee house. Both were avid folk musicians and dancers, and they absorbed skills and interests from a variety of arenas. On the whole, they brought to Bloomington tastes more eclectic than many were accustomed to.

Pat and Paul also differed from other arrivals of that era in that almost from the beginning they embraced the dance group as essential and important to their social and cultural well-being. And more than others, they came to Bloomington with confidence, charm, energy, and ideas. Perhaps this sprung from Paul's experience as a recreation leader at a church camp, perhaps from Pat's experience with North Carolina clogging, perhaps from Paul's upbringing in a small Indiana town where dance was an important social activity. They had genuine savvy in old-time music and dance culture but were not a part of the eastern and southern folk festival social network as were others. Indeed, they brought to Bloomington important community traditions that were only beginning to be associated with old-time music and dance revival.

One such tradition that they would successfully import was the sunrise May Day celebration in Ann Arbor. They had attended the early morning song and dance ceremony in 1977 and liked it enough to make copies of the song sheets. In Bloomington the next year, not long after their arrival, Paul decided to introduce the practice to the morris dance team. So he proposed hosting a party at their house, to be devoted in part to singing practice. They lived in Unionville, some ten miles from town, in a house too small for dancing, and Pat recalled being warned that parties without dancing were not common. The party was successful, however, and the reluctant morris dancers arose May Day morning before sunrise to greet the spring at the Monroe County Courthouse Square. The ceremony had been advertised for the public, but Pat recalled that only two spectators showed up that first year.

In years to follow, there was more enthusiasm and more attention. "Rise Up Jock," "Country Life," and other ritual songs popularized by English folksong recording groups became standard fare, and a sizable crowd of loyal supporters came at sunrise to listen and watch. One year, someone began the practice of decorating with morris ribbons the torch of the statue above the south door of the courthouse. By the mid-1980s, the team had scheduled morris performances at several locations and a party at the end of the day, amounting to an exhausting day of performance and celebration that began at sunrise. Because May Day might fall on any day of the week, it competed with work and other weekday obligations. Thus the impact of extending the sunrise experience into the day was to visibly interrupt Bloomington quotidian life with unauthorized celebration and to appropriate the rhythms of the body with merciless fatigue.

Eventually, the local newspapers took an interest in the celebration and sometimes used it as a feature story or photograph on an otherwise uneventful day. The attention from the local media gave the team and the dance group an added attachment, an even faintly totemic one, to the Bloomington community. The team's symbols that were adopted from civic artifacts as well as the use of the courthouse square as the pre-eminent site of the celebration made unprecedented inroads into the public sphere.

This was an appropriation of the civic sphere. It began at dawn, at a time when the workday and nightlife dispositions of civic authority were at their farthest remove. Moreover, the adopted civic symbols—blue for "Blue-mington," the fish from the courthouse weathervane—stood only ironically for any substantive sense of civic community. What *was* substantive was the intense celebratory spirit that the team initiated in the quiet of dawn and then infused into Bloomington's quotidian habits throughout the day.

Old-Time Music and Dance

20 DARE TO BE SQUARE

In addition to his involvement with the sunrise May Day celebration, Paul Tyler was also an experienced caller of southern squares and perhaps the first in the group to embrace squares deliberately as an alternative to contras. It was not that Bloomington had any antipathy to squares—which had, after all, been Barry Kern's trademark as a caller—but the group seemed to have settled into a set of stock preferences that Paul challenged. Somehow, the issue of how many of each to do had not arisen.

For all their similarities—both are essentially figure dances or set dances, describing mostly floor pattern movement of dancers arranged in sets—contras and squares are fundamentally different dances. Squares require a fixed number of dancers (usually eight) in a set. So dancing a square necessitates enumeration, most noticeably when dancers in the last unfilled set must coerce reluctant dancers to join or give up and sit out unwillingly. Couples in a contra set or line—"as many as will," so goes the saying—join at the bottom end until the line is full, and then start another line. Contra sets are usually large—the length of the room—so that many dancers interact. In a square one normally interacts only with the three other couples in the set, suggesting a closed community with fixed neighbors and codes of conduct. According to many contemporary dancers who have tried both, the social perception of each of the two is profoundly different.

When Mary Dart asked dance leaders nationwide why dancers preferred contras over squares, predictably, these structural features were given as the reasons (1995: 179). Still, however tempting this functional reasoning might be, it is important to note that it was the particular vision of community—egalitarian openness—that prevailed in these dance groups that made the effortless inclusiveness of the contra so attractive. One could use the same logic in favor of the square if the preference was for sustained, repetitive encounters. It is also worth noting that the Southern Appalachian "big set" incorporates most of the same attractive features as contras and has long been accessible to dancers in dance camp instructional programs. Yet it is practically nonexistent in revival community dances and has never been promoted as a more fulfilling synthesis of the two forms (see Jamison 1993).

Contras were also notoriously easy to learn, choreograph, and notate at a time of widespread expansion of dance communities. An experienced dancer, for example, could easily jot down the figures of a contra as it ended, finishing in time to get a partner for the next dance. An ambitious caller could throw together some new combination of contra figures, give it some sentimental name, and call it a "composition." Widely varying results in composing gave rise to an increasingly acute aesthetic consciousness, rapidly adapting the contra form to the social-interactional tastes of the new communities. Experienced callers and dancers consistently referred Mary Dart to the "story line" or "social plot" of a contra, reflecting awareness of complex social and physical relationships associated with roles, figures, and transitions between figures (1995: 108–10). With this acute sensitivity, contra choreography over the 1970s and 1980s was designed around the desire to extend dancer interactions beyond traditional limits (even in complex ways such as by involving more than the minor set of two couples) and also to provide, overall, a "balance of opposite sex and same sex, one-to-one, and group interactions" (106).

Composing was a novelty at first: when Dillon Bustin wrote "Anne's a Bride Tonight," it was a rare event to compose a new dance. But in

Old-Time Music and Dance

1983, the publication of Larry Jennings's encyclopedic *Zesty Contras*, with many of its 500 dances newly composed, opened the door for many to write their own dances. By the mid-1980s, new compositions predominated at dance events, and good composers were becoming known as celebrities. Ironically, one of the first to complain was Ted Sannella, who during the 1980s introduced his dance composition workshops with the question, "Why compose new contras?" "Philosophically," he once phrased it, "I feel there are enough dances out there; we really don't need new dances because there's a wealth of material" (Sannella 1986: 28).

The barrage of new compositions might have led to stratification—a realism of particulars—among contra enthusiasts, as those who kept pace had the upper hand at dance events. But what kept everyone on equal footing was that the new compositions were based largely on the same set of twenty or so figures. Callers and dancers still could abide by the inviolable principle that dances must be accessible to beginners, and teaching must still consist of the brief "walkthrough." For composers, this was a happy compromise: as Mary Dart facetiously computed, the number of compositions logically possible with the twenty figures was 390 million (Dart 1995: 83). Equally facetious was the "bad contra contest" first held in Chicago in 1983, which toyed with the composition craze and its propensity to patch together figures willy-nilly. The rules required that entries fit a standard tune, draw from existing figures and use more than one, and be "theoretically danceable"—all, ostensibly, with the idea of providing a legitimate test of the contra aesthetic (see Dart 1995: 121).

There was also—in distinguishing contras and squares—the issue of the role of the caller. Dart's experts noted the purity of the relationship in contras between dancers and musicians, and also the freedom to improvise that self-structured contras provided dancers. And there were also community issues, which were felt particularly in sustained communities like Bloomington. Callers had come to be servants to the community, efficiently yet unobtrusively providing the dances that everyone liked. Callers such as Bill Meek had become known for "calling from the floor," taking their place among the dancers, rather than a position of prominence with a microphone on stage. (There were no

Dare to Be Square

cordless mikes at the time, as there are today.) This kind of servant-caller was probably a local development, since, traditionally, country-dancing masters could be strict and authoritative—Tolman and Page referred to "birch-rod authority"—regardless of the form or level of difficulty of the material (1937: 18; see also Spalding 1993: 237–40).

The simplicity of contras did not always preclude showmanship, and some contra callers became known for extravagant instruction that kept dancers waiting. There was always discontent over this practice, and Chicago again took the lead in undermining it with inverted humor. The Breaking Up Thanksgiving weekend instituted a "five-minute rule" for teaching dances, with a committee of children keeping time. If the dance did not start on time, the children briskly pulled the caller off stage with a "hook."

In contrast to contras, southern squares required constant prompting. In most traditions, merely filling this need constituted something of a performance; in some, callers gained charisma for flamboyant styles and for facility with improvised verbal "patter." For example, a contra dance instruction might state, "Active women lead your partner around the inactives." "Translated" into traditional square dance patter, this same figure might well become "Chase that rabbit, chase that squirrel, chase that pretty girl 'round the world."

And there were historical considerations that favored contras. Contras were derived primarily from English longways set dances and squares from French quadrilles. Contras were among America's earliest popular dances, quickly taking on their own "Americanized" identity (Tyler 1992a: 127). With rising political tensions, particularly during the War of 1812, prevailing anti-British sentiment brought disfavor onto the "country-dance," as it was called, in most areas. It was then, according to Ralph Page (1973), that contras settled into rural New England among reclusive pacifists. Later, in the nineteenth century, there was intense pressure to adopt any of several new dance forms that swept over America in waves of popularity. Apparently, it was primarily stubborn resistance to change that kept contras alive (Page 1976: 9, cited in Dart 1995: 10). But one need not even take this account as fact: it was Page's historical voice that propelled the contra revival at the time it confronted the post-WWII dance audience.

According to these historical accounts, it should hardly be surprising that the revival of contras in New England in the 1960s and 1970s would come on the wings of counterculture ideology, as Richard Nevell (1977) later concluded. Neither, perhaps, should it be surprising that the revival of squares derived from the cotillion form would have flourished in the atmosphere of nationalism during World War II and the Cold War. Indeed, the revival of squares was associated not so much with small communities or cultural "islands," as Tolman and Page had called them, but with the expansive club square dance movement. Contra revivalists knew well the capacity for aggressive rigidity of the postwar square dance movement, which operated through a network of organized "clubs" and explicit doctrine. Even as late as 1986, Indianapolis dancer and dance historian Eddie Grogan still characterized this as a difference aligned with postwar ideology:

> Old-time dancing in America today is carried on by two distinct groups, the Western square dance clubs and the country dance revivalists. Both groups exist side-by-side and are both products of middle class American culture of the latter half of the twentieth century, but many of their values, aspirations and aesthetics contrast sharply. These two groups typify the reactions of two different generations to traditional American dance. . . .
>
> The clubs came of age in the 1950's, the era of the "Corporation Man" and no-limit growth. Their club structure with its officers, committees and "levels" of dance attainment, is corporate and hierarchical in nature. The country dance revival, on the other hand, came of age in the wake of the "counter-culture" and radical movements that have come to characterize the 1960's. Some revivalists are veterans of that era and some are not, but the habits and outlooks of most are tinged with the anti-authoritarian attitudes of that time. (Grogan 1986: 6)

Nor was it simply that club square dancing required expensive uniforms, graded lessons, certificates of achievement, set partners, and club membership. In the 1950s, club dance callers spearheaded a movement to eliminate live music because of its unreliability and because a caller could make considerably more money without the expense of a band. And there were also troubling encounters between the two worlds. When the massive National Square Dance Convention met in Indianapolis, Bloomington dancer Jim Johnson was ushered away by an armed guard while attempting to deliver some magazines to a vendor. At a large public event in Chicago, a contra caller was said to have had her microphone jerked away from her by a square dancer on the premise that she was calling without a "license." And it was becoming known that square dancers had been lobbying to have the U.S. Congress recognize square dance by law as the "national folk dance" of America (see U.S. Congress 1984; Mangin 1995). These accounts constituted a part of the ideological boundary by which the old-time music and dance revival was defined.

But square dances also had deep roots as community tradition, and it was in this sense that Paul and others in Bloomington enjoyed them. Many Bloomington dancers did prefer contras, but without much controversy, squares eventually took their place as a genuine part of the repertories of the best callers. In fact, the Bloomington dance was never referred to as a "contra group" as became common elsewhere, and except for a brief period in the late 1970s, there were always callers who called squares. Years later, some Midwesterners were bewildered when the issue became divisive nationwide with the publication in 1989 of a confrontational article by North Carolina dancer Phil Jamison in the old-time music publication *Old-Time Herald*. Often known by its subtitle, "Dare to Be Square!" the article outlined the structural advantages of squares and unleashed the frustrations of those weary of the relentless and uncritical appeal of what Jamison called "contra-mania."

Uniquely, he said, squares featured the spontaneity of patter calls and of dance figures called on the fly. Musicians were in most cases free to play "crooked" tunes outside the AABB melodic formula. Social interaction in the square was repetitive and sustained for longer periods than in contras, providing a more intimate dance encounter for veterans and a more integrative experience for newcomers. Squares were shorter in duration, so there could be more of them in an evening—and less chance a new dancer would sit out for long periods. And squares were technically simpler and less intellectual, providing fewer barriers to a sustained and intimate social experience. Because of all of this, Jamison believed that with squares, the caller, musicians, and dancers operated as a more unified creative organism (1989: 23).

It is odd that for Jamison and, as I observed it, many others, north-south rivalry did not play a part in the relationship between squares and contras and also between the music associated with each. In fact, contra-mania spread in all regions, and squares endured in cultural pockets where they had been established earlier. As a North Carolina square caller, Jamison felt alienated by his own local dance as much as any other. Foremost, it was the Knoxville, Tennessee, dance weekend where many from the South and from neighboring regions first experienced the intoxicating lure of the big-ball contra dance.

Jamison also wondered if the decline of squares might be related to disturbing changes in the character of old-time dance revival which occurred simultaneously with "contra-mania." This term came to characterize the rise in popularity of contras in the 1980s and also the differing tastes of the new proponents. Many new dancers did not have the historical curiosity that was definitive of the folk music boom. And many now came to dances as consumers, to be entertained, so that bands had to "resort to gimmicks to keep them satisfied" (1989: 23). Because of this, musicians had become alienated from their own communities; many only attended dances when they had to play.

It would be over-reaching, of course, to suggest that a resurgence of squares could rescue old-time dance revival from this social alienation. Historically, early contra revival groups were, to a fault, paragons of organic community, and today's contra revival veterans complain of many of the same ills that Jamison observed. What's more, the "square-mania" of the 1950s club dance movement was a great deal more consumer oriented than anything Jamison could have observed of contras. Nonetheless, when 1980s "mania" struck, contras and not squares were indeed the main object of desire, and they were well suited to a new dancer population that preferred greater intellectual challenge, more social distance, and less historical grounding.

Jamison's article was photocopied and passed around at dances, and it stoked the passions of those who liked squares everywhere. I remember seeing a stack at Breaking Up Thanksgiving in Chicago, where squares had enjoyed a loyal following from the start and where, at the time, a stock of very good square callers were at their peak of enthusiasm and confidence. My impression at the time was that Bloomington-generation dance groups still viewed themselves as hybrid old-time dance groups that had not yet been infected by contra-mania.

Recently, Jamison has written a retrospective of his article (2004), casting the debate in different terms, yet ever resolved that contra-mania has been an enduring affliction to old-time dance community. In the years between the two articles, he observes, enthusiasm for contra dance has indeed grown, and with it has come more outspoken intolerance for squares and sometimes also for old-time music.

The most important change in Jamison's retrospective involves a shift in the operative historical narrative. He examines a setting where contras and squares contended for prominence in New Orleans after the Louisiana Purchase of 1803 and before the War of 1812. In this setting, Americans had taken control of a city where French-speaking Creoles, who were wildly fond of set dance, outnumbered English speakers by as many as twelve to one. Political and cultural tensions were rife, and one frequent context for dispute was the ballroom. There Creoles preferred quadrilles (French *contredanses*, with set numbers of participants) while Americans preferred English longways country-dances. Ordinarily the issue was managed by quotas, eventually enacted into law, with set proportions of French quadrilles and English country-dances maintained in each event.

Jamison's account is impressive in the extent to which it provides historical depth to a distinction that has otherwise seemed a contemporary contrivance. But Jamison is also observant of the manner by which the Americans presumed upon the Creoles. In the 1804 incident called the "war of the quadrilles," six American couples added onto a longways set, insisting that the music continue to accommodate the new dancers. The band declined to continue, and violence erupted over the issue. This structural feature—the ability of the contra to accommodate "as many as will"—was then and is now the distinctive feature that accommodates the exuberant, cosmopolitan manner that constitutes contra-mania.

As Jamison admits, there are problems with attributing this historical foundation to contemporary contra dance. Much changed after the War of 1812. The enthusiastic Kentuckians who insisted upon extending their set later shifted loyalties decisively, as did many others outside of

Old-Time Music and Dance

rural New England. A century later Lloyd Shaw would conclude that squares were the prototypical "American" dance. Later, so also did club square dancers, who in the 1980s spearheaded the movement to establish the square as the American national dance. Against this backdrop, the New Orleans occupation was a thin historical sliver, with many decades of square-mania piled against it.

Jamison identifies a more likely influence in his insightful analysis of John Playford. He notes that in successive editions of Playford's *The English Dancing Master* (1651–1728), the number of longways dances prevailed increasingly upon other forms. Playford's influence extended to the American colonies, where English dancing masters taught the most popular dance forms. These dances formed the basis of the tradition that was reclaimed in the postwar revival. They also came to the revival directly from Playford via Cecil Sharp, who was acutely aware of Playford's formative and deliberate influence. Of Playford's fondness for the longways form, Sharp wrote that "he forced it into prominence to the exclusion of the earlier and less flexible types."

Jamison once believed that squares and contras could happily coexist in postwar dance communities. But now he has much cause to wonder if they are structurally and historically incompatible, and advocates the formation of a separate tradition of communities where the long-established affiliation of squares and old-time music can be enjoyed. This is without doubt a legitimate concern and reasonable conclusion. But my question here is, given the imponderable weight of history that lay before it, how and why was this unhappy marriage ever attempted in the first place?

The encounter at the stump in Bloomington presupposed no such separation of squares and contras. Indeed, it made worlds collide in an instant—contra dance and old-time music—based on the ability of each to manifest traditional community. Very soon squares were introduced, with the pleasure of community equally apparent as before, and in the innocence of discovery no one had cause to believe one dance form superior to the other. When each was embraced, it was embraced with curiosity, awkwardness, awe. As time passed, dancers and callers did develop preferences, and for reasons well known to most everyone, contras came to predominate.

Dare to Be Square

All along, however, community prevailed, and with it an enduring regard for friendship over style and a distaste for any programmatic atmosphere. After Barry Kern, a steady sequence of capable and influential Bloomington callers became outspoken advocates for squares—Paul Tyler, Frank Hall, Mary Beth Roska. Later Bridget Edwards moved to Bloomington from Baltimore, bringing with her a contagious and forthright fondness for squares. Among touring callers, Sandy Bradley and Bernard Chalk were among the most popular ever to visit Bloomington.

It is of possible relevance that Bloomington felt a direct historical link to New England and to the more catholic attitude of dance tradition there. In the 1970s, the New England origins of contra dance were known and respected to a greater extent than today. Dancers knew that Dillon learned to dance there and knew of Dudley Laufman from his trip to Bloomington. Sweet Willie, Eddie Grogan's tragic hero, made his pilgrimage there and was love-struck partly because Fair Nancy embodied the spiritual authenticity of her region. Other real dancers made this pilgrimage also. I remember hearing of Paul Tyler's trip to Concord, New Hampshire, which Paul and I thought a formative site. Ted Hall and I stopped at a dance outside Brattleboro, Vermont, on the way back from Pinewoods. We experienced dance as deeply connected to place—not as a disembodied structure. Squares and contras were not to be compared on a common scale.

Moreover, New England provided an apt historical model for the experiment combining the two. Ralph Page—a genuine cultural ancestor for the contra revival—had an outspoken fondness for squares. His chapter with Beth Tolman is called "Hats Off to France," and it admiringly recounts the efforts of the French dancing masters who came to America with French troops during the Revolution. The quadrille that they brought "so fascinated everybody that it immediately took hold and spread like measles in a kindergarten" (Tolman and Page 1937: 58). The figures Tolman and Page include in their examples "are those called by contemporary New England prompters and have never before seen print" (60).

It was this historical narrative that enabled the originating spirit of community dance revival in Bloomington. The account that passed through Ralph Page to Dudley Laufman had depicted contras as allied with rural life and as fundamental to a worldview that linked dance to organic community. In this worldview, contras and squares were not at odds but were natural allies in the formation of community.

It is even possible that the structural distinction between contras and squares—which provide Jamison's strongest argument for separation—was important to the type of organic community imagined in Bloomington. Openness, which contras so famously facilitate, was an important component in Bloomington community. It provided a connection to the folk revival at large and to the counterculture, and it was important in its juxtaposition to conventional locality. New dancers provided affirmation for the community and intrigue and excitement within the social network. Openness was also an express component of postwar intentional community and was taken to extremes in some communes. More broadly, social openness was considered a key alternative to the alienating structures inherited from the 1950s.

But there was a countervailing reclusiveness, a core of intimate familiarity, that was not to be yielded. For this reason excessive recruitment of new dancers—advertising—was discouraged. There was clearly a social formation, apart from but not outside of the dance, that the phrase "breaking into the group" described. This interiority was not mapped by social status, such as the "center set syndrome" suggests, but familiarity. It was a psychological bonding that came from common experience, self-revelation, and consonance of values. Its absence in contramania is one of the key characteristics by which veteran dancers are repelled.

So there was a counterbalancing social effect among squares and contras and among the adherents of each. But this was not the most important reason they were both embraced. Foremost, the absence of either would have necessitated an intolerable exclusion—of part of the community, of a regional affiliation, of a key source of ideas and of spiritual authenticity. And it would have necessitated the act of exclusion itself, the very antithesis of postwar intentional community.

When Fred Park used to extol the virtues of what he called "antique social dance," it was to extract from it the powerful rapprochement of self and other. This was foremost a physical, emotional, and spiritual

Dare to Be Square

rapprochement, but it implicated, by design and by default, the historical and cultural rapprochement that self and other entail. And it was
also a rapprochement of the other of dance—the authentic other of
traditional community—from which the contemporary self had become
estranged. This was why instruction of this type was thought necessary
and fitting: to learn to dance was to experience the emergence of a kind
of community that the prejudices of contemporary consciousness pre-
cluded.

21 THE SHUFFLE CREEK CLOGGERS

Pat Gingrich's dance experiences pre-dated her years in Detroit. A native of North Carolina, she had studied nursing at the University of North Carolina at Chapel Hill, the site of the vibrant old-time music community associated with the Fuzzy Mountain String Band. At about the same time in nearby Greenville, the youthful Green Grass Cloggers were merging traditional dance steps with revivalist tastes and values, creating a new dance style in their wake. Just as community square dance revivalists adopted community dance styles and attitudes and rejected club square dancing, just as the old-time music revival first arose at a distance from the fiddle contest movement, so also did the clogging revival look directly to traditional southern step dancers, such as Willard Watson of North Carolina, and rejected an established revival—competition team clogging—as too rigid a model (Jamison 1987–88, 1988, 1995). The term "hippie clogging" was used occasionally to distinguish the traditional step dance revival from competition team clogging. One early team that took this approach was Chapel Hill's Apple Chill Cloggers, a spin-off group that closely preserved the style and ambiance of the Green Grass ensemble. Members of the Apple Chill performing team led freestyle clogging and square dancing at the Station, a Chapel Hill bar, which, for a while, Pat attended.

By 1978 when Pat and Paul moved to Bloomington, clogging was common fare at folk festivals and dance camps and was a featured category at some traditional fiddle contests. Indeed, many Bloomington dancers knew some kind of traditional step dance. But there had been no sustained effort at organized clogging in Bloomington, and the reasons for this may have been structural. Traditional clogging, it seems, was most commonly found in one of three performance modes: (1) an improvisational embellishment to a walking step during figure dancing, (2) a category of individual or group competition, or (3) a display form presented with "precision" coordination by set ensembles called "teams." According to Gail Matthews-DeNatale (Matthews 1983), in western North Carolina where all three forms have had a lengthy coexistence in the same region, the first (embellishment to walking step) was the oldest and persevered only because proponents of the old style retained staunch conservative attitudes, resisting change. Traditional dancers described this dance form as every bit community social dance and explicitly regarded modernization as loss of community. So it would seem that the old style would be precisely the type of structure suited to old-time dance revival groups. But this was not what was being promoted in the old-time clogging revival. What the Apple Chill model suggested, at least to Pat and others at the time, was a structure not that dissimilar to morris dance: a non-professional team that practiced and gave occasional performances, with membership open to community members.

It should be said that in these formative years there was little awareness of the structural underpinning of clogging or any other of these dance styles. Probably because of their folk qualities, they just seemed naturally to go together with contra dancing, old-time music, morris dance, and so on. It may well also have been that open membership was merely a useful expedient to getting a team started where none existed. Still, with these principles operative, Pat began teaching freestyle clogging in 1978 on Wednesdays just before the Wednesday Night Dance. Soon after, she moved the meetings to Sundays at Studio Space for the Performing Arts on Fourth Street. During that first year her class cohered to the extent that Pat could book a performance engagement at

Old-Time Music and Dance

the Indiana Fiddlers' Gathering for June of 1979. It was in preparation for this performance that the notion of an organized team arose. The team's name, taken from the name of the road near Pat and Paul's home, was the Shuffle Creek Cloggers.

During those early years there were many personnel changes in the team. The group that danced at Battleground comprised, in addition to Pat and Paul, Teresa Broadwell, Frank Hall, Martha Marmouzé, Anne Reese, and Mark Rosenthal. Dillon Bustin was recruited on the morning of the performance as the eighth dancer. By 1981, in just three years, the team had used over thirty different dancers! For Pat, this meant teaching old routines repeatedly to new dancers.

The group performed infrequently at first. Its first festivals included the Battleground Fiddlers' Gathering, Kentucky Music Weekend in Louisville, and the Oliver Winery Festival in Bloomington. The latter venue was shared with the morris team, so those who danced both morris and clogging had to shuttle in and out of their costumes several times during the day. The first dance routines were, as was the prevailing style then, square dance figures performed with a limited variety of steps. There was the "Indiana Star," which Pat derived from the Apple Chill Cloggers' "Carolina Star," and there was a routine composed from the square dances "Texas Star" and "Bucksaw Reel." Choreography at that time was a group effort; practices were often devoted to trying out new figures and assembling them into routines. Initially the group danced in unmodified shoes as a gesture of authenticity, but later added taps to enhance their impact in performances.

With the frequency of personnel turnover and poor attendance at practice, the team's preparation for jobs had increasingly depended on Pat. During a particular ebb in momentum in April of 1982, she began considering giving up the team by rejecting bookings. But a phone call from Frank Hall changed that plan. Frank was winding up his affairs with Easy Street and was considering career alternatives. Although he had danced infrequently with Shuffle Creek, he was developing an interest in dance as a profession. His professional aspirations provided the needed boost of momentum, so the more ambitious team members closed ranks and made commitments to performance and practice schedules. In addition to Pat and Frank, there were Cliff Emery, Jana

The Shuffle Creek Cloggers at Battleground, 1980. During their early years, the team wore calico dresses, jeans, and unmodified shoes. From left, Ann Prochilo, Cliff Emery, Linda Higginbotham, Brad Leftwich, Reen Dobie, Mark Rosenthal, Pat Gingrich, Paul Tyler. Photo courtesy of Dillon Bustin.

Rygas, Paul Tyler, and Tamara Loewenthal (from Pittsburgh, where the Coal Country Cloggers were the resident team). During the summer, the team recruited Mary Beth Roska, who had danced with the Wild Goose Chase Cloggers in Minneapolis.

Practice sessions were held twice weekly, in the mornings, beginning in May of that year. The team entered several clogging contests and began booking jobs more deliberately. In addition to the Indiana Fiddlers' Gathering, the Oliver Winery Festival, and Kentucky Music Weekend, they performed at the Indianapolis Zoo, at the Lebanon (Indiana) Ham Days, at the Four-Wheel-Drive and Off-Road Show, and at a convention in Louisville.

In 1983, the team hired Amy Novick as booking manager, the first Bloomington dance group performing ensemble to use a salaried manager. The group's schedule became increasingly busy. Included were performances at the Winnipeg Folk Festival (1984), the Edmonton Folk Festival (1985), Wheatland (Michigan) Folk Festival (1984,

Old-Time Music and Dance

1986), Hiawatha (Michigan) Folk Festival (1986), Irish festivals in Milwaukee and Boston, and a weeklong workshop at Wolf Trap Farm Park (Vienna, Virginia, near Washington, D.C.). Their repertoire soon expanded to include Irish step dance, rapper, morris, French Canadian step dance, and English clogging. Inspired by a 1984 jazz dance class and unaware that modern dance was having a similar influence on tradition-based teams elsewhere, Pat composed an ambitious dance routine to Pete Sutherland's "Poor Man's Dream." In 1985 the group produced a Step-Dance Weekend, which offered advanced instruction in clogging, Irish step dance, and traditional tap dance to participants from across the country. In 1986 the team added three new members to the five—Abby Ladin from Baltimore, Bob Gingrich from Chicago, and Tom Kendrick of Minneapolis.

This impressive success became possible, in part, when the team's organic ties to the dance group were severed. As an extension of the Wednesday Night Dance, the team had incorporated by default the most important of its organizational principles—open membership, democratic decision making, balanced participation. When the team was professionalized, strict artistic and performance standards eventually gained precedence over the inherited performance practices of the community. Some of these same issues continue to haunt traditional step dancers in western North Carolina, where the long transition from social dance to public display has produced stylistic and ideological enclaves that must compete for support within a common populace (Matthews 1983). For some in Bloomington this was a painful process, particularly since it was not clear at many points whose aspirations were to be followed. Eventually, after the departure of several of those whose original ties were formed under the implicit auspices of the Wednesday Night Dance, the fallout from this transition was largely forgotten. Later, the group changed its name to Rhythm and Shoes, was reborn into the step dance revival, and there achieved widespread success and notoriety.

In some ways these were inevitable structural changes. In the late 1970s when Shuffle Creek was successfully operating as an extension of the dance group, many dance communities had a performing clogging team. In a very short time, particularly in the Midwest, most had disappeared. And in the same locales, morris dance was often seen to thrive and grow, always as a non-professional institution. It seems that after the glow of its antiquity had faded, community team clogging ultimately placed too many demands on its venues, on its dancers, and, most of all, on its organizers. And it could establish neither the aesthetic autonomy nor the deep connection with ritual transition and contemporary values as did morris.

22  THE OLD LIBRARY

During the late 1970s, Frank Hall, Ted Hall, and Bill Meek began calling and by the end of the decade would be the busiest callers at the dance. In June of 1979, the dance bought its first sound system for $348. It may be difficult for readers to imagine that the group endured seven years without sound amplification, but indeed that was the case. A new informal music group called C-band was meeting, with Ted Hall on guitar, Toby Bonwit on piano, Bill Meek on fiddle, and Stan Sitko on hammered dulcimer. The first dance group T-shirts were designed by Margie VanAuken—a dancing lady and fiddling kitten printed on yellow and later blue cotton and used for the jacket design of this book. The Bloomington dance became a stopping place for touring callers and bands. Financial records show that through 1980 the group had hosted Sandy Bradley, the Highwoods Stringband, Jim Morrison, Tracy Schwarz, Jon Sundell, Bernard Chalk, Pete Sutherland, and Claudio Buchwald.

The Wednesday Night Dance, meanwhile, was facing a challenge. In late 1978 Parks and Recreation decided to use the Jukebox for ceramics classes. When the ceramics equipment was moved in, the dance had to move out. From then until 1980 dancers relocated several times, unable to find a suitable home. For a few weeks it was in the Center for University Ministries on East Third Street and, for a longer time, at Hunter School on West Second. On several occasions it was held at the Unitarian Universalist church. It had a fairly long stay in the empty space above what was then Court Furniture on Fourth Street downtown. The second story there had a beautiful, springy wood floor and was leased for artists by a group called Studio Space for the Performing Arts. The building was later demolished and replaced with a parking garage. Finally, one memorable and thankfully brief location, Ted Hall recalled, was Scott Andrick's barn on rural Bethel Lane across from Marlin School.

The dance was upstairs in the loft; you had to climb a ladder to get up there. There was hay piled around, so after a valiant cleaning effort, water was sprinkled on the floor to control the dust. At one point someone was calling a dance with a down-the-center-four-in-line figure, which meant that the cumulative weight of the dancers went down the center also. This caused a significant sway in the building, enough that the musicians stopped playing, and Tom Stio grabbed onto a post. The dancers and the building survived, but, for the remaining meetings in that loft, no more dances were allowed that included that figure.

In 1980, the dance at last found a stable location. The county had recently undertaken a renovation of the historic building at Sixth and Washington that once housed the Monroe County Library. The building was to be converted into a county museum. Partial funding came from CETA (Comprehensive Employment and Training Act), the Carter-era employment program that funded on-the-job training for new workers in skilled trades. Some from the dance group took jobs in the restoration under this program. There was a finished basement in the building, featuring an open room with a small stage that was to be rented out to community groups. Like the best of previous dance spaces, the building was located along the civic-campus corridor. Better yet, it was across the street from Rapp's Pizza Train, a half-block from the Boys' Club, and within walking distance from the residences of many others who lived in the area west of the campus. Except for four supporting poles and hard, tile-over-concrete flooring, it was perfect.

Indeed, most dancers loved this space. Eventually, the group arranged

Old-Time Music and Dance

to store the sound system in a locked closet, eliminating much hauling and setting up during the winter months. Occasionally the museum would display on the walls artwork by students from the Monroe County Schools, where some dancers' children attended. And there was a subtle sense of common purpose with the historic significance of the building. But in spite of this, relations with the proprietors became strained. A can of paint disappeared, and the dance group was held responsible, largely by default. Then, despite years of continuous Wednesday night use during most of the year, the proprietors several times double-booked the hall and gave it to other renters. This was all the more upsetting since the dancers considered themselves model tenants, participating in benefit performances, making prompt payments, and cleaning the hall far more extensively than the rental agreement ever specified.

Finally, in 1986, a movement to relocate the dance began to swell. Harmony School, an alternative school that several dancers' children attended, had recently acquired an old public school building with a gym attached. The gym's acoustic qualities were not good, but it had a springy wood floor. After satisfactory preliminary arrangements were made to use the gym for dancing, proponents of the move scheduled a test dance there on a Wednesday night. A vote was taken afterward, and the group voted to relocate to Harmony School, where it has been ever since.

The period of dislocation and the ongoing tension with proprietors must have contributed to the existential atmosphere of the dance, confirming its estrangement from the mainstream. Although no official affiliation was ever sought with any venue or any proprietor, the potential for a relationship of extended loyalty was probably immense. Dancers yearned for proprietors to share in their sense of purpose and were hurt when rifts occurred. But this kind of alliance was not to be, and the prevailing distaste for authority was only amplified by the consequences of homelessness. What would have happened if the group had entered the 1980s allied with some proprietor is not known. As it turned out, much effort toward fostering community that might have come from such an alliance was instead diverted toward celebration. If anything, this was the mission that emerged from the period of dislocation.

Dancing at the Old Library, Christmas Day, 1984. From left, Spencer Mackall (seated), Les Chih, Jean Farmer, Paul Johnston, Cynthia Bretheim, Amy Letson (on fiddle in background), Eloise Clark, Ted Hall, Ken Bardonner, Bonnie Gordon, Jim Johnson (on guitar in background). Photo courtesy of Bill Baus.

It also fueled loyalty toward those in neighboring communities who were attempting to start dances. In 1979, a group in Indianapolis began a Tuesday night dance at the Hummingbird, a spacious bar in the northeast suburbs that featured folk music performances. The earliest group of dancers included Altha Cravey, Georgia Cravey, Eddie Grogan, Patrick Hauck, and Helen Rothfuss. According to Georgia Cravey, Bloomington dancers Susan Hollis, Ted Hall, and Bill Meek were instrumental during the early months in organizing trips to Indianapolis every Tuesday night to help with the dance. This was no small effort: two of the three were schoolteachers at the time, at schools in counties adjacent to Monroe County. After the evening with a drive of well over an hour

Old-Time Music and Dance

each way to and from the Indianapolis dance, they faced a lengthy early-morning drive to work the next day. Undoubtedly, they sensed a unity of purpose with the new group, for little else would have made the trip worthwhile. The Indianapolis dance thrives now with a core of talented musicians and callers. In October of 1985, the group began producing its own annual dance weekend, the Gypsy Moon Ball.

After 1980, many new callers and musicians became active in the Bloomington dance. Susan Hollis began calling in 1981 and quickly became important. Tamara Loewenthal, Pat Gingrich, and Mary Beth Roska began calling occasionally. Ted Hall, Brian Hubbard, Jim Johnson, Spencer Mackall, Mitch Rice, Gary Stanton, Tom Stio, Paul Tyler, David Weirhake, and I were among those who played music then. Rapp's Pizza Train closed in 1982. After about a year at Nero's on Walnut Street, the after-the-dance gathering settled into a pleasant stay at Leslie's Italian Villa, which opened in the Sixth and Washington location that had previously housed Rapp's. Once again, some group members, including Jane Henderson, worked at the restaurant, and its owners, Frank and Leslie Worth, became the group's friends.

In October of 1979 the dance group published its only newsletter, "BOTMDG News," claiming Grand Right and Left Publishers as publisher and Back Step Cindy as editor-in-chief. (BOTMDG is the acronym for Bloomington Old-Time Music and Dance Group.) The obscurity of this now-forgotten document surely illustrates the lack of sustained interest in Bloomington in organizational structure. The newsletter announced that the dance would move indoors to Hunter School on October 31 and reported on the continuing search for a permanent location. It announced that Toby Bonwit would replace Donna Doughten, charged with conspicuous absence, on the Gang of Four. Finally, it announced the upcoming "Breaking Up Thanksgiving" dance weekend at the home of Gene and Margaret Ritchie in the rural farmland west of Chicago.

23   SUGAR HILL

Breaking Up Thanksgiving was a weekend-long celebration of old-time music and dance beginning on the Friday after Thanksgiving. For a modest donation, floor space was provided for sleeping and some food for meals. But meals were mostly potluck contributions, especially leftovers from Thanksgiving dinners. Word was spread throughout the Midwest music and dance network.

At the time, there were old-time musicians widely dispersed throughout the Midwest. At festivals such as the Battleground Fiddlers' Gathering (near Lafayette, Indiana), the Eagle Creek Folk Festival (near Indianapolis), and the New Harmony Festival of Traditional Music (New Harmony, Indiana, near Evansville), they had formed a loose alliance. While few communities at the time had dance groups, many had old-time performing bands that were sometimes hired at these festivals. There were the Indian Creek Delta Boys from Charleston, Illinois; Company Comin' from Cincinnati; the Hotmud Family and the Corn Drinkers, both from southern Ohio; and the Chicago Barn Dance Company from Chicago. The Barn Dance included John Lilly on guitar, Mark Ritchie on banjo, and Mark Gunther, who had come to Chicago from Charlottesville, Virginia, on fiddle. As fulfilling as folk festivals were, musicians and dancers sometimes had to struggle with unaccommodating facilities and unsympathetic organizers to have satisfying jam sessions or dances. Why not, it seemed obvious to ask, simply organize an event devoted solely to old-time music and dance?

The earliest Breaking Up Thanksgiving weekends were extraordinary in their circumstances. Gene and Margaret Ritchie were not dancers but hosted the party because their son Mark had become involved in the Chicago music and dance community. For the Ritchie parents and siblings, this was an undertaking of immense sacrifice. I remember sleeping in an attic during one of the early years. It was a spacious room, yet as guests continued to arrive throughout the first evening, they would lay down their pallets one by one until the room was simply covered every inch with sleepers. This was the extent of the crowd. In the evenings when everyone was indoors, it was so crowded on the main floor of the house that it was almost impossible to move. The greatest risk to personal injury, as happened once to someone, was in sitting too close to a fiddler and accidentally being poked in the eye by the bow.

The Ritchie family members seemed to take it all in stride, allowing the chaotic weekend to unfold around them. Mark's siblings seemed unfazed by this assault on their privacy, on their time, and on their personal space. Once I arrived early to find Gene and Mark erecting a huge log post, which they had cut from a recently blown-down hardwood tree, in the basement to support the central joist under the dance floor. This seemed to me so poignant an affirmation of the loving, engaged family, of the profound value of our undertakings, of the usefulness of discarded things, and of the fundamental unity of all of these qualities from which so many in the postwar revival had been alienated. I don't think anyone at the time grasped how extraordinary it was for a family to host a weekend old-time music and dance party of more than a hundred guests for their son.

Although Breaking Up Thanksgiving was genuinely innovative, earlier weekend events outside the Midwest provided more than vague models. In the area around Lexington, Virginia, old-time musicians organized Breaking Up Christmas, a series of parties during the week ending with New Year's Eve. The event was based on the mountain "old Christmas" tradition as described in the fiddle tune and song made popular in the revival by North Carolina fiddler Tommy Jarrell and others. And near Ithaca, New York, a mid-summer Highwoods Weekend was held that year, organized by the Highwoods Stringband and friends. Both were loosely structured old-time music celebrations, but neither had the focus on dance that became the norm in Chicago. In featuring both dance and music, Breaking Up Thanksgiving established the first annual celebration that linked neighboring old-time music and dance communities, and in doing so left an indelible mark on what would become the ubiquitous Midwest dance weekend. When the Ritchies held that first party, there were no other dance weekends in existence. The term "dance weekend" had not entered the vocabulary of old-time revival at that time.

In Bloomington, Frank Hall and David Molk were among a small Bloomington contingent that attended the Highwoods Weekend in 1977. This was, at last, the final inversion of the Highwoods theatrical experience: without an authenticating stage performance, the ritual potency of the event drew more democratically from the collective and more broadly from the variety of informal musical and other activities. It was the imagined community to which Highwoods performances alluded. The weekend was held in a rural setting in the Finger Lakes region of New York where band members lived. The year I attended, there was an impromptu softball game and a screening of films on old-time music, including one on Uncle Dave Macon. There were informal jam sessions around the campsites, but no organized music performance that I recall.

With the popularity of Easy Street and increasing travels of other dancers, it seemed that a Bloomington party was in order. In 1979, the idea arose among the Easy Street circle of friends to have a large party on the rural land owned by Randy and Martha Marmouzé, Stan Sitko, and Toby Bonwit. A cluster of August birthdays was appropriated as the occasion for the party: Frank Hall, Martha Marmouzé, and Laura Ley—all astrological Leos. Randy Marmouzé recalled that the grove of maple trees over the hill from the site of the first party inspired the name for the event, Sugar Hill. Undoubtedly the raucous old-time tune of that name, popular in Bloomington and elsewhere, contributed also.

Close to a hundred people showed up that year. It rained, and the

Old–Time Music and Dance

dance was moved from the not-yet-roofed house to the workshop. Donations were collected to pay for fried chicken prepared by Randy. The next year was much the same, although the roof was finished and the dance was upstairs in the house. James Chiplis suggested printing T-shirts, and they were designed by Margie VanAuken and sold at the event. Admission was charged, and Michael Wagner attended the "gate."

One Bloomington dancer who attended that first Sugar Hill was Tom Morrison. Tom had little previous interest in old-time music and had only been dancing since early that year, but he was quickly consumed by the experience. Even after such a short exposure, he wanted to organize an event of his own—something, he thought, that would combine the workshops featured at the Indiana Fiddlers' Gathering with the community atmosphere of Sugar Hill. With encouragement from Ted Hall and others and much help from Linda Handelsman, Tom organized the first Swing into Spring in April 1980, at McCormick's Creek State Park. He financed the event and would even have paid for it had Teri Klassen not announced a collection to reimburse him. For the first two years, Swing into Spring was one evening only, and then it expanded to a full weekend.

McCormick's Creek State Park is a spacious and densely wooded park in Owen County situated among deep ravines cut by McCormick's Creek. Its serene natural features were chosen as the site of a nineteenth-century sanitarium, which was later donated for use as a public park. Set in a wooded area, Camp NaWaKwa, where Swing into Spring was held, consists of four buildings, each with around thirty cots for sleeping, and a fifth structure with a large kitchen and meeting room that housed the dance events. Workshops were scheduled during the day on Saturday. In the early years Bill Meek would usually offer "Improve Your Contra," Nancy McKinley sometimes led a wildflower hike, and Mark Feddersen developed a nifty "Old-Time Band" workshop. Each band gave a short performance at dinner, including, according to Mark's instructions, someone from the band telling a joke. For the evening dance, bands and callers rotated in shifts throughout the night.

Sugar Hill, meanwhile, was approaching a crisis. In 1981, Randy and Martha finished their house and did not want to host Sugar Hill on their property that August. In June, at the Battleground festival, with Sugar Hill expected in August as the next major event of the year, dancers began taking stock of their options. Driving back to Bloomington from Lafayette, Susan Hollis, Jana Rygas, and I devised plans to try to keep the event going. During the week that followed, Susan and Jana began looking for another site. They both had been Girl Scouts in their youth, and it was this connection that led them to the magnificent Camp Dudley Gallahue. They were able to reserve the camp for Sugar Hill, and the three of us joined others to organize the event.

Susan and Jana, deciding to provide meals for the entire weekend, planned menus and food purchases. They talked with scout officials and scrutinized camp regulations to find a way to make them palatable to dancers. Michael Wagner and I organized the gate, and Frank Hall helped with promotional flyers. Jim Woods designed T-shirts, and Doc Welty and Nan Coffin printed them. Frank Hall organized bands and callers, and Ted Hall was in charge of cleanup. As this more complex organizational effort unfolded, it enabled a new, informal organizational structure within the group.

Mark Feddersen sketched a map of the camp to guide dancers around the complex of buildings in the camp. This map, along with the schedule of events and camp rules, was compiled into an information sheet that was handed to dancers when they arrived. I had drafted a list of camp rules we were to follow, and I was surprised at some of the corrections Mark made to my draft. He had separated the list of rules into two sections. The first section, titled "Rules of Camp Gallahue," consisted of a short list of simple proscriptive commands such as "No smoking." The second section listed eight "Additional Suggestions from Sugar Hill Folks" and employed a kind of folksy language that might seem on the surface not to have been said in earnest: "Sugar Hill is a family event, so please be safety-conscious if you have (or are) a kid." Or: "Park cars in the parking lot and leave them there for the weekend. These country roads are dusty! And please don't park on the grass." Number seven: "Remember that Sugar Hill is an all volunteer effort—no one gets paid and everyone pays to get in. So please do your share to make it a success." And the last on the list: "Enjoy the camp and come back next year!"

In fact, in their degree of earnestness, their relative effect was quite the opposite—and this provided me with a lesson in natural morality that I will never forget. The first section compiled rules that were meant primarily to be acknowledged and observed—both by the scouts and the dancers—as the rules of the camp. No one smoked at dances, and it would hardly have been taken seriously to have sincerely proscribed it. Mark even drew one of his signature pinhead figures (which in other places were depicted as dancers having fun) beside the list, pointing a hand at the three rules. The second section, in contrast, mattered a great deal. Thus its appeal was not to a higher authority, but to the convergence of interests that everyone shared and in the real freedoms that participants should be willing to sacrifice to be able to use the camp.

Sugar Hill organizers were soon preoccupied by weekend's rapid growth in size and intensity. Like the original Sugar Hill and like Swing into Spring, the renewed Sugar Hill maintained its volunteer system of operation. Over the years innumerable people contributed, and with increasing numbers the event came to depend even more on a broad base of support. In 1986, the three hundred or so dancers attended Sugar Hill from twenty-five states and three foreign countries. It is difficult to overstate the impact of Sugar Hill on dancing in the Midwest. At a time when the dance movement was rapidly expanding, here was the utopian dream articulated in its glory. For dancers from newly organized dance groups, this might be the first large dance they attended; for musicians and callers, this might be the first opportunity to play or call away from home, with some of the finest callers and musicians in the nation.

Many dancers arrived Friday night, making the winding trek over several miles of gravel road in the moonlight of rural Brown County. At the gate, their admission was collected, and they were issued a large plastic cup and urged to keep it throughout the weekend to conserve resources and cut down on trash. Then the dancer was handed the "job book" and asked to choose a job—preparing or cleaning up after a meal, cleaning the camp on Sunday, or whatever. It became widely understood that there was not a single paid staff member, so that the work of putting on this huge undertaking had to be spread among all the participants. Without ever getting out of the car, dancers had been offered a stake in the ideals—resource conservation, natural morality, and communal labor—that propelled the event.

Because parking was restricted to the area near the gate, there was a half-mile or so walk to the dance farther down the gravel road. During the walk the dancer was certain to encounter others and not know, in the darkness, if they were strangers or old friends. With new dancers, some of whom might have had little idea what they were getting into, this long walk in the dark must have raised the sense of disconcertedness to unimaginable heights. Then, suddenly, over the crest of a hill, the landscape erupted into sound and light. A most unusual building, faintly resembling a large boat, built split-level into a hill and appearing almost to hang out over the adjacent lake, brightly illuminated the scene. The upper floor had a full wrap-around porch and was bustling with people, inside and out. This was the dance: a rainbow of brilliant colors on a vast, empty canvas of darkness.

To get inside, you had to traverse a small ditch via a "gangway" of sorts, then walk around a piece of the wrap-around porch, then pass through one of two doors on either side at the top of the sets. Everywhere there were crowds of people talking. On the dance floor, every dance expanded to fill the space, and then a little more. Signs read, "It's crowded! Please sit out every other dance." Every flat surface was packed with plastic cups, each labeled to identify the owner. "Please label your cups and reuse them," another sign read. Yet another, "Sugar Hill prices low because you help," had attached a small announcement of a vastly more expensive dance weekend in another city. Another read, "It is rumored that the dancing goes on all night," and had a small clipping from a TV listing for the movie *The Zombies of Sugar Hill*. Gene Hubert later wrote and published a dance with that title.

Truly, the dance never ended. It simply kept going, and going, and going until there was no one left to play or dance. Callers and bands were scheduled until around 2:00 A.M.; after that the mike was open to anyone who was still awake. It became well known that the better dancing was late, past midnight, when muscles were limber, when the less committed dancers were gone, and when the floor was no longer crowded. Some dancers would nap early and dance late. During the mid-1980s, it was not uncommon for the dance to go past daybreak.

Many Sugar Hill veterans have affixed in their memory the sounds of Lotus Dickey, then in his seventies, playing at daybreak, having outlasted all the younger fiddlers.

Meals consumed much of the labor during the weekend. Each was prepared by a crew of ten or so volunteers and was supervised by someone who knew what the menus were and where the materials and equipment were stored. There were separate crews to set up the table space before and clean up after. No one had ever cooked for three hundred people, so menus evolved through trial and error. Watermelon was served once, and was decisively banned thereafter by Ted Hall, who hauled away the garbage each year in his truck. Once Tom Morrison contracted with a local farmer to plant corn so as to ripen and be harvested on the day before Sugar Hill. It turned out to be field corn, so everyone had a good laugh at Tom's expense. Vegetarian dishes were provided conscientiously and prominently. Some cooking crews tried to work together year after year. Some dishes became classics, such as Cindy Levindofske's scones, Jim Johnson's French toast, and Tamara Loewenthal's biscuits.

There was a small afternoon dance on Saturday, but most people spent their day at the beach, either swimming, paddling around in canoes, or playing volleyball. Musicians gathered in the shade for jam sessions. On one especially hot day, a group of swimmers supported a trash can lid on some floats as a table and played Euchre in the shallow part of the lake. Once some musicians gathered on the dock, and Paul Tyler called a square dance below in the lake. Children chased the ducks and played in the sand. One year, after a rain, they found an irresistible mud hole to play in. A section of the dinner line might suddenly transform itself into a massage line. Those with long hair might trade off making French braids. Often someone who could juggle would perform informally before or after dinner on Saturday. In later years, when Marc Nadell was organizer, he arranged for a large pontoon boat with a slide. Jim Woods painted a huge banner that was used for many years. For a few years Gail Patejunas made sketches of Sugar Hill people and activities. Everywhere, volunteer photographers snapped pictures for the Sugar Hill calendar, which Tom Morrison and Tom Stio compiled for nearly a decade after I began it in 1984. They customarily assembled

Dance lines at Sugar Hill, 1985. From left, in the two front sets, Sara Roos, unknown, Kathy Anderson, Peter Moxhay, Teri Klassen, Kevin Enright, Amy Letson, Steve Csik. Photo courtesy of Tom Morrison.

the group just before dinner for a large group photograph. One year, during the evening dance, I hung a bed sheet out over the lake and showed films. One was John Cohen's *Musical Holdouts* (1975), featuring the Highwoods Stringband and a scene of Brian Hubbard playing on the streets of Berkeley, California.

By the end of the 1980s, most every Midwest dance community had some kind of annual event. Some derived much inspiration from Sugar Hill; others were based on entirely different models. Sugar Hill seemed always to bear the standard in lack of structure: so much happened, so little was planned. Each year the group would invest around $4,000 on food and supplies, with no assurance that anyone at all would attend. There was no pre-registration. No musicians or callers were scheduled or advertised. There were no scheduled activities during the day. There was no staff. There were rules to follow, but no way to enforce them. Each year, Sugar Hill essentially bet the farm that people would come and work to make it all happen. In its essence, Sugar Hill was an extraordinary wager on natural morality and authentic desire.

Jam session at Sugar Hill, 1987. From left: John Hatton of Lansing, Michigan (guitar); Paula Bradley of Cincinnati, Ohio (banjo); Kathy Anderson of Dayton, Ohio (banjo); and Dan Gellert of Elkhart, Indiana (fiddle). Photo courtesy of Tom Morrison.

As dance weekends sprang up elsewhere, many followed other models—such as the influential Knoxville, Tennessee, weekend—often because dancers preferred these alternatives. Dancers would hear popular bands and callers at camps and other weekends and would organize weekends to bring these well-known bands and callers from great distances to perform. Organizers of new weekends faced a daunting uncertainty if they considered promoting a weekend with absolutely no callers or bands to advertise. And where Sugar Hill once shined against a vast canvas of darkness, a new weekend would be measured against a busy calendar of stiff competition. By the end of the decade, the historical and social foundation on which Sugar Hill was built had lost much of its vigor.

For some veteran Bloomington dancers, the die was cast when Sugar Hill left the Marmouzé property, where it had sprung from a small group of old-time music friends. Indeed, the three who instigated the

Water euchre at Sugar Hill, 1983. From left, Patrick Hauck, Mary Beth Roska, Amy Novick, Ann Prochilo, David Harris. Photo courtesy of Tom Morrison.

Sugar Hill revival in 1981 had not been an important part of the mid-1970s "golden age" in Bloomington. Only Susan had attended the event at the old site, and I was then the only old-time musician of the trio. Moving the event to a public place, however remote, made it more accessible and less strictly aligned with the old-time music community. Consequently, just as veteran old-time musicians were shifting their interests elsewhere, Sugar Hill was being transformed in subtle ways to accommodate the tastes of recent converts to the fast-growing Midwest contra dance scene.

In most ways, little was different about the 1980s wave of newcomers. But one key element was significant: before 1980, there was a wide-spread and sometimes irresistible passion for playing old-time music. Now, calling, composing dances, organizing events, and a host of related lifestyle matters were rapidly being absorbed into the aesthetic realm of the old-time music and dance scene. The new Sugar Hill—with its huge and magnificent setting, its daunting logistical demands, and its tempting recreational possibilities—provided ample fare for this new appetite. The new organizers believed wholeheartedly that they were called to duty by the community, but there may well have been an enclave of veterans who were alienated by the changing tastes and the evolving music and dance atmosphere that the new Sugar Hill represented.

24 YOUNG AUDIENCES

Many musicians who played at the Bloomington dance had other performing outlets that accommodated old-time music. In the 1970s, old-time concerts were held at the Gables restaurant and the Monroe County Public Library, and Easy Street played a weekly engagement at Rapp's Pizza Train. In the 1980s, the Daily Grind coffeehouse and the Second Story bar featured folk concerts. But none of these could match the enduring relationship dance musicians had with Young Audiences of Indiana.

Part of a national organization, the Indiana chapter of Young Audiences presented many kinds of performances in educational settings. Its association with dance group artists began in 1974 when Dillon Bustin saw a television announcement soliciting auditions from prospective artists. He and the Rain Crows put together a program, but it was initially rejected with the suggestion, he recalls, that it be more humorous. A second try was accepted, and over the 1974–75 school year, the Rain Crows became the first dance group ensemble to work for Young Audiences.

In its essence, Young Audiences operated as a booking agency that compiled an annual catalog of artistic performances and workshops for

Indiana schools. To be listed in the catalog, artists like the Rain Crows had to design detailed programs and perform them at an audition. If approved, the program description was listed in the catalog of Young Audiences shows, which was sent to schools throughout the state. Schools could then schedule the program through Young Audiences. Administrative expenses were donated or publicly funded; artists' fees were standardized and paid by the schools for each show performed. Frequently schools would choose those programs which reinforced their curriculum. Most of the old-time music programs were presented to assembly-sized elementary school audiences and supplemented fourth-grade study units on Indiana history. Each program was forty-five minutes and was essentially musical theater, with a pre-determined title, dramatic structure, and repertory of songs and tunes that were linked thematically to the skit. In small communities, the local newspaper might send a photographer to the performance and run a short front-page story on the performance.

In 1975–76, a group made up of Kathy Connors, Bob Herring, Mark Feddersen, and David Molk performed, and in 1976–77, Easy Street began the first of seven years of school work. In 1982–83, Frank Hall and Mary Beth Roska performed with Easy Street as "Hot Feet." The following year Paul Tyler and I joined Mark Feddersen and Teri Klassen for Easy Street's last year, and the Shuffle Creek Dancers performed with Linda Handelsman and Tom Sparks. In 1984–85, the Sugar Hill Serenaders were formed with Lotus Dickey, Teri Klassen, Paul Tyler, and me; Linda Handelsman and Brian Hubbard performed with the Shuffle Creek Dancers. In 1985–86, Karen Billings replaced Teri in the Serenaders. During their tenure as performers, some of these artists earned the largest part of their income from Young Audiences performances.

As an organization explicitly devoted to "cultural programming," Young Audiences was notably unintrusive in matters of aesthetic judgment. The administrators understood very well what devices were effective with school-age audiences and would offer helpful suggestions if the need arose. There were also annual workshops in which some veteran school performer would present materials on performance and program design. But all of the programs whose design I observed or had a hand in were accepted, mostly with little or no comment. And these comprised a wide variety of subjects and styles—skits with various kinds of audience participation, instrument-making workshops, programs on Indiana history, and so on.

On the other hand, the practical demands of working in school settings exacted unrelenting pressures on inherited aesthetic principles, so that for us the end product was often some new generic mutation of traditional culture. This pressure was entirely democratic, of course, and came either directly from the audience in the form of unengaged listeners or from the schools in simply not selecting acts that were not designed or presented well. And this was surely a consequence of the structural relationship between Young Audiences, the schools, and the overall status of the arts. Young Audiences, after all, was designed explicitly around conceptual gaps in the curricula and staffing of mainstream schools—gaps produced by the chronic neglect of the arts and humanities and the manner of thinking in which they were conducted. Folk revivalists were, almost by definition, adept at crossing into and out of the separate worlds of mainstream and traditional arts. It is little wonder, then, that dance group performers were so successful at adapting their music and dance to this alien setting.

Folklorists, of course, have long taken a dim view of this kind of circumstance since what is demanded in theatrical savvy is often precisely that which is unnecessary and undesirable in traditional performance. During my performing years, this dilemma was brought into sharpest relief in circumstances involving folksinger and fiddler Lotus Dickey. Lotus was an Indiana native and a highly regarded performer in folk music circles nationwide—he is covered in detail in a later chapter. Yet he had little success in Young Audiences performances without some kind of scripted role provided by others from the dance group.

In one circumstance, Lotus had been selected as a candidate for a school residency, and I accompanied him to the daylong selection meeting where artist-candidates were displayed to representatives from those schools that had received artist residency funding. This was an intensely competitive event, demanding the highest in entrepreneurial skills. By informal networking, artists had to quickly navigate a chaotic social scene to identify prospective schools and lobby for selection. Later,

Old-Time Music and Dance

school personnel watched a fifteen-minute-or-so sample performance by the artist, looking not merely for artistic talent but also for the ability to engage and manage a classroom of young children, perhaps in the absence of teachers. These qualities are not normally associated with traditional performance, and they certainly were not intrinsic to Lotus's performances at Orange County social gatherings, or for his family, or even for folksong audiences that in recent years had found him so compelling. But there were other candidates competing for folk music residencies who were very savvy in school politics and school performances. In short, Lotus was competing, almost helplessly, against professional "folk" performers.

This not to suggest that either was more deserving than the other. But the experience of those of us who worked with Lotus in the schools was that it was very difficult for him to break through the pedagogical membrane that prevailed in school culture. And it was all the more difficult at this event because there were other competing versions of folk culture in circulation that demanded far less from audiences. That is, over the course of much of the century, Lotus had studied the music of the best southern Indiana performers and had composed songs that spoke to a lifetime of southern Indiana experience. Folk revival performance, in contrast, was adept at *referring to* traditional life—with and without actually experiencing it—at precisely the cultural remove that worked well in pedagogical settings. At the dance or at regional folk festivals this was not a problem since there was already a prevailing understanding of this process and an appreciation for traditional folk culture. But here, entrepreneurship and democracy set folk culture in direct competition with a synthesized version of itself, undermining the very pedagogical transformation that any traditional performance would have sought to enact.

In actual performances, we as Young Audiences performers used every device imaginable to synthesize and convey traditional experience. One long-running Easy Street skit featured the song "Stay on the Farm," about the temptations and frustrations of city life. It played explicitly upon the rural-urban conflict that runs through much old-time music and vernacular theater. It employed formulaic devices from hillbilly humor and stock hillbilly attire, including overalls and tattered hats. Possibly the most popular Young Audiences segment was Easy Street's fiddle contest, with several students selected from the audience to act as judges. Another that the Sugar Hill Serenaders developed was a skit built around the theme of vernacular learning, with Lotus Dickey as the master teacher and Paul, John, and Teri as his stubborn pupils. Its finale was a humorous parlor song, "Quack, Quack," that Lotus remembered from his youth. While Lotus taught the students the simple harmony lines, their teachers were offstage learning the melody. Their unexpected appearance onstage to sing a silly song with the students never failed to meet with the most uproarious approval.

In these examples, the key theatrical device consisted in inverting the student-staff hierarchy—"involving" students in authoritative roles or casting teachers in scenes of comic inversion. This would seem to have had little to do with music tradition, but in fact it was precisely the kind of symbolic power old-time music revival sought and wielded over contemporary life. It always sought to grasp and subvert the authoritative structures at work in audiences. Across the gulf of the proscenium arch of school performance, the immediate view may have been of the authority of the teachers. But lurking in the distance were the conventional structures of contemporary life that suppressed the vitality of traditional music. It was the compelling power over these structures that folk revival musicians enjoyed, and it was this quality the Bloomington bands honed to perfection during these years in the schools.

Throughout this period of a dozen or so years, dance group ensembles—often with two groups operating simultaneously and including some fifty or so shows and workshops a year—amassed upwards of a thousand performances, many to audiences of two to three hundred children. Adding to these impressive numbers the fact that teachers sometimes molded their curriculum to the performances and local newspapers sometimes reiterated the message, one can conclude that the dance group introduced much of a generation of Indiana school children to their particular version of old-time music and dance. What the students learned from the experience was another matter, of course, for they may well have had little in their experience to meaningfully contextualize the music. On the other hand, it may have been significant to some that they heard old-time music played by young, talented, casually dressed adults who were having a very good time together. This concept of "old-time string band" would have derived from the strain of thought that ran through Highwoods to Easy Street and elsewhere: a kind of social prototype, an ideal world that musicians were able to visualize and re-create together by reassembling images and sentiments that had adhered to the music in so many dances, jam sessions, parties, and festival campsites.

25 LITTLE BLOOMINGTON

Young Audiences of Indiana provided an unusually good climate for this kind of performance: there, encoding sentiments and values into the music was important because school audiences generally were far removed from the native world of old-time music. In other stage performance venues, however, one found an audience of peers. Local bars, restaurants, or coffeehouses, for example, might sponsor folk music one night a week where a band could hope to build a following that built on a core audience of friends. Occasionally, someone would sponsor a concert in an auditorium, but there a larger audience was needed. Performing for hire at weddings or other ceremonies could be lucrative and short in duration. But in these settings the music was generally incidental to the occasion, so the satisfaction for the musicians was largely mercenary. The most highly prized venues were folk festivals, where earnest followers of folk music and old-time music were self-selected. There the machinery of authenticity and status operated at full capacity.

Folk festivals, in fact, played a significant role in the authentication of old-time music, probably due to the close historical links at crucial stages of development. The Newport Folk Festival featured the New Lost City Ramblers soon after their founding; both the Highwoods

Stringband and the Fuzzy Mountain String Band made formative appearances at the National Folk Festival during the pivotal years of the early 1970s. According to Mac Benford, the "approval of the folklorists" nurtured the early career of the Highwoods Stringband and prestigious folk festivals like the National Folk Festival provided them an audience that appreciated their unique mission (1989: 23). The original formation of old-time music revival as a privileged link with memory culture and as a source of ascribed authenticity gave folk festivals their special significance.

This profound relationship endured throughout the 1980s even after several festivals, small in number but high in prestige, adopted a "no revivalists" policy that excluded young bands whose exposure to old-time music had come through folk revival channels (see Wilson and Udall 1982). This practice and the protest that followed may have been avoided had old-time musicians developed institutions of self-authentication native to the style. In bluegrass, for example, there emerged an abundance of festivals, awards, and magazines, all catholic in scope. As a consequence, institutions such as folk festivals that catered exclusively to traditional bluegrass were viewed positively, as helping protect a vital historical core of the style that might otherwise be neglected (see, e.g., Snyder 1986). In contrast, old-time music remained curiously dependent on folk festivals and on external authentication.

Indeed, in 1989, long after the precipitating events of the 1970s, the "no revivalists" issue exploded in the pages of *Old-Time Herald* almost as soon as the magazine was founded. The debate raged for seven of the first thirteen issues, attracting twenty-five printed contributors and covering a period from February 1989 to October 1990 during which no other issue came close in consuming readers' attention. At the center of the debate was the Highwoods Stringband, whose martyrdom—in having been embraced and then rejected by traditional music festival organizers—had by then become prototypical. Highwoods' status as heir to an antique guild surely foreshadowed the disposition and understanding of other folk festival confrontations throughout the 1980s, some involving Bloomington dance group musicians. The compelling resilience of this issue and the uncommon importance of folk festivals in old-time music culture is an apt measure of the extent to which the old-time music movement was motivated by authenticity. I do not mean this in a critical way: ultimately, it is a testament to the stature of old-time music as moral discourse.

In Indiana, these issues formed only a distant backdrop to a quartet of regional festivals that, much in contrast to the controversial national festivals, had managed to integrate folk revival motives into programming as a means to amplify, not undermine, the high regard for authentic tradition. Those festivals which were regularly supported by the dance group included the Indiana Fiddlers' Gathering near Lafayette, the Eagle Creek Folk Festival northwest of Indianapolis, the New Harmony Festival of Traditional Music in New Harmony, near Evansville, and the Metamora Canal Days festival in Metamora.

All were warm-weather festivals that staged most performances outdoors. New Harmony was particularly important during the mid-1970s due to the historical affiliation with the utopian community there and to the strong representation of Bloomington performers onstage. Of the four, Metamora was most closely tied to local community and attracted Bloomington performers largely because Randy Marmouzé grew up in the area. New Harmony and Eagle Creek were short-lived. Metamora still holds Canal Days and still programs traditional music, but Bloomington participation declined gradually over the years. The Indiana Fiddlers' Gathering, with strategic proximity to Bloomington, Indianapolis, and Chicago, still programs folk music and attracts Bloomington performers.

The Indiana Fiddlers' Gathering, known colloquially by the name Battleground, was begun in 1973 as an event honoring a local fiddler who at the time was in failing health (Hallman 1997: 30). The audience of 300 that first year grew to 10,000 by 1976 as the event took on the classic eclectic qualities of outdoor folk festivals. Dance group festival-goers typically made an annual pilgrimage and camped together in an area one dancer facetiously called "Little Bloomington," as if an ethnic neighborhood. Some brought along lawn ornaments to display, again facetiously, near their tents. Jam sessions ran late into the night and attracted musicians from old-time music enclaves throughout the region. Dancers nurtured a cordial relationship with the building custodian for the performers' dormitory, not far from the favored camping

Jam session at the New Harmony Festival of Traditional Music, 1976. From left, Ted Hall (standing), Brian Hubbard (fiddle), Randy Marmouzé (banjo), David Bailey (fiddle), Teri Klassen (guitar), Anne Reese, and Melissa Leavell. Photo courtesy of Teri Klassen.

area. On the night before the festival began, there was sometimes a party hosted by one of the Lafayette dancers who had a large house. On the Sunday evening afterward, friends from all points would sometimes gather for a final meal at a restaurant before they dispersed for the long trip home.

These Indiana festivals were wholeheartedly regional events, drawing audiences and performers mostly from Indiana and neighboring states. The program, even on Saturday evening, was never packed with national touring acts, although always there were some. Once, Battleground staged a reenactment of a country music radio jamboree that had long ago been broadcast in the region. Advertising, if there was any, never seemed to reach the dance group. Instead, word spread informally, and people went for the festival itself, not because any particular performers were to be there.

Usually some from the Bloomington group had an important role, either as advisers, emcees, recruiters, workshop instructors, or performers. While Bill Thatcher was working on a film of the Roane Mountain

Hilltoppers, the band was invited up from Tennessee. When Dillon Bustin was researching traditional Indiana dances, he arranged to perform them. On the day of the performance, he recruited some Bloomington dancers who were there as festival-goers and walked them through the simple steps. Most years, Dan Gellert of Elkhart would perform a set with his current playing companions and then play late into the night at the campground. Lotus Dickey, in his years as an active folk music performer, would most always play a set with his current Bloomington accompanists. I still listen to a tape from my first Battleground, 1977, of a jam session with Brian Hubbard and Dan Gellert fiddling at the center. The intensity and facility of their playing swelled with each tune and reached heights that I had thought unimaginable. I still count this as one of the formative musical experiences of my life.

In good weather, the evening programs at Battleground would attract a thousand or so, easily filling the space on benches and on blankets on the ground around them. The stage was no more than a canopied platform with a back wall, so there was no backstage inaccessible to onlookers. Consequently, artists gathered on the sides of the stage and watched the performance or huddled behind the stage to tune their instruments. Generally artists performed one evening set on the stage and may or may not have had other additional duties in workshops during the day. There was a sound amplification system and an attentive sound engineer, seated on a platform fifty feet or so in front of the stage, who tended the mixing board. Outside the entrance gate, vendors in booths sold short-order food, tapes and records, T-shirts, crafts, and instruments.

Although it went by the term "Fiddlers' Gathering," suggesting an atmosphere of informality and an exclusive focus on fiddling, Battleground took its organizational cues from large outdoor folk festivals, such as the Newport Folk Festival or the National Folk Festival. These models were adopted while Dillon Bustin was program director (1976–80) and were continued by Paul Tyler after him. As their centerpiece, they had main-stage evening variety shows moderated by an emcee, with several simultaneous and less formal performances or workshops during the day. Their programs featured hired folk performers or ensembles who performed short sets and overall were meant to suggest the

Old-Time Music and Dance

Easy Street at Battleground, 1981, during one of the daytime sets. On stage, from left, Randy Marmouzé, Teri Klassen, Mark Feddersen, Bob Herring, Frank Hall. Photo courtesy of Tom Morrison.

American or regional folk cultural panorama. The design of the program was surely amplified by the substantial contingent of experienced festival-goers who were well versed in the festival ideal that permeated certain strata of American culture.

Yet, the facade of cultural spectacle was in some ways transparent. Particularly for those who had joined the Battleground "family" by attending frequently, it was really not all that difficult for competent, tradition-minded performers with some experience to be invited to perform at least once. The sponsors, in fact, depended heavily upon the advice of program directors, musicians, folklorists, and others. Generally, if seasoned ensembles or performers had an interesting repertoire that drew upon and showed respect for traditional material, and if they displayed a modicum of marketing skills, they might well get on the program.

Even Battleground's modest efforts at multicultural representation were enough to suggest a diverse nation. But this was a gathered diversity, its emphasis on represented perfection and not on perfect representation, on the quality and not the accuracy of plural America. Aficionados of Anglo-American string band music probably outnumbered other contingents, and in this respect the event most lived up to its name, "fiddlers' gathering." Still, at least by the late 1970s it was not a fiddlers' gathering but a folk festival, one which carved out a primitive commonwealth from its admittedly narrow range of interests.

In this, followers of old-time music, bluegrass, contest fiddling, Celtic music, blues, songwriting, and a few other styles managed to articulate a simplistic yet sincere commitment to cultural diversity. It was most tangible in stage performances where the distinctions in musical style were broadest and where song lyrics generally professed compassion and tolerance. But there was also a peaceable union throughout the park—in the diversity of jam sessions or in the subtle yet important lifestyle differences in the various camping areas. For example, the tenters in "Little Bloomington," situated in an area prohibiting camper trailers, were less bothered by this proscription than the bluegrass followers in RVs would have been. Overall, this bland mélange of part-unplanned and part-scripted circumstances of difference—inherited from folk revival festival tradition—was an enactment of a localized diversity. Limited in practice, it was boundless in ideal.

It may have been significant for loyal followers that the festival itself was ultimately the province of the park board—a somewhat disinterested party—and was not created to advance the cultural agenda of any particular advocacy group. Thus participants found much of the festival accessible, yet they were always a step outside its governing structures. This led to occasional conflicts between the board and its appointed organizers, but it also shielded the festival family from the quagmire of internal strife that organizational power can invite.

An even more important source of heterogeneity was that the festival had operated for many years as a local fiddlers' gathering and already had a sizable contingent of museum volunteers and local enthusiasts affiliated with that design. The folk festival model brought its own audience along, thereby juxtaposing idealistic youths against the conservative-minded locals who were already there. Moreover, to a program once honed around local tastes, festival performances introduced racial diversity, political themes, and, foremost, a host of styles and genres. By necessity, various audiences with entrenched investment in the festival had to find a way to share with one another the event, the physical space, and the invested symbolism.

Thus, for a variety of reasons, the social world of the ongoing festival family was split into contingents according to their interests and their vision of the event. None was coterminous with the design of the festival; instead, the participants adapted to "official" structures they could never truly possess. Often these worlds were in striking parallel: for example, there was likely to be an informal jam session at the campground concurrent with the evening main-stage program, appealing exclusively to those who didn't want to attend the concert. But these were not exactly in conflict. Organizers respected the festival family ethos enough to give repeated return engagements to those who most fully articulated it—musicians such as Dan Gellert, or Lotus Dickey, or Garry Harrison, or Mark Gunther—even when they did not entirely articulate the display ethos, such as by appearing onstage too casually dressed. Indeed, the gathered momentum of the festival found these two worlds increasingly entwined.

So closely bound were these two distinct festival modalities that there evolved an underlying theory of culture that motivated their integration. For example, even in its staged display, the festival did not pretend to engage in representation of authentic tradition in its purest sense, nor were festival-goers exactly passive onlookers. Although authentic tradition was a genuine concern, the festival's approach to this ran counter to the drift in 1980s folklife festival philosophy. In this period, the pedagogical goals of festivals were thought to be in explicit and inevitable conflict with the social ambitions of experienced festival–goers (e.g., Camp and Lloyd 1980: 72–73). To counteract this circumstance, the most privileged festival spaces were often reserved for a direct encounter with staged traditional practice (e.g., Wilson and Udall 1982: 16–23). Battleground presumed no such conflict and nurtured its festival family just as it did traditional performance.

Instead, Battleground implicitly presumed a crucial strain of cultural value *shared* among its participants. Thus the notion of community suggested by festival performance was not merely the locality from which the performers came. Rather community was an idea, often at odds with modern life even in the localities of origin of traditional performers. At home and at the festival, for "traditional" or "revivalist" performers, community was an ongoing dialectic with social forms that might undermine it. Festival-goers were drawn to the event with the vague hope of engaging this cultural dynamic—one not situated wholly within the bounds of the festival. Traditional community was an all-embracing community of estrangement, and the festival was designed to foster particular social relations that emerged from the event.

From this vantage, the broadly inclusive qualities of the festival were not seen as a betrayal of local traditional practice. Yet neither were these festival qualities indiscriminate: they suggested a broad purpose of stimulating an ongoing dynamic of tutelage of wider-than-local scope. This was in visible abundance throughout the festival—in the learning of new tunes, in the appearance of loosely formed ensembles where performances were vehicles to indoctrinate initiates, in the variety of skill in jam sessions and in the esteem given to the most skilled. The consequence was to establish a visible dialectic whereby the status of older performers drew its strength from the attention of the younger ones. A contemporary organizer still takes care to note that the festival "fosters an atmosphere where older musicians teach the younger ones" (Hallman 1995: 30).

Hopefully, this was an ongoing dialectic, and the festival an affirmation of and not a departure from cultural practice at home. There, far beyond the reach of official culture, the festival ethos inclined the will of festival-goers toward the well-being of some generalized cultural other—helping elderly neighbors, working for social justice, improving depleted farmland, restoring old homes, and so on. It was this ongoing dialectic that gave Battleground its distinctive empowering qualities—in contrast with commercial festivals designed around the prestige and talent of the performers, or with festivals designed around representation, where status was controlled and conferred primarily or exclusively by the organizers.

The delicate management of these perplexing and ineluctable issues at Battleground gives some appreciation for the peculiar way the festival

Old-Time Music and Dance

operated. At Battleground, as with so many contemporary folk festivals, there were at once two festivals operating in dynamic proximity. One was a festivity, a celebration of an ongoing festival community; the other was a staged display ostensibly representing community tradition at home. Borrowing terms from performance theory, the former involved an "integrated audience"—a type of collective with enduring relations to the event and with one another. The latter involved an "accidental audience"—one whose relationship to the event was determined by the structure of the staged display—ticketing, performance schedules, audience behavior, and so on. But at Battleground the two modes were not viewed as adversarial. Rather, the overall effect of the festival was to stimulate the status system of the ongoing Battleground family. It did this by fostering the ongoing integrated festival audience and then deflecting the entrenched inwardness of its community outward. The effect was to draw the accidental audience into the dialectic of status of the integrated audience and reclaim the achievement of those traditional artists estranged by the encounter with the dominant culture.

Festival campground ghettos were then and still are common occurrences at old-time music festivals. They illustrate the extent to which old-time music events, more so than folk festivals in general, incorporate integrated audiences. It was important at Battleground that both types of audiences were encouraged and nurtured, and that they were able to interact freely and meaningfully. Battleground enabled and displayed sustained relations with performers and provided many routes by which members of the accidental audience could engage the community of integrated relations. It could be said that musical genres lend themselves to this kind of integrated display, but this is in part because old-time music revival community itself emerged from integrative audience behavior.

This dual semiotic at Battleground provided for the segregation of some functional components of the event—the informal structure of the festival community on the one hand and the finances, infrastructure, and public relations on the other. For the most deeply involved participants, it may even have provided a performance medium—staged display—that local performance practice did not always provide, one where group values could be articulated and refracted to an attentive audience.

Little Bloomington

But, in truth, the double semiotic prevailed everywhere: even "Little Bloomington" jam sessions attracted casual onlookers, who were then exposed to a wider array of community symbols—such as jam session social structure, informal conversation, food and drink, casual dress, lawn ornaments, and control over the nature and duration of performance—than could ever be attained in the genteel world of the stage.

Festival-goers who were inclined toward this life navigated the symbolic maze of the festival with little difficulty. Cathy Maris, an Indiana native who attended the festival for the first time in 1975, had done English country-dancing and was attending bluegrass sessions when she encountered the Bloomington jam sessions at Battleground. Captivated by this "Bloomington sound," she moved to Bloomington in 1978 after a couple of visits to the dance. For Cathy, as for many others, Battleground was scarcely passive entertainment: it was a conduit to a life-changing experience, one by which she passed easily through the protective veneer of display.

One can scarcely imagine any other setting where the ethos of the dance group could have imposed itself so wholly upon the world from which by design it was estranged. And here, moreover, was representation in its purest sense, a fragment of partially embedded dance group life illuminated by a stolen ray of stage light.

26 EIGHT MILES FROM TOWN

I remember a special excitement that surrounded those Rounder recordings of the Highwoods Stringband and the Fuzzy Mountain String Band. As a teen I had begun a modest collection of pop-rock LPs, but later, via folk revival channels, I had added a hefty complement of County reissues, vintage country LPs from bargain bins, bluegrass and contest fiddle records I bought at festivals, and folk revival recordings on both mainstream and independent labels. Like many others, I still have them—on homemade pine board shelves, a shrine to a period that remains the spiritual linchpin of my life.

The route to this eclectic destination had been a twisted one. In my youth, even in central Alabama, my musical experiences had arisen within a rigidly stratified culture. As much because of propriety and class, rather than lack of talent, not a single member of my extended family—spanning three generations and more—ever played a musical instrument. Nor did any of my friends, nor, to my knowledge, anyone in their families. Against this backdrop, I went at age eleven with a school friend to see *Twist around the Clock* at a local theater and experienced for the first time musical culture as an empowering and liberating force. There was little question, then, of what music I would come to call my own.

I did not know then the powerful capacity of rock music to erase its influences, to appear "contemporary"; nor did I know the way this blended with local elitism to obscure from my awareness the richness of living musical culture that was so close around me. To this dismal circumstance, the folk revival arrived as an epiphany, a unifying consciousness that gave me a strange power over the blinding self-absorption of pop and elite culture. I remember browsing for 78s in antique stores in the early 1970s and coming upon Willie Mae Thornton's "Hound Dog" at a shop not a mile from where I grew up. I remember bringing it home, setting it on the turntable, and switching to the 78 rpm setting. I am certain I knew no one outside of folk revival circles who even used the 78 rpm setting, and this alone fused the folk revival experience to the extraordinary event that was about to unfold. When I set the needle on the disc and Thornton belted out that signature opening phrase, "You ain't nothin' but a hound dog . . . ," I learned in a rush of excitement and anger how one of the defining anthems of rock music and of my own youth was appropriated and, by extension, how smoothly the cultural isolation of rock iconography had meshed with the racial elitism of my upbringing.

Few others around me seemed to be having these experiences of historical epiphany, so I increasingly found my way into folk revival circles, where musical diversity was a kind of worship, though often at arm's length. There I found others who identified with pop music for its cultural resistance and with folk music for its historical power. This, I imagine, is how it was that monuments to self-absorption like the Beatles recordings could sit on the record shelf so comfortably close to those "poor substitute" recordings of the Bogtrotters. Indeed, it was not at all uncommon to encounter in the homes of folk revival friends LP collections with this same perplexing taxonomic strategy. And as is so often the case with displayed material culture, the recognition of something so unique and complex, yet at the same time so familiar, surely smoothed our way to deep rapport.

In my collection of recordings, the distinctive presentation and purpose of each type of recording gave clear definition to its category. The pop industry, of course, knew very well how to appeal to and manipulate the values of youth culture. Beginning around 1968, pop music executives had begun allowing young rock artists to design their own record jackets, obscuring the barrier between youth musical culture and the grownup recording industry. Consequently, like much of the music itself, rock album covers were a feast of symbolic self-reference that provided the industry a means to acknowledge only the least threatening and most self-absorbing facets of youth politics. Indeed, an urban legend thread emerged around reports of provocative record jackets that were withdrawn from circulation by nervous company executives.

In contrast, the presentation of old-time music was crude and quaint. Folkways and later Folk-Legacy had surely defined the presentational extreme with their thick, barren, black jackets. County used archival promotional material, vintage photographs, or quaint drawings. The RCA-Vintage series featured icons of country living—acoustic musical instruments, or backdrops of ornamental corn or hay bales. Only Vanguard acknowledged the iconography of the folk revival, using photographs of folk concerts or festivals. Generally, whereas pop recordings asserted their cultural presence, many folk and old-time LPs denied it, deflecting their own cultural status with mechanisms of self-effacement that were at the time fundamental to folk revival presentation.

Rounder changed these conventions dramatically. If LPs in the pop market were able to validate youth culture, Rounder found a way to visually and structurally affirm the folk revival as a youth movement using images that were vivid, intimate, and specific. Their first two releases articulated decisively the new consciousness of old-time music revival. One was *George Pegram*, featuring the two-finger banjo style of a traditional Appalachian musician; the other was an eclectic mix of old tunes and songs from a young Boston bluegrass band, the Spark Gap Wonder Boys. Charles Wolfe has described the impact of these recordings in this way:

> Both LPs were actually released on the same day—October 20, 1970, and the pairing was in a way, curiously symbolic of the Rounder philosophy. One was a carefully produced field recording of a well respected traditional musician; the other was a carefully produced field recording of young revivalist musicians who were carrying on this

Eight Miles from Town

tradition. In later years, other companies would focus on doing one direction or another, but Rounder would manage to successfully straddle the fence and redefine old-time music in a refreshingly broad sense. (1995: 36–37)

And in the manner of recordings of traditional musicians, the Spark Gap recording even came with a lengthy set of liner notes.

Very soon, Rounder found that conventional sales networks would not accommodate small esoteric companies, and they were forced to bypass record stores and sell directly to their customers:

> By [1972], too, the Rounders were becoming familiar sights at festivals around the country, setting up shop in their old VW bus, and selling their records to fans firsthand. "We would have almost all of our records with us in the van," Ken [Irwin] recalled. "And we had to keep the mail order going. So about every day we would call in and check our messages. If there were any orders, we'd take down the address, go to the local radio station, say, 'Do you have any record mailers you don't need?' put the records in, address them, and drop them off at the post office. We were into recycling long before it was fashionable." (Wolfe 1995: 60)

Consequently Rounder quickly absorbed and was absorbed by the most active component of old-time revival—those who attended and performed at festivals. Like the best folk music companies, Rounder itself became a part of the movement—a fact confirmed by the packaging, the labels, the marketing strategies, the catalogs, the sales booths at festivals.

So, by default or design, Rounder was soon positioned as a formative influence for old-time music revival. In displaying the sedate and reverent posture of Fuzzy Mountain or the vivid abandon of Highwoods, they provided not merely music but also a visual map for the meaningful experience of it. Suddenly, old-time music came to life on recordings, not as the memory culture of the *Anthology* but as a component of a living movement. In its own way, by suggesting the means of an authentic contemporary experience of old-time music, Rounder resolved the inherent contradiction of recorded old-time music that Rich Nevins had seen as fundamental. Where Nevins in his words and other companies in their presentation had suppressed the potency of the recording as

Old-Time Music and Dance

mere substitute experience, Rounder graphically situated its recordings of contemporary old-time music within the realm of usable authentic experience. Consequently, its effect was to affirm not merely the music but also the broader social engine of the old-time music revival.

Of all the qualities routinely touted as distinctive and superior in LPs, their capacity to display bold, visible jacket covers reigns supreme. As an extension of social discourse, however, LPs were notoriously un-wieldy. They were fragile, bulky, and easily damaged by heat or improper storage. They could be produced (or reproduced) only in large runs on specialized equipment. And the device that played them was even more unwieldy, requiring a level, motionless surface. In retrospect it is sur-prising that social experience could be extracted from such a device as the record player. And it is ironic that as the old-time LP came to full flower in those memorable Rounder titles, it presaged the necessity for a far more suitable recording medium. Slowly yet steadily, the dauntless, sociable cassette made its way into the cultural nexus of old-time music.

In the 1970s, before studio recordings were released exclusively on cassette, cassette technology was developing its own aura as a vernacular medium. Aspiring old-time musicians used portable cassette recorders to tape jam sessions, concerts, and older-generation fiddlers. At festi-vals, it was even possible to see microphones, sometimes attached to long poles, penetrate the center of a popular jam session. Some musi-cians loathed this intrusion, but cassette technology seemed perfectly designed to articulate the widespread view that this was the people's music. And surely everyone in the revival, at one time or another, had been at both ends of the microphone.

The earliest cassette recorders were crude instruments, so the most serious collectors at first used high-quality quarter-inch tape on un-wieldy reel-to-reel machines. I once took my quarter-inch deck to a small bluegrass festival, only to find that forty or so others had done the same. They were allowed to use some tables just below the side of the stage, where the recorders were stacked three-or-so high and all hooked together piggy-back—with one's output leading to another's input—leading through a mixer to a set of recording mikes taped to the loud-speaker mikes on the stage.

But the cassette was portable and could be played in the car, so many musicians simply adapted their tastes to accommodate the medium. And if its aural capacities seemed substandard, so, in the age of reissues, did the 78s. The Highwoods Stringband, after all, had released *Fire On the Mountain* (1973) with a photo of the band recording outdoors, defiantly mixing live to two-track (as opposed to recording each instrument on a separate track and mixing later) at a time when multi-track recording appealed to the highest aesthetic tastes in pop music circles. There were even aesthetic reasons, then, for the attraction of the rough-hewn sound that cassettes offered. Then, in the early 1980s, when Sony began producing the Walkman Professional, it became possible to make very good live recordings on cassette. This was entirely appropriated technology, of course: the small, portable Walkman machines were meant to appeal to the walking and jogging craze, and old-time musicians bought them to record jam sessions and learn tunes.

It is difficult to say who in dance circles released the first studio recording exclusively on cassette. But suddenly, they were everywhere. The first that I remember was *Eight Miles from Town* (1982), which Pete Sutherland brought to Bloomington when he moved there in the 1980s. Soon after, he, Dillon Bustin, Malcolm Dalglish, and Grey Larsen recorded *Root Crops and Ground Cover*, an unusual half-length cassette (including a quartet version of "Gardening") packaged in a small envelope designed to resemble a seed packet. John Hatton, a guitarist from the Lansing, Michigan, area, began bringing a sales display case to Sugar Hill filled with nothing but cassettes. So also did traveling bands, when they visited the Wednesday Night Dance. The design of the portable cassette display case, usually homemade from quarter-inch plywood to fit a particular vehicle storage area, was a matter of demonstrable achievement.

In 1984, Marimac Recordings was founded in New Jersey by Larry MacBride to produce and distribute old-time cassette reissues from the sizable collection of 78s owned by his associate, Frank Mare. The low startup cost of cassette production was clearly an attraction: MacBride at first rented recording equipment and dubbed copies in the evening at home, using "a timer at the dinner table to let him know when the dubbing was finished" (Jackson 1995: 27). After the mid-1980s MacBride turned much of his attention to the "established community of talented younger musicians" (26). When his employer relocated Mac-Bride to the Chicago area in 1987, Marimac became the chief recording outlet for the old-time music revival in the Midwest. From the company's founding in 1984 until mid-1993, the year of MacBride's untimely death, Marimac produced only cassettes and distributed them by catalog and through other old-time music revival channels.

Cassettes were so accessible, in fact, that in some cases their distribution did not really suggest a marketplace at all. In dance circles many excellent cassettes were financed, produced, and distributed by bands themselves, who brought them to camps and on tours and hawked them during the break in the middle of a dance. Under such circumstances, buying a recording from a group of friends who had produced it was an odd mixture of ritual consumption and homage to friendship. The emotional investment might span this gamut entirely—anticipating the enjoyment of good music bought and sold, anticipating pleasurable associations connected with the dance event, and even paying respect to the friends who made the recording. While much of this logic of self-production was entirely pragmatic, there were surely some who enjoyed the erosion of the stock of fetishism that had accumulated around LPs. Some of the populist idealism associated with the cassette resurfaced as resistance—sometimes on antiquarian terms—to the emergence of the compact disc and its imminent invasion into old-time and other folksong markets. Until CD playback equipment and production costs fell within the modest means of most old-time and dance musicians, cassettes had a brief run as the vaguely acknowledged "people's medium."

Self-production, of course, was entirely dependent on a breed of small recording studios that has flourished since the 1970s. "Homegrown" studios—Bloomington had one by just that name—arose everywhere, some specializing in acoustic music as a small part of their business. With cassette technology and folk-friendly studios, any band or artist might be tempted to put together a collection of tunes, record them locally, order a few hundred copies with a stock or custom "J-card," and sell them at dances and festivals. I remember watching a local studio duplicate the first recording of our band in high-quality "real time" (the same speed as playback, as opposed to high-speed duplication). They simply loaded blank cassettes into a bank of ordinary cassette decks and turned them on all at once to "record." As digital technology became more accessible and less expensive, it also became more acceptable in folk and old-time circles. Studios or engineers might encourage artists to use the most sophisticated technology. In 1990, our band recorded a cassette in Cincinnati, and we were persuaded to use digital technology for the master tape. Our total outlay for 300 cassettes was just under $1,500, or $5 for each cassette, divided approximately equally between studio costs, J-card and booklet printing, and cassette duplication. But we might well have gotten by for less.

It is worth noting that even with the important role that recordings played in old-time dance music, there was not the slightest interest in using recordings in place of live music at the dance event itself (see Herman 1995: 7). If a recording contained instrumental dance music, which some but not all of these did, it might actually say so, particularly if it contained uninterrupted "dance-length cuts" that were considerably longer than the three minutes allotted most popular songs. Such a recording would be of limited appeal outside dance circles but within them would be used as practice music by callers, cloggers, or even small groups of dancers. Novice callers were known to practice in the car on long trips to dances. Again, cassettes served these particular needs well since they could be played in the car or on "boom boxes," which, unlike LPs, did not jump off track when the floor shook from dancing. Still, in the vast majority of cases, people just put on the music and listened, hoping to bring something of the thrill of old-time dance to some less pleasurable occasion.

In some ways, the rise of the cassette was an industry nightmare. Surely in the history of sound recording there had never been a format on which packaged studio recordings and self-made recordings would freely mix to the extent they did with cassettes. A dancer's or musician's automobile tape box might well include recordings by popular artists on major labels, dubbed cassettes of selected titles or complete LPs, production cassettes of old-time dance music bought at festivals or dances, and live recordings made at jam sessions, dances, workshops, or performances. In my career I made numerous fiddle "learning tapes" of favorite tunes; the best was a collection on a single cassette of nearly a hundred dubbed excerpts of my favorite tunes, each played only once through, that I used to expand my repertoire.

Stripped of the rich visual iconography of LPs, the car tape box was instead a catalog of personal experience. Sharing a ride to a festival or dance weekend, one might inquire about a tape crudely labeled "Glenville '82" and get a firsthand account of an unusually good jam session. Even production cassettes would most likely have been bought at dances or festivals, perhaps after a memorable performance by the artists. But cassettes were almost never bought in stores, and this gave them an existential aura distinctly different from the imposing LP. In all respects, though most notably with taped jam sessions, the cassette reintroduced and amplified the status of recordings as a "poor substitute" for musical experience.

Sometimes LPs were dubbed to cassette to pass on to friends as gifts. But they were never sold, and there was certainly no black market of pirated folk cassettes. A friend of mine whose tape box had been stolen from her car was especially bitter because, as everyone agreed, the tapes would probably be tossed in the trash. Dubbed copies were also important because cassettes often "wore out" from repeated use, exposure to the elements, and rough treatment and thus had to be replaced.

Still, in the 1980s, with the rise of a class of professional and quasi-professional folk artists, an outspoken anti-pirating movement arose in folk music and old-time music circles, supported by dramatic anecdotal accounts. In some ways this was an abrupt shift from a cultural movement that celebrated the free exchange of dubbed 78 rpm recordings, amateur field recordings, and appropriated materials for revival performance. Using old-time music as an example, John Cohen long ago argued the case for a separate standard for folk intellectual property:

> It is unfortunate that all payment for a copyrighted song goes to one specific claimant or another, when, in truth, many have been responsible in the evolution of a folk song. In this sense, the songs are the product and expression of the community; and, if they are the property of many people, it is odd that one writer or publisher should be allowed to claim them. (1964a: 37)

The conversion experience of folk revival performers from their self-proclaimed status as recipients of dispossessed culture to protectors of entrepreneurial rights surely counts in the old-time revival as a post-modern moment. Surely also was it ironic that the anti-pirating movement could assert so distinct a moral voice in folk music circles, where in pop music the Grateful Dead and others established anti-commercialism and the primacy of live performance as a kind of moral high ground. Each, in fact, arose where its opposite prevailed. Dillon Bustin recalls that a tape of a single performance of a song he wrote and performed, "Shawnee Town," was circulated throughout the East Coast folk scene—and subsequently recorded and performed by others. As many others would also do, he took this not as piracy but as an affirmation of his stature as a performer and writer.

In the cassette market that developed in dance circles, there were structural barriers that left little incentive for pirating. The value of a recording as a token of friendship with the artist or as a souvenir of a pleasant experience was simply too great. In such cases the ritual act of buying the recording directly from the performers was what infused it with that value. Where recordings were available both from performers and in shops and catalogs, it was not unknown that a purchaser might make a point to buy directly from the performers so as to acknowledge the purchase and to assure that the performer got the full markup. But there were practical considerations also: production cassettes were not that expensive to begin with, they made poor master tapes because of the noise introduced by playback machines, they were often non-standard lengths, and the J-card and notes were difficult to copy. And perhaps foremost, purchasing directly from performers was supremely convenient. All of these concerns had their effects subliminally, as an extension of the experience of dance community, without evidence of an underlying moral-code.

As a medium of communication, the cassette was readily adaptable to the social habits of old-time music and dance revival. The broadcast media, in contrast, was not so flexible. Televised old-time music was unheard of, and old-time radio shows were rare enough that many followers knew by reputation the shows that were broadcast in localities nationwide. In 1977, however, the dance group gained some access to radio when Gary Stanton took over the campus folk music radio program that had run since the 1950s. The program was broadcast once

Old-Time Music and Dance

each week on the National Public Radio affiliate, WFIU, which was operated by Indiana University. The program was designed for a broad folk music audience, but the concerns and tastes of the dance group frequently figured into the playlist and the presentation.

He conceived the program, called *Music Down Home*, around an informal atmosphere, with imaginary friends close at hand. "We were a family—the listeners and I," he later wrote, "and many of the ideas for programs and music for programs came from the people who listened" (Stanton 2000). Partly to overcome shyness, he invented a broadcast personality—the "Radio Ranger." Throughout the program's run, ensembles from the dance group made regular guest appearances, performing live and discussing their music. He routinely announced events of importance to the old-time music scene. Musical selections drew from a wide range of folk and ethnic recordings, but regional and local music and vintage recordings constituted the bulk of the playlist. At some point he devised a contest whereby listeners could phone with answers to a weekly trivia question, often on the subject of vintage old-time recordings. The prize was a "Radio Ranger" button with a likeness of this fictional character.

The program was targeted at the broader Bloomington folk music community, but the dance group took special delight in the personal connection to Gary. Routine announcements or discussions with guest musicians might innocently allude to personal affairs of dancers. But the significance of the music may have been even greater. The jarring contrast of Charlie Poole and the North Carolina Ramblers, the first selection played, with the station's prevailing classical format boldly asserted the group's esoteric musical tastes into the range of aesthetic options in a city that loved music. It was a prominent point of exposure for the dance group and its music.

27 THE PIANO CONTROVERSY

Through the 1970s, the aesthetic conventions that unfolded after the meeting of Miles and Dillon held in check a familiar, redundant old-time sound at the dance. But with exposure to dance music elsewhere through travel and recordings, the range of musical interests began to expand. Even some whose tastes had been forged by the old-time music revival were now experimenting with or returning to other styles. In some cases, this was reflected at the dance. Many were attending camps, where evening dance bands were most always driven by accordion and piano. After the Knoxville, Tennessee, dance group founded its dance weekend, often featuring New England contra music and dance, Bloomington dancers usually assembled a carload to go down each year.

In the early 1980s, the band Swallowtail from Amherst, Massachusetts, passed through Bloomington and played the Wednesday Night Dance. Then, in 1984, caller and concertina player George Marshall left the group to form a pared-down Wild Asparagus, the most widely traveled band of the 1980s. This was the first dance band I ever heard that did not have a fiddle, and I remember anxious concern in Bloomington when it became known that this feat was to be attempted. For

Bloomington and perhaps other Midwest locales, the transition from Swallowtail to Wild Asparagus was significant.

By its appearance, Swallowtail grew from the New England tradition of informal dance bands, a full sound with ample personnel, its repertoire predominantly old chestnuts. When the band began experimenting with modulations in key, tempo, and dynamics, as well as changes in instrumentation, however, it marked a departure from the community-oriented sound by which people in other regions had been introduced to contra dance. Even in New England, Swallowtail is today a historical bridge leading to a sound too old-fashioned for contemporary tastes.

Wild Asparagus was a spin-off of Swallowtail's most ambitious elements. The band featured only three musicians, played from an eclectic repertoire, used unconventional instrumentation (concertina, oboe, piano), and improvised wildly. George Marshall was the caller and also played concertina. For many, this was not merely a stylistic change: rather, it introduced a new dynamic of showmanship between musicians and dancers. The three musicians were also well organized and well suited for a life on the road and traveled extensively to local dances.

From these and other sources, there was a gathering interest in Bloomington in New England–style music. In fact, so appealing was this sound that a small resistance movement grew, fearing it would erode the decade-old tradition of old-time music at the dance. The key issue was the piano: the dance hall did not have one, and putting one in just might open the floodgates. The debate smoldered for a time, and then the matter was abruptly settled. One night the dancers arrived at the hall to find that the hall owners themselves had put a piano onstage. In the years to follow, it was used by some bands. As often as not, however, the old-time sound rang out.

But the die was cast, and in Bloomington and elsewhere, old-time music and what some in Bloomington called "New England dance music" (or sometimes "Celtic music") were becoming distinct alternatives. There were indeed key differences. With piano and accordion as its foundation, the New England sound featured discernible and sometimes dramatic harmonic progressions, signaling shifts of energy so in-

The Piano Controversy

tense that dancers responded wildly. These harmonic formulas were multiplied manyfold by medleys, key changes, and sometimes even instrument changes. And innovative keyboard players such as Peter Barnes of Boston were ceaselessly on the lookout for new cadences that would achieve these effects. Often the theme of these novelties was to increase the tension away from the tonic chord, almost teasing the dancers, so that the urge to return to it alluded loosely to the sense of returning to the "home" position in the dance.

In contrast, perhaps in defiance, old-time music purists seemed to be drifting toward a sound in which melodic interest and harmonic movement were sacrificed entirely to unbridled rhythm. Often only the simplest chord progressions were used, even where the melody might have suggested otherwise to many musicians. The key element of this fundamentalist old-time sound seems to have been harmonic restraint built on subtle rhythmic complexity, played in endless repetition, mantra-like, to achieve a kind of transcendent state of consciousness. The key contrasting instrument was most likely the banjo, played in drop-thumb style to produce a hypnotic syncopated rhythm.

Because in this "frailing" style the banjo only approximated chords and melody, it was definitive of this and only this style. In fact, since Pete Seeger, old-time banjo pedagogy had most often excluded any discussion of harmonic structure or even diatonic (and certainly not chromatic) melodic structure, and some banjo players never developed these skills, even if they used them on other instruments. In their place, banjo players acquired a keen facility with a particular set of melodic formulas common in old-time tunes and could articulate them rhythmically to achieve the old-time sound.

Bloomington had a core of old-time purists, but what they embraced was more a personal style preference than a resistance movement. At the Bloomington dance, musicians were, as often as not, open-minded about the sound, and in the early 1980s, one might have heard popular old-time tunes played on whatever instruments the musicians liked and had available. In short, there was a tradition of eclectic taste in the dance group that included an uncontroversial interest in traditional New England tunes. The rising popularity of New England dance bands, however, seemed to be accompanied by an enthusiasm that was less open-minded.

Oddly enough, while Bloomington worried over the effects of a piano in the dance hall, the concern elsewhere was whether old-time music was at all appropriate for contra dancing. And surprisingly, the issue was raised not by dancers but by purist old-time musicians, perhaps worried that stage practice at dances was pressuring old-time musicians to compromise too much. Particularly in the image projected by the Fuzzy Mountain recordings, the definitive performance setting of old-time music revival had been the jam session, which placed few, if any, performance demands on musicians. Through much of the 1970s, the Bloomington dance featured what was essentially an old-time jam session transplanted onto the stage. New 1980s callers, oblivious to this background and sometimes entirely unfamiliar with old-time music, were placing increasing demands on bands—specifying tempo and meter, or calling for familiar New England tunes. An inexperienced caller might, for example, learn a dance from Ted Sannella's influential *Balance and Swing* (1982)—an instructional book for beginning callers—and expect that Sannella's suggested tune was the *only* tune appropriate.

In part, this was because the old-time music revival and the dance revival, once happily wedded in places like Bloomington, were saturating the calendar with separate institutions. Dance communities, dance weekends, and dance weeks, once few in number, were becoming so numerous that some dancers were no longer drawn to fiddle contests or old-time music festivals. But the most debilitating threat to this happy marriage was largely invisible: the declining romantic impulse, which held traditional sources, authentic style, and direct tutelage by traditional masters in the highest of regard. Even while old-time music continued to be played, sometimes with facility unachievable in the previous decade of discovery, its system of values was being eroded by a rising tide of formalism.

New England style musicians must, then, have seemed shameless in the way they understood and exploited formal qualities of their music. Indeed, many understood the music very well and why and how it

The Piano Controversy

worked for dancing. Here, for example, is how Massachusetts musician David Kaynor described contra music for Mary Dart:

> The good band and the good caller consists of being able to identify *when* to take off on a flight of fancy, *when* to do something really repetitive, when to do the bare minimalist playing, when to get extravagant, when to play just the absolute simplest version of a tune because the dancers are confused and they need everything orderly. And then say, the dancers have it. The dancers are in the groove. Let's go wild. (Dart 1995: 38)

In the old-time bands that thrilled dancers at the Jukebox during the 1970s, such concerns would have been inconceivable. It is not difficult to imagine how pressures to respond to these concerns—from dancers, callers, and other musicians—riled old-time musicians. But the more serious threat was not the rise of new performance pressures, but the erosion of values that had propelled old-time revival. A fiddler might once have been held in high esteem for mastering the bowing for, say, the Stripling Brothers' "Wolves a-Howling"—now it was unlikely at the dance that anyone would have heard of the Stripling Brothers.

Probably by the mid-1980s, repertoire lists used by New England bands began appearing indexed or categorized according to the effects the tunes had on dances—smooth or bouncy, fast or slow, and so forth. Tune choice and style of playing were then matched to the figures of the contra—abruptly truncated accents for the balance figure, smooth sixteen-beat phrases for weaving figures, minor keys for the "gypsy" figure, decreasing and then increasing volume to mimic down-the-center-and-back (Dart 1995: 40–41; Herman 1995: 8–10). In contrast, probably as a result of jam session etiquette and also in deference to banjo players who had to retune for each key change, old-time lists were most always organized by musical key. Some old-time musicians, defiant in their response to emerging pressures to please callers and dancers, clung to narrow definitions of old-time music. Some ignored callers' or dancers' tempo preferences; some insisted upon "crooked" tunes (those structured in other than the "straight" or "regular" four-by-eight bar, AABB arrangement) for contras, annoying some callers and dancers who expected the music and dance phrasing to match (Dart 1995: 114).

Old-Time Music and Dance

My band was generally very adept at adapting old-time tunes to the evolving dance music aesthetic. But once we were pushed too far and played a cruel trick on a beginning caller. Clearly under the spell of *Balance and Swing,* the caller asked for a specific tune for the contra she was teaching—a tune we didn't know. Rather than make a fuss, we consented, but then launched into some old-time favorite that we knew would do just as well. She had no idea what Sannella's recommended tune sounded like, of course, and the dance came off just fine.

Perhaps the surest sign of the widening gulf between contra dance and old-time music was the writings of Phil Jamison in *Old-Time Herald.* His 1989 complaint, "Dare to Be Square!" had called for a resurgence of southern squares, partly to curtail the intoxicating popularity of contras, but also to provide a better environment for the fast tempos, irregular structures, and informal performance practices that were fashionable in old-time music circles. In 1991 he addressed the matter more directly in "Make 'em Want to Dance! How to Play for a Dance." In this, it was not so much the advice he gave, which was all very helpful; rather, it was the way he characterized the relationship between old-time music and dance. "Playing for dances," he wrote, "is also an opportunity to expose the general public to old-time music, which hopefully they will come to embrace" (1991: 10).

Dancers as the "general public" that needed to be "exposed" to old-time music? This was an extraordinary and disheartening assessment of old-time dance revival, which so recently seemed inextricably wedded to old-time music. But it was also a perplexing strategy. Jamison might have instead looked to bring into the authorized scope of "old-time music" bands and musicians who had long been wedded to dance in the Midwest and South, and he might have acknowledged the legitimate claim New England dance musicians after Ralph Page had long ago staked in the term "old-time music." Instead, he wrote for an old-time music audience with the narrowest of interests, deeply alienated from dance.

In time, stylistic trends in old-time music played into this controversy, which was felt in dance circles as a kind of formalist response. The stylistic strain known as "bug music" drifted throughout the movement in the 1980s, championed by such bands as the Tomkins County

The Piano Controversy

Horse Flies, which included former Bloomington residents Jeff Claus and Judy Hyman. The style featured stripped-down melodic formulas, deliberate avoidance of harmonic movement, and a pulsating, hell-bent rhythm, which seemed to exaggerate, sometimes to absurdity, the fundamental elements of old-time music. *Old-Time Herald* reviewer Dale Morris called the Horse Flies' first recording "progressive" old-time music and warned readers that "if you are an old-time purist, straight and true, you may not care for it" (Morris 1987: 32). But, commenting on "Bloomington Breakdown" (a Strawberry McCloud piece) and "Benton's Dream," he added: "The dance floor beckons on these two tunes, for the music quickly gets into your feet."

Sometimes old-time style also attracted wickedly irreverent, even cynical, theatrics. Band names may have been the most visible layer of this cynicism. Inventing band names, even under ad hoc circumstances such as fiddle contests, became an art of finessed irony. For a time, our band played under the name the Razorlickers, an irreverent play on "Skillet Lickers." We "bought" the "rights" to the name for one dollar from former Bloomington fiddler Lucy Freeman, who was briefly a passenger in our van on the way to a job. She had used the name with some friends at a fiddle contest. We were not really committed to this, of course. But those who genuinely embraced the form added to this sparse style an extraordinary aura of tongue-in-cheek existential despair.

Although contra dance was far from central to the concerns of this style, it may well have helped to resolve some of the divisive tensions that had arisen. The Horse Flies, in fact, became popular at dance camps and special events, and dancers from all points seemed to have discovered in their music some element of old-time music that other dance music forms lacked. The style was not that difficult to imitate, so bands could register its influence substantially without always having to commit to its austere principles. In this way, old-time music became a formal alternative to New England music. But this came at the expense of its romantic aura, alienating "old-time purists." Those whose success had been earned by investing in the romantic impulse might not have been pleased by this turn of events.

On the whole, the old-time versus New England dispute had widely varying effects depending on what local tastes and habits had preceded it. In Bloomington, and in same-generation communities such as St. Louis, Chicago, and Urbana, traditional stage practices were firmly grounded in old-time stage etiquette, and squares were not at all unpopular. There, dancers and musicians seemed satisfied with the range of musical options that were being explored. In 1987, veteran Bloomington musician and dancer Teri Klassen, whose tastes in old-time music run conservative, described for *Old-Time Herald* a Bloomington scene with an uncontroversial variety of styles:

> If it's Wednesday in Bloomington, there's a square dance. Actually, more contras are called there, always to live music, and often to Southern old-time music, although occasionally to Cape Breton or New England styles. (1987–88: 25)

Indeed, many old-time ensembles adapted pleasantly to the changing needs of dancers; likewise, many dancers appreciated wholeheartedly the unique advantages that old-time music brought to the dance experience. The lion's share of traditional old-time tunes, after all, featured the "regular" AABB melodic structure that was ideally suited for contra dance.

Bloomington's ongoing fondness for old-time music was also a key link to local and regional musical culture. During the early years, the informal dance band was a comfort zone for local musicians. Even bluegrass musicians would occasionally sit in. Later, it was the presence of a well-established old-time aesthetic that provided a hospitable environment for Strawberry McCloud and later Lotus Dickey. Lotus personified the Bloomington aesthetic better than anyone: he had deep roots in old-time tradition, but like the best old-time musicians he had eclectic tastes and versatile technique. His fondness for banjo and guitar were no more remarkable than his interest in hammered dulcimer and piano.

Ultimately, the dance hall piano meant that new options had been made available. In Bloomington, the New England style found its ablest proponent in Linda Handelsman, a versatile keyboardist who adapted the idiom to a wide variety of formal and informal ensembles. Her band, Scotch on the Rocks, formed with Emily Humphries-Baer of Lafayette, Indiana, and Norb Spenser of Louisville, Kentucky, emerged at music sessions at the 1980 Winter Dance Week at the Campbell Folk School.

Lotus Dickey and Pete Sutherland play for a dance during the mid-1980s. Photo courtesy of Gary Stanton.

The following year they were the featured band at the Knoxville dance weekend, which itself became a pivotal venue for the spread of New England style music in the South.

Even in Bloomington in 1980, however, Linda's tastes were not remarkable. Through the 1980s it was not uncommon to hear bands that included concertinas, accordions, hammered dulcimers, flutes, and tin whistles. Some of the more influential musicians were Kate Dunlay, a Cape Breton–style fiddler; Linda Breitag, a versatile fiddler who ex-

Old–Time Music and Dance

celled at French-Canadian style; Peter Moxhay, who played New England dance style; and Pete Sutherland, a New England fiddler who enjoyed a variety of styles. Malcolm Dalglish and Grey Larsen came to Bloomington as established Celtic-style recording artists and sometimes played in dance bands. Often, what resulted was a hybrid form and an innocent unconcern for the turmoil that raged elsewhere.

28   THE BOOK

In Bloomington, these differences in style paled against what was the
only genuinely divisive issue the dance faced throughout its early history: the local status of bands, callers, and dancers as artists. The informal "open mike" arrangement, installed very soon after the dances began, had endured with widespread satisfaction throughout the 1970s.
By the 1980s there were rumblings of dissent, however, and a call from
some quarters for the scheduling of set ensembles. Some would even
have charged admission at the door and paid bands and callers.

The rise of this sentiment coincided with several changes in the participant population of the dance. For one thing, most dance communities elsewhere paid bands and callers, generously so in a few places. In
such settings, bands and callers could approach semiprofessional status,
sometimes earning a reliable portion of a modest income. As musicians
and callers from other communities moved to or passed through
Bloomington, and as Bloomington's own veteran musicians began playing in other communities, they were exposed to these contrasting
norms. Consequently, some began to call for a more structured dance.

Bloomington had achieved its initial sense of community at a crucial
historical moment, when organic community was forged out of cultural

self-reliance against a backdrop of passive consumer entertainment. Democratic musical participation—most prominently the jam session—was the ritual centerpiece of this movement. But contra dance as a holistic dance and music event, with similar levels of participation and fulfillment in both roles, had evolved as an even more perfect articulation of organic community.

For those propelled by this ideal, the essential pretense of such events was that there were no passive roles—the more one participated, the more one was fulfilled by the experience. Whatever benefits were achieved from aesthetic practice were created by and dispersed throughout the whole community. It was designed as a mutually created, mutually experienced aesthetic work because it was meant to celebrate the holistic aesthetic lifestyle. At its boundary with the outside one might expect to surrender all expectations of passive entertainment. So, to have replaced this initiation with an admission table, as some wanted, would undermine the organic experience.

Throughout the period of development of egalitarian dance communities, however, there remained nationwide an equally viable strain of folk revival community that continued to be constructed around display events. In these, there was a division of labor—quasi-entrepreneurial "folk artists" supplied the cultural raison d'être for the event while a complex system of organizers, volunteers, and aficionados exchanged labor, time, and money for derived authenticity and passive aesthetic pleasure. It was surely this influential model that inspired the movement to reimbursement bands and sometimes also callers, for never did the discussion involve a systematic inventory of the variety of skill and labor involved in maintaining the community.

This model might well have been a great deal more influential in Bloomington, in fact, had the demise of the Folk Club and coffeehouse scene toward the end of the 1960s not allowed Bloomington's unusually strong penchant for unmediated community to develop in relative isolation. Still, at its core the debate was neither about mediation, display, representation, nor entrepreneurship—all of which most everyone endorsed and practiced in other settings. Rather, it was about the dance itself as the articulation of community—about where, for example, music stood within the social and cultural locus of the group. Was musicality in its essence drawn from the cultural stock of the group, as it once had been, or did it come from elsewhere?

Compounding this conflict locally was a less visible but equally influential force: beginning during the 1980s, the population of new dancers was made up of those with increasingly fewer ties to the counterculture and less awareness of the historical significance of the music. New dancers did not always know that Easy Street had been forged from the cultural substance of the dance itself and from old-time music revival. At the same time, the friendship bonds that for some had been the sole basis of community were being stretched to unacceptable limits. It may even have been that Sugar Hill and Swing into Spring were the catalysts for this shift: as much as they seemed to be extensions of the dance itself, they were not universally supported by the old guard after Sugar Hill was moved from the Marmouzé property and became a public event. Supporters of reform spoke of a lack of "respect," as if an acknowledgment of past accomplishments was not being passed on to the relentless waves of new participants.

As the 1980s began, however, resistance to reform was widespread and extended to the staunchest veterans. The thought of losing the principle of participant equity was important to some: if callers and bands were paid, *everyone* who contributed should be paid—those who operated and maintained the sound system, cleaned the floor, opened and closed the building, published the Orange Sheet, and so on. Ted Hall used to say, not entirely facetiously, that it was the dancers who should be paid. But the greatest abomination was the prospect of a physical barrier—an admission table—that would restrict free and informal movement into and out of the dance. And conservatives had on their side the political structure of the dance, which made no provisions for structural changes without a general referendum. Until the end of the 1980s, the group indeed held only three general elections: the Gang of Four election in 1976, the change of location vote later in 1986, and this referendum on bands. Truly, the Gang of Four seemed to serve only to deter, and never to facilitate, significant change.

In October of 1983, reformers began discussing the principle of scheduling bands and, as a separate item, paying them. Frank Hall, the leading proponent of changing the system, drew up a written proposal.

A date several weeks hence, November 9, was set for a vote at the beginning of the Wednesday Night Dance. During the intervening weeks, debates were intense at parties, at the dance, on street corners, or anywhere. There was no official membership in the dance, so anyone who attended the meeting was allowed to vote. Although the issue itself was intensely divisive, there was not even a hint that either side had usurped community trust by packing the meeting with supporters. When the votes were counted, the first proposal (scheduling bands) succeeded and the second (paying bands) failed, both by wide margins. The principle that seemed to have been newly accepted was that the stage was no longer open at all times—that an ensemble could, with the blessing of the group, become a band, and for its scheduled period exclude others from the stage.

Once this was established, the logistical adjustments were inconsequential. Some volunteer kept a schedule "book" of upcoming bands. To prevent a fiefdom from forming around any individual, the job was passed along periodically to someone else. The original term was three months, but this was only loosely followed. The business of scheduling was normally conducted during the dance itself by making announcements that bands and callers were needed or by making rounds, asking specific individuals to sign up. Most schedulers also phoned those who attended infrequently in an effort to attract their participation, but the system clearly favored those who attended the dance. Still, some musicians and callers attended only on the evening when they were scheduled to perform. Scheduled bands began playing each week at 9:00; the period before that, as well as the entire first Wednesday of each month, was still "open."

This system proved vastly successful in providing for stylistic experimentation, so much so that among the early problems was a complaint that too little conventional old-time music remained on the program. There was never any presumed linkage between scheduling bands and the rise of New England music—Frank Hall, in fact, was well known as a proponent of the old-time style. The new system enabled the kind of planned arrangements that favored the New England style, but this went largely unnoticed. When the complaint about too little old-time music was made, the volunteer scheduler merely took note of it and for a time gave preferential treatment to old-time style bands. Without doubt, those musicians who were more comfortable in informal ensembles got less playing time, and those who wished to be paid were still denied this. Until a decade later, this divisive issue was put aside.

In fact, the period of the mid-1980s developed its own mystique similar to the innocent and formative "golden age." By this time, dance groups had arisen across the Midwest and across the nation. Among them, Bloomington seemed a holdout from an earlier age, unconventional in its ways, alive with its own historical purpose. It was from this historical consciousness that the notion of a written history emerged— when history, ideology, and style were very near the surface of experience at the dance. This was no more than a gathered circumstance, not any kind of historical ascendancy. Yet with this qualification I began two decades ago to record as best I could the nexus of experience that was the dance. At its center was the weekly dance, which I was attending regularly.

29 COLLECTION TIME!

This book was undertaken from a particular historical perspective. It was 1987 when I first drafted this narrative and printed it in the Sugar Hill calendar. Most of the issues and people discussed here had their influence before this date; most who came after are omitted. I have followed some thematic threads past that date when it seemed helpful. This chapter describes a typical dance at the time I began the narrative. To give readers a foundation for the issues discussed in the book, this chapter ought to have come sooner. But I felt that it could not precede its own formative influences, and have left it until now. In keeping with the overall approach here, the focus is on the holistic organizational effort—the articulation of community—and not merely on the music and dance per se.

As was the case with so many dance communities in the mid-1980s, habit, tradition, and some vague will to carry on guided so many of the logistical necessities for the Bloomington dance group. To a visitor, a dance would have appeared to operate almost by intuition, with no pre-determined structure. Personnel would shift routinely in and out of habitual roles. Some aspects of this logistical practice were unique to Bloomington. In fact, whereas dancing itself became increasingly standardized across groups nationwide, community organization was notably localized. In relocating to a new group, adjusting to the dancing itself was not that difficult. But if a dancer brought too many structural expectations along, finding a comfortable niche in the organization could be more difficult.

Generally, infrastructural differences had much to do with the way particular dance groups were founded and who founded them: Bloomington's counterculture roots became less common as new groups arose from circumstances contemporary to the 1980s. The best way to understand this is to examine what it might have taken to bring together a typical Wednesday Night Dance. For appearance, I have organized the discussion into sections, but this is not to suggest that the dance itself was so strictly partitioned.

Setting Up. The dance officially began each Wednesday night at 7:30, and at about this time the sound system arrived and the door was unlocked. For many years, the sound system was stored at Ted Hall's house, so each week he brought it to the dance in his car along with the key to unlock the door. Most likely the few who arrived at 7:30 would help set up the equipment.

At the time, operating the sound system was not considered a specialized role—anyone was allowed and even encouraged to learn its basic operation and adjust the settings when necessary. The equipment itself, one might soon learn, was public property. Later, concerns were raised that there were too many people adjusting the sound, but in the beginning no one wanted to create a bureaucracy over something that could be managed much more simply. If there were serious problems with the equipment, they were usually passed on to Jim Johnson, Roger Diggle, Gary Stanton, or Ted Hall.

In winter, the dance was held in the gymnasium of Harmony School, an alternative school where some dancers worked or had children who attended; in summer, it was held in an open-air shelter at Upper Cascades, a city park. Many Bloomington dancers missed the old hall, the Old Library, from which they recently moved, citing its "warmth." The acoustics were noticeably poorer in the new building. Poor acoustics, uncomfortable temperature and humidity, poles that supported the roof (and got in the way of dancers), poor relations with proprietors or

Old-Time Music and Dance

neighbors, and poor flooring could each spoil the effectiveness of a hall. Yet poor conditions were never entirely debilitating: on a given night, determined dancers could overcome even the most daunting obstacles to achieve good dancing. In such cases, setting up meant transforming a physical space into a properly prepared ritual space.

Transporting the sound system week after week could be a demanding job. Yet, because the dance emerged as an informal social event, volunteers were not paid for this or for any other work. Even in dance communities where callers and bands were paid, sound operators most often were not paid unless they owned the system. But like dancing itself, and like so many other work-like activities at the dance, setting up or helping with the sound system had intangible rewards. All tasks had the same volunteer status, so any could confer deep involvement in the communal ideal—the sense of one's re-creation that marked the shift to involved participant. For a new dancer, sound setup could quickly neutralize the perceived emotional distance from the experiential ideal and from the physical space. If there was a "backstage," this was it. Yet it was still a job, and for those who did it every week, its relentless demands eventually could and did take their toll. "Burnout" occurred, and jobs such as this had to be passed on. At the time, transitions were handled informally by asking around to see who might be willing and able to take over.

The new winter dance hall also differed in the size of the stage. In previous locations such as the Old Library and the Jukebox, the stage was only slightly elevated, a small step up from the floor. In the new site the stage was more than waist-high, with a curtain and stairs on either side for access. At first, musicians and dancers insisted that the mikes be set up on the floor, eliminating the distance and the barrier of the proscenium arch. Over time, bands increasingly preferred using the stage, and eventually this was the norm. This may well also have been an imperceptible but important shift in the function and status of musicians, but I never heard any discussion to this effect. Bands generally could sit (and only rarely stand) where they wanted.

Talk during and around setup might consist of the week's events: news of group members, recent travels, that evening's band and caller, news from outside the group. If newcomers were present at this time, they were easily noticed and were quizzed about how they heard about the dance and where they came from. By 8:00 P.M., there would be enough people for several conversations at once, and soon after that, a crowd sufficient to start a dance. Musicians might have begun playing informally. At once, someone would notice the crowd and cajole a caller to teach a dance. Someone would call out, "Line up!" and stand with a partner at a spot recognizable as the top position of a contra set. From there, a single set would form for what would surely be a straightforward contra. As dancers arrived during that dance, they would take partners and fall in at the bottom. Having missed the instructions, they would watch the dance and expect other dancers to help them through until they learned it.

The Dance. This first dance and the next one or two to follow were effectively preliminary experiences. Newcomers were sometimes advised not to show up at 7:30 when the doors open—that the dance "didn't really get going until around 8:30 or so." In part this was because beginners were more likely than veterans to have arrived on time; in part it was because new couples might have to be coached through the figures a few times before they caught on. But there was another important reason.

Dancers spoke of halls as being "too small" or "too big." Overcrowding—a logistical matter—was mainly a measure of the ability to dance without danger of collision or injury. But undercrowding pertained to ritual matters and measured the ability of a crowd to "fill up a hall." It had to do with the ability of the dance to rise to the expectations implied by an empty space. A dance in an undercrowded room was an effort: a dancer in such a situation had to work at dancing rather than have dancing work on the dancer. Sets spread out so that figures covered too great a distance. With space to move, dancers were too easily tempted to employ exaggerated and unnecessary movements. Consequently, they were prone to arrive late for important figures. In communities where extremely large halls accommodated much smaller crowds, barriers, such as a row of chairs or a drawn curtain, were sometimes used to limit the space. The Bloomington dance used the whole room, and at some point on each Wednesday night the space was sufficiently filled.

Old-Time Music and Dance

In the mid-1980s, the period before 9:00 as well as the entire evening on the first Wednesday of the month was considered "open mike"— anyone could volunteer to call or play. This was usually accomplished by the callers taking turns, though there might have been only one caller present during the first hour who wanted to call. It may also have been that no one stepped forward to call, so some urging would be necessary to get a dance going. It was scarcely an annoyance for things to come to this, since generally someone would rise to the occasion without too much delay. Indeed, it was during this hour when novice callers could try their luck with a new dance, or when veteran callers who might otherwise have retired from calling were pressed into service by necessity. There was usually an abundance of able callers active in the group, a circumstance that the open-mike arrangement undoubtedly helped create and foster. In other dance communities open-mike events were not as well supported as those with prearranged bands and callers, but even in the late 1980s Mary Dart observed that in Bloomington attendance on nights organized under each of the two arrangements was relatively even (1995: 182).

Musicians eventually began taking turns also, respecting an unspecified limit on the number of musicians playing and the prevalent style being played. Musicians who were accustomed to playing together usually did so. In earlier years there was a more competitive spirit on the stage, possibly because so many old-time musicians were learning to play. But over the course of the 1980s a more cooperative spirit emerged, possibly enabled by the scheduling of ensembles. Stage time had become a less-valued resource than it once was, partly since many people enjoyed dancing and talking.

In Bloomington, many dancers would sit out dances. Some dropped by only to talk and did not dance a single dance. When the group considered collecting an admission charge at the door (rather than passing the hat for donations), this fact was brought out in opposition. Jim Johnson and Nancy McKinley for several years brought farm eggs to sell and collected empty egg cartons that dancers donated. Those with gardens would bring extra vegetables at harvest time. Things to be bought, sold, borrowed, and lent among dancers were "brought to the dance," having been put off until Wednesday when a convenient meeting was certain. Tom Morrison once brought a television to the dance to watch an important Indiana University basketball game. Rides were arranged for travel to festivals and weekends, dates were made, meetings were arranged, parties were planned. People told their life stories, exchanged hugs, flirted, made friends, fell in love, broke up, and consoled one another.

Young children ran free on the edge of the dance floor and sometimes had to be restrained from the perilous space too near the dance sets. Dancers sometimes played with the children, sometimes watched them for the parents, but rarely or never expressed displeasure over their presence in the room. If anything, the children of the dance closed the circle long ago breached by the WWII generation who had abandoned folk culture. Children who were "raised in the dance" might someday be those who would carry on the work of the community.

In Bloomington and other dance communities, asking and being asked to dance did not carry the great social import that mainstream society sometimes attributed to it. A dance with any partner was expected to be fun or at least charitable, and both postures were advanced with ease and sincerity. Thus one rarely turned down a dance when asked, and only did so by offering a plausible excuse. To decline one partner and accept another was a serious and noticeable affront both to individual and community, and rarely happened.

If asked to dance and already obligated for the current dance, one could agree to "the next one" or even "the one after." If the waiting list got too long, there might be a moment of comic relief acknowledging inequitable popularity. There was also a danger of forgetting an obligation as well as confusion over whether waltzes or mixers, for example, counted as a dance. Such a circumstance could cause offense to a neglected partner.

Generally, women asked men to dance as often as the reverse. This practice was reinforced by its contrast with mainstream social dance decorum and often had to be explained to beginners. If there were unequal numbers, women danced with one another; in increasing but lesser numbers men did so also.

Occasionally, as a novelty, men and women would switch roles in a dance, sometimes only for a brief moment. More often at special dances, men would wear skirts, citing as reasons keeping cool, enhancing dance movements, and transcending gender rigidity. Generally, in instances where gender stereotypes were so challenged, there was an intent both to enhance experience through reversal and to routinize the reversals to the point where they were divested of their significance.

On the dance floor, etiquette, particularly regarding relations between men and women dancers, was in constant negotiation, with the twirl as the most potent issue. Callers lectured on it. Articles in newsletters were cut out and posted on the wall. Men who danced the women's role executed exaggerated twirls, presumably enjoying for the moment one of the more salient aspects of the woman's part; women who danced with them might complain of their uncompromising demand to be twirled when dancing as women.

At 9:00, on all but the first Wednesday of the month, the open-mike time ended and the featured local ensemble took over. This might be an experienced band that performed in venues outside the dance, or an experimental ensemble that worked up a set, or a group cajoled over their protests into playing. They may or may not have adopted a band name. Sometimes no band was arranged, and the informal group kept playing. The caller might or might not have worked with this particular set of musicians or this style of music. This shift from open mike to featured band was accomplished with only a brief pause in the flow of activity; it was not identified as a "break." There might well be a shift in energy, however, as a result of the new and possibly more intense style of music.

Collection Time. At some point in the evening, between dances, someone who felt a momentary flash of responsibility would initiate the collection procedure. This was often done when, it was estimated, the most people were at the dance, and thus the most money could be collected. Truly, no one was designated as responsible for the collection, although in practice it was usually initiated by one of several people who were accustomed to handling the money. That person, or someone else at that person's insistence, procured a hat or something like it, yelled "Collection time!" and went about collecting money from everyone in the room as the sets formed for the next dance. The average contribution was about $1. In the mid-1980s, the total had to reach $45 per week to cover the rent and other expenses. If it appeared that too little money was collected, another pass might be made later. On rare occasions, no one remembered to take up the collection.

The money was kept by Ted Hall in a bank account and was used to pay rent on the hall, to cover the initial purchase and upkeep of the sound system, to pay touring groups who came to Bloomington approximately eight times a year, and to cover miscellaneous expenses incurred by individuals in service to the dance. When touring ensembles performed, dancers were more generous and the collection considerably larger; even so, it was often padded with money from the treasury to pay touring bands.

Around 1985 the facility rent and sound system expenses had risen faster than the weekly collection, and those who watched the bank account noticed that it had begun to dwindle. In response, I put out a financial report and called for increased financial consciousness and more generous collections. The plea was heard, apparently, since group coffers soon stabilized. Most often, however, few knew or cared about the details of the financial arrangements, although Ted on several occasions distributed photocopies of the books during times when their contents needed to be known.

Collection time was also announcement time, although the annoying din of conversation during the collection compelled some to wait for the calm just prior to the next dance. Anyone who so wished might step up to the mike and announce anything of interest to dancers—invitations to parties; upcoming concerts or other events; honors, birthdays, or other causes for personal celebration; appeals for help in personal crisis; travel arrangements to out-of-town events; sales of records, tapes, books, or anything; upcoming meetings of B-band, Sacred Harp, or other groups; introductions of new or visiting dancers; or requests for help with group events. Often a line formed on the stage to wait to use the mike. Generally, the importance of this personal use of the stage was respected both by speakers and listeners: announcements were brief and informative and complaints about delays rare.

Many announcements of events were reiterated by accompanying flyers—these were placed in stacks on the stage and were brought with the sound system each week for continuous distribution. Dancers from other groups promoting large events usually sent a stack of flyers by mail to be distributed at the dance. This, along with word of mouth, was the major form of communication for upcoming events. Until after 1990, Bloomington did not send mailings to individual group members; consequently, presence at the dance was an essential link in the information conduit and thereby in participation in the community.

Resumed Dancing. This break in activity was never lengthy and was not, as in other communities, actually considered a break. The band ordinarily did not leave the stage, and rarely did someone have to urge the beginning of the next dance. More often, impatient dancers began forming contra lines on their own even as the collection hat made its way through the crowd. Eventually the dance resumed and continued as before. However, especially if the collection was late and only one or two dances remained, this point marked a slight downward shift in energy in anticipation of the end of the dance. Some might leave early at this point. In any case, the dance continued until just prior to 10:30 p.m., when it ended. It was said that the 10:30 p.m. ending time was dictated by the rules of a facility the group once used. Occasionally, someone would suggest extending the hours to get in more dancing, but such proposals met with resistance from those who enjoyed going to the bar afterward.

Dancers knew which contra was the last and would sometimes take special care not to miss it. Because it was last on the program, bands might save their most exciting tune for that spot. Dancers might look for a partner they especially enjoyed dancing with, expecting that it would be a good dance. Good callers generally saved a dance that was interesting but not challenging; some would call a dance that could be easily memorized, and then join the set with a partner once it was going smoothly on its own. With a good band, excitement would build throughout the dance; when it ended, the crowd might erupt in wild and spontaneous applause. Indeed, there was no other moment when the band was so extensively acknowledged.

The Last Waltz. Except for rare and unscheduled polkas, hombos, and schottisches, the last waltz was the only dance of the evening where partners danced exclusively with each other during the entire dance. Much like contra and square dance, the rudiments of the old-time waltz could easily be taught on the spot, affording a beginning dancer a modicum of pleasure at a relatively small cost of effort.

In contrast with contras, however, the waltz was more inclined to articulate dyadic relations rather than roles as community members. For precisely this feature, it was distinguished—as a "couple dance"—from "set dances" such as contras and squares. Moreover, in its location as last on the program, it served to reintegrate couples drawn apart and into the community by both contra and square figures and by a code of etiquette that encouraged social mixing. It was even called, specifically, the "last" waltz. In some communities, there was sometimes opposition to the last waltz precisely because it undermined the freedom from role rigidity that dancers enjoyed in forms such as contras and squares.

More often, however, dancers happily tolerated the romantic capacities of the last waltz if they did not deliberately exploit them. For those who wanted to punctuate lingering romantic ties, the last waltz was an effective way to do it. Attached couples, for example, would frequently make stated or unstated arrangements to dance the last waltz together. Over time, others learned this and stopped asking either to dance the last waltz. The waltz could also confirm a mutual romantic interest or test a yet unverified one. Once at a waltz workshop, an instructor, with telling facetiousness, had dancers change partners frequently to prevent them from falling in love.

The waltz also served non-romantic interests. It was an opportunity for focused conversation, providing friends a chance to reaffirm a neglected tie or catch up on news. Pairs of women and, rarely, men would waltz together. Sometimes children would be included. Groups of more than two friends occasionally waltzed in a circle; sometimes the circle would grow in size until it was apparently open to anyone. In each case, the pivotal motive was more social than aesthetic, and the social impact was heightened by the position of the waltz as last on the program.

For others the waltz was dance, an expression of grace and physical control. As with the other dance forms, dancers would analyze skills, learn and experiment with new forms of waltz, regard graceful waltzers highly, and critique the quality of the music. Cajun waltz as well as European styles became popular as alternatives to the conventional and simple old-time step. Skilled waltzers sought out one another as partners. Generally, the potential of waltz as mere physical movement did not conflict with its capacity as a marker of romantic attachment. Each function, in fact, seemed to draw upon the ambiguity that the other provided. Nor did skill prevail over inclusiveness, for example, in such a way that an inexperienced couple felt their performance inadequate or unfulfilling.

The last waltz was socially reintegrative in other ways unrelated to form. It might have been preceded on the program by a recognition of the musicians and caller, affirming their talent and efforts but also bringing to closure their specialized roles. The caller, who had no duties during the waltz, usually rejoined the dancers and thus also the community. A din of conversation even among those dancing would break the spell of attention to the caller. Those not dancing begin putting their coats on, resulting in a bustle of reintegrative energy. Someone might even begin breaking down the sound system, leaving in operation just enough equipment for the remaining musicians. The lights were often dimmed for "atmosphere." When the waltz ended, scattered applause might greet the band, but it was considerably less robust than the applause after the final contra.

Breaking Down the Sound System. Soon after the waltz ended, perhaps during the applause, the lights were switched back on. Groups of conversations would form, with no apparent rush to leave. Those ultimately responsible for the sound system, particularly Ted Hall, hurried to put it away. A plea from Ted, "We need some help with the sound system," was issued, and a few people would respond and help. Instruments were put away; final business was conducted regarding things brought for exchange. Sound equipment was maneuvered around groups of talkers. Conversation during this period might well be deliberate, bringing some issue to closure, or might anticipate some future meeting such as going to the bar, to the dance next week, or to an upcoming dance weekend, party, or other event. Often those who had to close the building grew impatient and asked the last few stragglers to leave. Eventually they did, and the building was locked.

Swimming. During the summer, particularly during the hottest months, the call would quietly go out for an after-dance swim. If enough people were interested, a group of anywhere from five to fifteen would go to a local swimming hole. Swimming was not publicly announced the way other events were, although neither was it meant to be exclusive. It was a "backstage" event, one whose accessibility was understood but not advertised. It was generally promoted by asking individuals or groups of individuals if they wanted to go. New dancers, if they appeared interested, were invited to the swim.

The ambiguous accessibility of swimming went hand in hand with its flaunted disregard for conventional recreational practice. Swimmers would follow a dark and sometimes treacherous path through woods with healthy stands of poison ivy, all to participate in what was for most skinny-dipping. Because it entailed physical and social risk taking, it could be an effective way for a newcomer to gain entry into the group. It also entailed a vague ideological endorsement and allusion to sexuality, all the more vivid when the group of swimmers appeared en masse with wet hair later at the bar.

Kilroy's. At some time during the first few years of the existence of the dance, dancers began extending the event past its 10:30 P.M. ending by reconvening at a local bar. During the mid-1980s, the meeting-place was Kilroy's, a popular student-gathering place on Kirkwood just a block west of the campus. Thus each week after the dance ended, as many as half of those at the dance (perhaps twenty-five) drove to Kilroy's, pushed the tables together, and sat together for at least another hour's talk. During most of the 1980s, Bill Baus negotiated with management for special accommodations for the group. Kilroy's was unexceptional in their response but did reserve a block of tables during a normally busy time. They also were usually willing to turn the music down and regulate the temperature to the group's liking.

The practice of pushing the tables together endured a number of different settings, establishing it as a marked activity. Except for a few brief exceptions, settings with bolted-down or round tables were categorically avoided. Although a wide range of table arrangements was possible, the preferred pattern was the arrangement most similar to the contra formation of the dance—a long line of dancers facing one another across a table. Its importance seemed always in allowing "everyone" to sit "together," a circumstance that must have depended upon having a single seating unit and also the proximity of neighbors seated

Old-Time Music and Dance

across and to each side. In this way conversations might be briefly dyadic but not private, and there was a persistent inclination toward larger units of conversation. Until the late 1980s, other seating arrangements featuring smaller segregated groups consistently aroused discontent.

At the bar, unlike at the dance, the randomizing and circulating effects of the longways formation was reoriented. Romantic partners might well sit together, as would groups of friends, but gender here was of no regard. This provided a handy reintegrative device for musicians, callers, social cliques, groups of friends, and couples since it employed the same spatial structure that served to separate them in the first place.

The way that the seating formation at the bar most affected social structure was in the ease of sustained conversation. At the dance, distractions and interruptions were far too likely. But at the bar, there was ample time to explore many areas of interest, such as dance business, other dance events, personal struggle and triumph, involvement in romantic relationships, personal history, sports and news, and travel. One lengthy romance in which I was involved began when a friend sitting beside me left early, and I had a pleasant chat with his neighbor, who slid over from one seat away. Those who complained of lack of integration into the group were sometimes told that they would "get to know people better" if they went to the bar. Birthdays were generally celebrated at the bar; Leslie's Italian Villa used to donate a slice of cheesecake to anyone celebrating a birthday. Photos of vacations or dance events would be passed around the table for all to see. Once, when I was using the film *Country Corners* for a course I was teaching, I brought it with a projector to Kilroy's and was permitted to show it on the wall.

Beer was a vital component of the after-dance scene. The group never went to a site where it was unavailable, and it was generally preferred over other drinks. Beer was also important at parties and other informal events, but it was rarely seen at the weekly dance. In venues where it was proscribed by facility proprietors, it was occasionally an attractive "backstage" activity. Yet, anything more than moderate consumption was thought to impair social interaction or dancing. The prevailing practice, it was said, was to dance hard and drink lightly.

There was some suggestion that alcohol served in part to expand the scope of natural morality. In its capacity to inhibit self-control, alcohol

Collection Time!

could enlarge the role of spontaneous and natural good will in this free-spirited group. Once at a large outdoor gathering, an older local man who had apparently had a rough upbringing remarked that he couldn't believe that there could be alcohol at so large a party and not have fights break out. Indeed there were never fights, and there was actually some concern with the dangers of pent-up emotions associated with fastidious sobriety.

There were many who chose non-alcoholic drinks, and it would have been unacceptable if their tastes could not be accommodated at the after-dance site. The overall variety on the menu was a consideration, but not one as important as seating or beer. Some did struggle with alcohol addiction, probably more so than was generally known. Although passive cigarette smoke was a serious concern at events held in homes, it was grudgingly tolerated in bars.

Increasingly, drinkers cultivated a taste for good beer. Although at Kilroy's inexpensive domestic brands—bought in pitchers to share—were the most popular, even they were sometimes refused if they did not taste right. At parties, imports were always preferred. One group member started a business selling home-brewing kits, and some from the group took up the hobby and won or participated in national and regional brewing contests.

After Kilroy's. As at the dance hall at the beginning of the evening, there was a critical mass phenomenon which brought the event to closure. At some point, a number of people left at the same time, possibly all sensing that it was "a good time to go." If there was any more to the evening together, it was highly spontaneous and, consequently, would have vast integrative potential. In years past, a small dance might be held outdoors, a group might go for a late swim in summer or reconvene at someone's house or another bar.

30 THE RECLUSIVE MUSE

At the beginning of the 1980s, nearly a decade had passed since Dillon Bustin called that first dance in the green house and conjured up the spirits of old-time American dance. Dillon's interests had passed through several phases, and now he had turned to productions of works on southern Indiana. In 1983 he made a recording, *Dillon Bustin's Almanac*, of songs composed during his years of subsistence farming and rural life. A prominent theme was the way the exigencies of rural life— gardening, cutting firewood, and the assault of the seasons—coupled with the incomprehensible dissonance of the modern world led Dillon and other rural artists toward an evolving inwardness. This theme was echoed in a trilogy of documentary films made with filmmaker Richard Kane. In the films, he examined what he called the "reclusive muse" that inspired art forms produced by rural Indiana vernacular artists in response to a changing world.

In *Tough, Pretty, or Smart* (1981), it was Pike County and the band the Patoka Valley Boys, for whom old-time bluegrass music was a repository of community values in an atmosphere of rapid technological change. *Add and Mabel's Punkin Center* (1984), featured Add and Mabel Gray, who turned their general store into a museum of country collectibles, folk art, and local memories in southern Indiana. And *Water from Another Time* (1982) was a study of three southern Indiana folk performers. In the film, Dillon and Ronnie Moon were depicted driving through Orange County, visiting native artists known throughout the region for their exceptional talents. One, Lois Doane, was a self-taught watercolor painter, batik maker, and poet, who in her youth had worked as a housekeeper in the grand resort hotel at French Lick. And there was Elmer Boyd, an eccentric folk inventor and avid reader. The third artist, Orange County singer, composer, and fiddler Lotus Dickey, actually a late replacement in the film, was the most influential of all of Dillon's subjects. I return to Lotus in the next chapter.

A theme shot through these three works echoed Dillon's emerging views on folk culture in southern Indiana. These subjects were all rugged native artists who enjoyed few material rewards from their art, yet they persevered, under the most austere conditions, because their insights seemed to leave them no other recourse than to create. The style of the films was slow and deliberate, as each artist struggled to extract from his or her life and work the words that might reveal some underlying pattern. In each case, the motivating force of rural vernacular art was not the uncritical response to life's exigencies, not the passive inheritance of tradition, but a deliberate and premeditated nurturing of a local antimodernist ideal. Southern Indiana, in its landscape and in its circumstance, had drawn these people together and helped forge their ideals.

But what of Brown County? Similar in terrain, Brown County lay not to the south of Bloomington but to the east, and only a short drive south from Indianapolis. Nashville, its county seat, was virtually an antiquarian bazaar, an entire economy built around objects invested with the values of quaint rural life, sold and displayed in antique stores, country-style restaurants, craft shops, and eccentric museums. Nearby Brown County State Park had even adopted names for its buildings from a comic strip that had once depicted a fictional Brown County of quaint speech and colorful characters. Clearly this was a facade, but how did it really differ from the evolving fictions of native vernacular artists in the southern counties?

Dillon took up this question in his most deliberate work, *If You Don't*

Outdie Me (1982a), a book which recounted the events leading to Brown County's peculiar status as a site invested by outsiders with intense romantic sentiment. It focused on the life and work of Frank Hohenberger, an early-twentieth-century photographer who had captured the rustic ideal in Brown County and left extensive diaries of his experiences. In its earliest years as a romantic site, Brown County's appeal was merely scenic, the subject of landscape painters uninterested in the people of the region. But Hohenberger was not like the painters; rather, he was genuinely fond of the people. Consequently, they were most always the subjects of his photographs and written works.

Most of these works by Dillon Bustin were produced in the years just before the spate of publications that appeared under the banner the "politics of culture." Yet Dillon spoke to the deepest concerns of this movement. In Brown County, there were no extractive industries; the key motivating economic feature was the proximity of the region to Indianapolis. When the land was acquired for Brown County State Park, in part through the deceit of a local negotiator, there was scant protest; most were happy to get a good price for their nutrient-depleted soil. When the state hired a local man to enforce restrictions on hunting, there was widespread defiance. In fact, in 1925, as it was becoming apparent that Brown County was an attraction to outsiders, there was a local movement to "cultivate" the "tourist crop" (Bustin 1982a: 19). Indeed, while outsider artists served as unwitting promoters, it was the local people who developed the museums and shops that would come to define Nashville.

The crucial issue was cultural—how the region would be presented—and in this the locals had an acute and informed interest. Most were enthusiastic about any rise in the value of local commodities such as crafts, services, or produce. But they resented being depicted as bumpkins. It was exactly in this respect that Hohenberger was so unusual a figure. Hohenberger genuinely loved Brown County and its people. But in 1923, he began a column in the *Indianapolis Star*, "From Down in the Hills o' Brown County," depicting the people, using only thinly disguised pseudonyms, as quaint and colorful. Over the years, he grew even more fond of the people, but with each step closer, his imagination projected them two steps away. In the end, it was Hohenberger—who

The Reclusive Muse

died alone and was buried in Indianapolis, away from the people he loved—who most suffered the ill consequences of the romantic pact. As Dillon concluded, Hohenberger first endorsed the idea of a pastoral ideal in order to feel a part of a close community, yet he unknowingly alienated himself from that community forever (1982a: 134). Dillon's conclusion was that the crucial dilemma of cultural programming was existential, with existential consequences.

Taken together these works represent an unusually sensitive study of the vagaries of the antiquarian impulse. It was as if Dillon went to southern Indiana in search of some secret inaccessible to moderns like himself and found that the only people who knew this secret were those very much like himself. Others who were unconcerned or uncritical of their environment followed the paths of modernization with no resistance; those who cared deeply, like Dillon, were likely to invest their concerns in the prominent forms of vernacular art. Several years later, after he had left southern Indiana, his experiences would still lead him to an extraordinary generalization: "Folk culture is a conceptual knot of ideas—a mesh of utopian dreams, scholarly theories, popular images, and marketing strategies—all with the recurring theme of antimodernism" (1988: 1).

31  LOTUS DICKEY

By the early 1980s, Dillon Bustin was an infrequent participant in the Wednesday Night Dance; most dancers would not have been aware of the extent and nature of his publications. But the effects of his writings were felt thoroughly in the third subject of *Water from Another Time,* Orange County musician and poet Lotus Dickey. Increasingly through the 1980s, Lotus was an influential figure in the dance group by way of his fondness for it, his many friendships with dancers, and the recording and performing career he shared with so many dance musicians.

Born in 1911, Lotus had a rich musical upbringing. He sometimes said of his childhood that, as the youngest of five siblings, he more than the others absorbed the wealth of old ballads, hymns, and tunes that circulated in the world of the adults. In fact, several unusual circumstances might have contributed to this quality of his upbringing. When Lotus was an infant, his father gave up a life of labor organizing and socialist political action around Muncie, Indiana, all for a decisive and risky exodus to the remoteness of Orange County. There, where inexpensive, nutrient-poor land abounded and industrial development was rare, the Dickeys could escape the unpleasant excesses of industrial life. So, along with a few other labor refugees, Marion Dickey, at age fifty, shifted the course of his life, engaging head-on the relentless burdens of subsistence farming with the foremost hope of reaping its existential rewards. Indeed, years later, in spite of an upbringing that demanded unrelenting toil and little material prosperity, the Dickey children all recalled in their youth an "atmosphere of shared attainment and blissful contemplation" (Bustin 1995: 9).

Of all the children, it was Lotus who most bore the burden of Marion Dickey's utopian strivings. Born during the hopeful search for land, Lotus's name was taken from the symbol of the lotus blossom in the Bhagavad-Gita and effectively accumulated around Lotus, as Dillon put it, his father's "hopes for an unsullied life disengaged from the pollution and corruption of the industrial age" (1995: 7). Indeed, of the children, only Lotus grew up with no knowledge of the family's prior life. After the others left one by one for jobs or further schooling, it was Lotus who stayed behind to embrace the fullness of the burdens of the farm. And although the Dickey cabin had rung ceaselessly with music of rich variety, Lotus more than the others fancied the traditional old-time music played by local fiddlers.

Nor was Lotus's inherited antimodernism purely a matter of circumstance: his entire life, in fact, was a series of calculated choices in which tradition was measured against and brought into active dialogue with the exigencies of contemporary life. When Lotus reached his nineteenth year in 1931, his father was over seventy years old, the Depression had severely diminished wages, prices, and opportunities, and the family was still making payments on the farm. Lotus faced a "season of decision," as Dillon put it, and designed for himself a life charter to resolve the compelling urges and obligations that confronted him. He had enjoyed school and would have liked to follow his mother's advice to go to college. But after so fulfilling a childhood, he felt both an attraction and an obligation to stay near his parents, the farm, and the community (Bustin 1995: 5–6). When Lotus took a job that year at the basket factory near Paoli, working ten-hour shifts six days a week while helping manage the farm in his spare time, music became the tangible sacrament that endured through his life to restore his sense of unity and purpose.

In 1943, Lotus married and the next year became the father of the first of eight children, born between 1944 and 1958. In its second decade the marriage became strained and ended in divorce in 1963, and Lotus moved back into the log house of his youth to care, alone, for the six children who remained at home. Throughout all these events, he continued to measure and engage the exigencies of his life with poetry, songwriting, and fiddling. In 1981, in semi-retirement and with his children only recently all on their own, Lotus was visited by Dillon Bustin. "I'm 'Available Jones,'" were the words Dillon often recalled him saying as they discussed his prospects as a folk performer. Indeed, his transition to folk icon was abrupt: because of a last-minute cancellation, Lotus was hired on short notice for Pinewoods Folk Music Week. Only later did his relations with Bloomington dancers blossom. He began performing with Dillon and Linda Handelsman, and Paul Tyler encouraged him to come to the Wednesday Night Dance, where a lively old-time band would often form spontaneously around the two of them. He also performed with Bob Lucas, Pete Sutherland, and others and was a member of the Young Audiences ensemble the Sugar Hill Serenaders, which gave several hundred performances in Indiana public schools during the mid-1980s.

On the whole, Lotus regarded these events as circumstances of unqualified pleasure and good fortune. But they were not encountered, as Dillon Bustin has so astutely described, without some measure of dissonance and resolution (1990a; 1995: 16). Having emerged from a life of relentless toil—never, for example, having had a vacation in his life—he was perplexed by the degree of leisure that folk revival aficionados enjoyed at their celebratory events. But Lotus also found to his amazement an audience that could easily grasp the complex interplay between the motivating sentiments of his work and the formal qualities of traditional music genres he employed. In his life Lotus had accumulated a lengthy record of unfulfilled artistic aspirations, so the deep understanding afforded by his newfound listeners brought him unforeseen satisfaction and encouragement.

Naturally, Lotus's contemplative regard for his music had a compelling effect on those in the dance group who themselves were struggling to make connections between traditional music and various avenues of existential and leftist philosophy. Thus it was important that he preferred old music not merely because it was old but because its emotional

Lotus Dickey with the Sugar Hill Serenaders. This photo, taken in front of Lotus's cabin around 1984, was a publicity photo for the band for its Young Audiences of Indiana performances. From left, Lotus Dickey, Paul Tyler, John Bealle, Teri Klassen. Photo courtesy of Teri Klassen.

core resonated with his charter for life. He would commonly discuss traditional song texts as vivid events, speculating about the extraordinary courage of the pioneers or about the possibility that one could really die from a broken heart. Once, arriving at an Indiana University dormitory to pick up a fellow musician, he mused about his days as a laborer, digging the huge holes into which the concrete footers of that very dormitory were poured. Indeed, from this experience had emerged one of his finest songs, "Indiana, My Home Sweet Home" (Bustin 1995: 4, 15). If the Stohler father in *Breaking Away*—who also helped build the Indiana University campus—invested too much of his identity in the campus and the company, Lotus, in contrast, had been sustained modestly but dependably by traditional culture. Tradition seemed not to alienate Lotus from contemporary life, but to strengthen his purchase of it.

Perhaps for this reason, Lotus had developed a keen capacity for assessing the value of various contemporary cultural influences. He was an eager student of the mail-order tunebook that came with the fiddle his brother Cyprian ordered from Sears and Roebuck, of harmony lines drawn from hymns and parlor songs that his sisters played on the pump organ the family owned, and of fiddle tunes, played by Arthur Smith on the Grand Ole Opry, that he strained to hear as they pierced the night air over the radio. As a youth he even formed a string band, called the Skillet Lickers, with other young musicians in the area. His earliest attempts at songwriting were inspired by the style of Tin Pan Alley, particularly Irving Berlin, but this model was discarded from his active repertoire as the need arose for lengthier, more complex structures—such as ballads and biblical narratives—to express his personal sentiments (see Bustin 1995: 11 and passim).

In 1940, Lotus hitchhiked to Nashville, Tennessee, to audition, unsuccessfully, for the Grand Ole Opry; in 1969 he returned for an unannounced visit to the publishing office of the Wilburn Brothers, selling a composition after singing to the receptionists (Bustin 1995: 15). But the prosperous future to which he surely hoped this would lead was not to be. The country music industry was poised to explode in popularity, but its expansion was toward glitzy, urban forms. The old-fashioned compositions that Lotus hoped would ensure his songwriting success never sold.

In short, Lotus managed his cultural options with a steady eye to his antimodernist charter, bringing selected influences of popular culture into the realm of his life without giving himself over to the seductive world of consumption upon which they depended. He may have wished for the success he saw others enjoying, but he never adapted his poetic and musical idiom to the constraints that success demanded. Nor would he have been able to do so: the distinctive quality of his idiom was that he lived in the world of his songs, a world fewer and fewer would experience or find cause to celebrate. Over time, his song repertoire accumulated such a vivid abundance of personal and local significance that its outside contemporary influences seemed only incidental. Even as a fiddler, he maintained a staunch allegiance to his local and personal roots. Lotus held in highest regard unnamed tunes he had learned from local fiddlers—such as Albert Doughtery, John Coulter, Deck Ainsworth, and Allen Downey—and gave them names according to their source—"Albert Downey Two-Step #2," "Coulter's Rag," "Ed Fleming Waltz," and "Albert Doughtery Schottische." Always, the scope of his ideals was vast, but they were firmly anchored to experiences close at hand. For this, he became endeared to so many in the dance group.

Still, the stature Lotus earned as an artist within the folk revival came not only from his works but also from the sense of self that he had crafted and authenticated over the years. In his stamina or enthusiasm as a musician—one was never sure which—Lotus could easily outlast younger competitors. I recall waking one morning at Sugar Hill just after sunrise and hearing the dance band's last strains—Lotus had stayed up all night and had taken the last shift on fiddle. But he might compete in other ways. He had an acute memory and might engage his companions in reciting poetry learned in school, naming the U.S. presidents, or recalling the birthdays of his friends. He loved people; upon arriving in Bloomington he would sometimes sit down with the Orange Sheet and set about methodically to call his friends and let them know he was in town. In a community invented around antimodernist desire, Lotus had more of it than anyone.

One measure of the extent of his impact on the dance and on folk revival in Bloomington is the catalog of collaborations that Lotus accumulated. In 1985, he recorded a cassette of his traditional songs and tunes, *The Pride of Glencoe,* produced by Dillon Bustin and recorded at the home of Andy Mahler and Linda Lee in Orange County. Accompanying Lotus were many of his new musical associates—Dillon, Andy, Nancy McEntire, Linda Handelsman, Bob Lucas, Paul Tyler, and myself. In 1988, the year before Lotus's death, Bob Lucas produced a recording of Lotus performing his own compositions, *The Very First Time,* that Paul Tyler called the "zenith of [Lotus's] musical career." In 1992, Paul produced a two-volume collection of Lotus's Orange County fiddle tunes, with a biographical essay included in the accompanying booklet (Tyler 1992b). By the end of the decade, several from the dance group had written tributes to Lotus for folk music publications, including Dillon Bustin (1990a, 1990b) in *Country Dance and Song,* and Pete Sutherland (1989) and Bob Lucas (1990) each in *Sing Out!* Nancy McEntire designed and taught a course on Lotus at Indiana University.

In 1993, an annual tribute to him was founded, the Lotus Festival, a celebration of world music that soon became an important cultural event for Bloomington. As a component of the event, Grey Larsen organizes an evening concert of Lotus's music featuring his friends and family. In 1995, before the World Wide Web had become so widespread as today, Mitch Rice designed a Lotus Dickey homepage. But surely the most complete tribute was *The Lotus Dickey Songbook*, edited by Nancy McEntire, Grey Larsen, and Janne Henshaw, a book of transcriptions of 101 of his songs including recordings taken from private recordings made by fans all over the U.S.

There is no question that Lotus was a composer and musician of exceptional ability and that these qualities earned him his high regard in folk revival circles. But it is also the case that his motivating spirit was to resonate within the folk revival as nowhere else in American culture. Indeed, many of his followers became personal friends, so that even in revival circles his audience likely had an emotional connection as much with his life as with his music. What this connection entailed was a mutual regard for many unconventional life choices. Like others in the dance group, Lotus had eschewed more lucrative opportunities elsewhere to hack out a life in the austere but majestic southern Indiana hill country. But Lotus had endured far more than any Bloomington dancers and in far less prosperous times than 1970s and 1980s Bloomington. Undaunted by these imponderable obstacles, Lotus's passions remained steadfast, nurtured, in part, by his music. In the dance, Lotus discovered a world where it mattered a great deal that he had clung for so long to Orange County and its old tunes, that he had raised a family alone in a two-room log house, that he could render a lengthy "Barbara Allen," that he could recite the U.S. presidents in reverse order and reach 1900, or, mainly, that for most all of his adult life he might have moved to Detroit or Gary or Chicago and have vastly improved his material prosperity—but chose not to. In part because he shared these deep concerns with his dance group friends, it was the musical career crafted around a folk music audience that was more fulfilling than any other of his artistic ambitions.

32  BREAKING AWAY

When I inquired among Bloomington dancers to compile the facts surrounding the dance group's history, John Levindofske recalled an eerie yet half-forgotten scene from the summer of 1978. He remembered that summer watching from the second floor out the Walnut Street window of Bloomington Music as a film crew below worked on scenes for *Breaking Away* (1979), a feature film about Bloomington written by playwright Steve Tesich and filmed there on location. The scenes he no doubt saw were those filmed around the Monroe County Courthouse. The courthouse and other sites of local import served as a crucial physical and symbolic backdrop to the narrative. As dancers each week paced the contours of practiced community, this potent meditation on Bloomington as locality and community was unfolding around them.

For the longest time I viewed *Breaking Away* as a clever, innocent, coming-of-age film set in a time and place both familiar and dear to me. As the world changed over the course of the 1980s, however, *Breaking Away* seemed to retain its vitality while, simultaneously, the motivating spirit of the Wednesday Night Dance receded into the past. As that gap widened, the film became emblematic of the seismic shift in worldview, in Bloomington and in American culture in general, that was curiously imperceptible at the time the film was first released. This shift had everything to do with the formative conditions of the dance. For this reason I devote a chapter to the film, depicting it as a kind of prelude to the cultural watershed that some dance veterans were later to feel.

When *Breaking Away* first appeared, Bloomington viewers naturally took great pleasure in the vivid and flattering depiction of their area. Indeed, the film drew astutely upon local places that had long served to engage the symbolic tensions that defined the Bloomington experience. Squarely upon this symbolic foundation, the film superimposed a harmless comedy in which an underdog protagonist overcame great odds. Less perceptibly, the film exacted a transformation of cultural values that echoed, reinforced, and localized a broader shift taking place in American society at the time. This transformation had a profound impact on the reception and experience of folksong revival in America. It is for this reason that *Breaking Away,* in the way it refigured the cultural setting of the dance, warrants attention here.

An early sequence from the film was enough to signal the theme of locality. On a summer's day, four recent Bloomington high school graduates arrive at one of the old abandoned limestone quarries, a familiar though unauthorized swimming hole for locals. One is singing "Bury me at the A&P" to the traditional tune "Bury Me on the Lone Prairie" (a song Lotus Dickey, in fact, loved to sing), and the viewer soon learns that the existential despair appropriated from this reference is meant to approximate the feelings they have confronting their future in the local service and retail sales industry. Like Lotus Dickey at this age, they face a "season of decision." Forced to strike some compromise between obligation, opportunity, and ambition, they seek to alter their immediate surroundings to suit their spiritual and intellectual longings.

One of the four, Dave Stohler, earns his protagonist status by his fixation on Italian bicycle racing. It is immediately apparent that it is not mere sport but, somewhat like the folk revival, an adopted cultural alternative to his apparently drab prospects as a townie. So he studies Italian, addresses his pet cat and even his parents by Italian names, belts out arias at every idle moment, dreams of racing with Italian cyclists, and views Indiana University coeds through the foggy lens of operatic romance. Indeed, the first half of the film follows his pursuit of the affections of a coed, undertaken in the guise of his Italian persona. In truth, it is less genuinely a romance than a test of the validity of his persona and, it turns out, of the validity of adopted authentic identity in general. For the time being the scheme works—so well that his companions and the whole narrative momentum of the film cling to it also.

But there is more: Stohler's father had invested the whole of his own identity in the toils and aspirations of the limestone industry south of Bloomington. The best of his life, in fact, was spent cutting stone for the buildings at Indiana University. One night, standing under the overhang of the university library, he spells out for his son the origins of his despair: "When I was finished, the damnedest thing happened. It was like the buildings were too good for us. Nobody told us that. We just felt uncomfortable, that's all." Now he has quit stonecutting—because of layoffs? his recent heart attack? for a better life?—and works as a used car huckster on South Walnut Street, exacting his revenge on the apparently gullible Indiana University student population by advertising unreliable cars as "English Major," "Graduate School," "Magna Cum Laude," and "Senior."

Unabashedly, the film carves out its territory of class struggle rooted in town-gown relations. Dark comedy pervades the Stohler household, cloaking its rootlessness with a veneer of half-hearted worry over the father's health and the son's ambition. Food appears effortlessly at mealtime, and the family's stoic mother mediates as the two males squabble over the menu, as if a stereotypical food tradition—ethnic Italian or middle-class American—could revive or destroy their broken spirits. But rollicking dialogue masks the film's agony: Dave's father hoped to pass on to his son a great tradition, but now he can only bestow the self-denying sense of duty he earned from a craft that has apparently betrayed him. Dave now bears the burden of both his own success and that of his father—in a world where even his father could not succeed.

From this source—from what Dave sees of himself and of his future through his father's eyes—the historical depth of the four friends' despair is established, and Dave's personal utopia of Italian ethnicity is given fragile credence. But from there the film takes an unusual turn. In

1979, Dave should have found refuge in ethnic and folk identity. By the mid-1980s, southern Indiana stonecutting would become a celebrated folk craft, nowhere more eloquently than in Scott Sanders's *In Limestone Country* ([1985] 1991). But like a hero from some other time, Dave is curiously isolated and pins all his hopes on competing with an Italian racing team that will soon race near Bloomington. His father refuses him permission; but his mother intervenes in his favor, showing him a passport she has saved, having hoped to travel abroad someday when she is freed from the invisible bonds of the postwar domicile.

This ascendancy of the feminine is the most crucial moment in the film. Dave had stood against his father in the previous scene when some hapless customers had returned a defective car to the lot: "We're poor but we're honest," he had exclaimed, invoking the mythos of utopian ethnicity, and had demanded that the customers receive a refund. Thus the gauntlet laid down by the film for the upcoming race is one not of victory but integrity. At risk are all the assembled feminine elements by which Dave had distinguished himself—opera, cuisine, leg shaving, and ethnic utopia as an alternative to masculinized social status and success. When at last Dave races with the Italian bikers, however, they are merely ruthless competitors and force his bike into a ditch during the race. The imagined community that had become his personal salvation has betrayed him. "Everyone cheats," he tells his dad after the race; "I just didn't know it." "Now you know," responds his father. Without a complaint from the narrative voice, this brings an end to any investment the film has made in feminized natural morality. And without a complaint from the audience, who might have recoiled in horror at the ease with which Tesich let Dave's source of strength slip from his grasp.

Conveniently, this existential nadir follows almost precisely the eruption of a brawl with fraternity members in the student union. In a brilliant act of containment, Indiana University president John Ryan defies long-standing tradition and dictates that the annual campus bicycle race, the "Little 500," allow one (!) "cutter" (stonecutter, or townie) team. It was widely known in Bloomington that Ryan played his own character in the film, marking a departure from narrative fiction at the very moment town-gown relations were being reconfigured. Having dispensed with ethnicity, the film now resurrects the same crisis of identity as contest. Indeed, the entirety of ethnic utopia is transformed and reduced into this single "team" which enters the competitive marketplace as a token equal of college fraternities.

This time between the two races is *Breaking Away*'s liminal hiatus, when received ontological stability is out of kilter. When Dave reveals his deceit to Kathryn, she is moved not by confessed deceit nor by the emergence of truth, but by the loss of transcendent identity: "Who are you?" she asks. "I haven't a clue," Dave answers. Unredeemed by his confession, he then returns home to remove all of his Italian paraphernalia from his room. Cleansed of his guise, he walks with his father under the Indiana University library overhang, where they come to terms with their ambitions and disappointments. In this transitional moment, Tesich shifts the arena of confrontation from the abandoned quarries, a popular local site for existential atonement (see Sanders 1991: 3–12), to Indiana University, where the products of the father's labors have apparently lain inaccessible to him. Now with his father's encouragement, Dave will attend Indiana University in the fall and thereby repair the breach that has plagued both of them.

There is, of course, much to be said for this father-son reconciliation and as much also for his father's accounting for his past, but it only alters and does not solve the existential dilemma of the film. The corruption of ethnicity—the asserted fact that "everyone cheats"—remains undisputed, so the quality of the boys' angst must shift from internal conflict to external obstacle. They discuss their options, and Dave, desperate for existential resolution, concludes that they must beat the frat boys in the Little 500 in order to salvage his identity. This crucial shift— from experiential purity to tangible reward—defined much of the course of popular culture in the 1980s. Ethnic fantasy, the dream of authenticity, the utopian quality of sport—all dissolved into radical individualism and naked competition. This shift, of course, only hastens the narrative toward its now foregone conclusion: they must win the race. The boys practice hard, do indeed win the race, and father and son embrace in triumph as mom looks on. The origin of Mr. Stohler's despair, his resolute cynicism, his alienation from the fruits of his life's work, the gnawing absence of collective authenticity in being a townie, the opening of the feminine in the discourse of the family, and the deeply embedded father-son schism to which all of this led—all are condensed as symbol into the outcome of the race and as substance into Dave's plans to attend college.

It is possibly important that the film was once two scripts, fused together at the behest of the producers—one about class struggle in the shadow of Indiana University, the other about an Indianapolis cyclist who crafted an Italian identity. One can only wonder if the outcome of the adopted ethnicity and the motivation for the town-gown class showdown might have preyed less upon each other in separate scripts. And screenwriter Steve Tesich did actually attend Indiana University, in 1961, when town-gown relations were apparently strained much as the film depicted. Tesich was born in Serbia (Uzice, headquarters of Tito's army) in 1942 and was summoned to East Chicago, Indiana, in 1957, by his father, who until then was presumed by the family to have been killed in the war. His period of immigration was chronicled in the more tangibly autobiographical *Four Friends* (1981), in which he and his East Chicago companions sought to transcend the oppressive existential moorings of post-WWII middle-class identity. This film echoes and helps explain the themes that run through *Breaking Away*.

Four Friends intermittently broods over Tesich's vacuous father, who, like the Stohler dad, embraces work as duty and self-denial. For contrast, one need only compare the Dickey household, where hard and relentless work was accomplished with fulfillment and balanced with an abundance of music and spiritual nourishment. Consequently, the sons in *Four Friends* find themselves adrift in the anomie of the 1960s, pulled toward mind-numbing middle-class obligation at one moment and the seductive lure of unbridled counterculture freedom at the next. Moreover, Tesich himself, as also his character Danilo, is in the unusual position of sharing with his father his status as first-generation immigrant. So *Four Friends* quickly defines itself not merely as personal struggle but as a generational meditation on America. Opening with his train ride into East Chicago, the film there and throughout juxtaposes Tesich's immigrant odyssey with the signature strains of Dvořák's "New World Symphony."

Tesich plays Dvořák's studied optimism against a similar melodic strain, "Georgia on My Mind" (composed in Bloomington by Hoagy

Carmichael), representing the impulsive, undisciplined desire of Romanticism's darker side. These latter qualities are personified in the heroine, Georgia, serving as a beacon of freedom—as Lady Liberty—for the conflicted young men who adore in her what they lack in themselves. "School's ending, kiddos," she exhorts in an early scene, "and it's out into this world with us all. We are poised and ready to fly!" But Tesich's father, on hearing his son wants to attend college, sternly warns, "You are like many I knew—you want to hide from life. You will see—life will find you and step on you—it will happen!" Indeed, the friends are incited to extraordinary will power, yet they are only able to accumulate experience without tangible success. Georgia manifests the extreme of this quality: set on being a famous dancer, she can only chant the words "Isadora Duncan," without showing any evidence of working toward her goal.

As in *Breaking Away,* ideology lurks around the film without providing the context for the freedom and success for which the protagonists strive. *Four Friends* is brutally anti-historical, traversing the chronology of the 1960s at a distance from any motivating conditions for its signature events. Tom joins the army and worries that he may be killed, Danilo is a pacifist with conscientious-objector status, but Vietnam is never mentioned. The women of the film, especially Georgia, possess qualities the film struggles to celebrate, but they remain passive heroines, alienated from the boldness of feminism that ought to surround them. On the way to visit Georgia in New York, Danilo passes his African American friend Rudy in a bus headed for a voter registration drive in Mississippi and only in the nick of time swerves back on course to avoid following it. Danilo even toys with his own Slavic ethnicity, sharing a brief relationship with a retentionist lover. But he is oblivious to ethnicity as a creative force and, after a brief visit from Georgia, falls again under her siren spell. Indeed, the entire film is defined by passive internalization of observed injustice until a closing scene when Danilo at last takes on Gergley, the school bully turned local bigot, in a fight, vomiting on him just before they both fall exhausted.

Danilo awakes from his bout with Gergley in a strange house where two Vietnamese children—Tom's daughters, the daughters of war—are watching the 1969 lunar landing. Here is the film's resolution in a nutshell, America at once triumphant and exhausted, with no more to show for its dreams than a fleeting image on television and children to care for. From this, the four friends, who have strived throughout to integrate the creative self with the dizzying cacophony of unachieved ideals that tempt but never satisfy, can only surrender to the circumstances they inherit. Danilo, now "Citizen Prozor," has become an American at precisely the moment in the film that "American" is no longer something one can become.

So *Four Friends* cannot triumph: instead, it resolves the frantic tension between utopia and reality by occluding history, by abdicating ideology and sinking all hope into the singular world the friends have together endured but not created. "I'm so tired of being young!" Georgia sighs in the end, prepared at last for an improbable marriage to Danilo. Likewise, Danilo has relinquished the desire for her that has propelled much of the film. Now exhausted—she of her self-destructive energy and he of his self-denying fascination for her—their marriage can proceed as mutual submission. Now, having personalized ideology, obscuring its historical imperative, the film renounces the past as a stage of life—"being young"—that the four have passed through and transcended. Surely this is the first and most powerful stroke of the historical closure of the counterculture.

If *Four Friends* is a confrontation with ideology, *Breaking Away* is an appropriation of it. In the closing scene, the film joins Dave during his first day at college. A pretty coed drops a notebook and, alluding to his meeting earlier with Kathryn, Dave picks it up for her and spontaneously assumes a foreign accent to impress her—this time French. The film has replayed a scene and thereby set the viewer above the existential channel of its narrative: one could chuckle condescendingly. But this palpable comic incongruity is in truth ironic distance: *Breaking Away* has ceded the vast territory of idealism in which its first act was wholly invested. The film is a veritable road map of hegemony: one discourse completely envelops the logic of the other around a common text.

Four Friends ends with an equally eerie scene. After an unexplained narrative hiatus, the four friends are back at the Indiana dunes (on Lake Michigan) around a roaring campfire, each with spouses, some with children, all apparently done with "being young." In the fire, engulfed in flames, is Tesich's immigration trunk with all the belongings of his significant past—all, that is, except the flute that one last time plays the fragment from the "New World Symphony." Tom, the only Jew of the four, is Tesich's odd choice to announce historical closure: "Someday we might look back at all this and"—he pauses, making way for comic incongruity—"not remember a thing!" One could wince at such a remark, but Georgia will soon move things along. "You know what we've never done?" she asks Danilo. "A lot of things," he responds, at last getting it right. "You've got it, kiddo!" she answers.

Clothed in historical obligation, *Four Friends* repudiates history. Its characters glibly withdraw from issues they themselves have raised. Initially Tesich conflates the capacity to externalize America as an ideological object with his own immigrant desire; now, as "Citizen Prozor," he becomes American by embracing the culture of forgetting. It is against this particular modality of forgetting that I have adopted my historical cause. Like Dave Stohler's fragile utopia, the circumstances about which I have written seem quaint and impractical. Is it possible or even desirable (and if so in what manner) to restore the discursive authority around circumstances that are being constantly replayed as tokens of themselves? This dilemma propels my book.

I remember watching *Breaking Away* in 1979 with alarming naïveté. Like other dancers and Bloomington residents, I took a personal interest in the familiar scenery that critics lauded as verisimilitude—the courthouse square, the quarries, the campus fringe housing area. Dave's initial meeting with Kathryn takes place at the western end of the campus, not all that far from the renowned stump, where, like the meeting of Dillon and Miles, a serendipitous, symbolically charged encounter might occur. The Stohlers were depicted as residing on Lincoln Street, where several dancers then lived, where in an early scene the camera froze breathlessly on the house Paul Tyler and Pat Gingrich were soon to buy. Even the A&P supermarket, which the film introduced as the resting place for the spiritually dispossessed, was an after-hours cultural scene just beyond the campus fringe, where local youths engaged in playful verbal competition in displays of wealth, power, and cunning outdoors before the community (see Leary 1980).

But there is a foreboding tragedy in the way the film insinuated itself

Old-Time Music and Dance

into the same town-campus corridor where the dance then had established its own sites of symbolic significance. For here—not just in Bloomington but in other dance communities as well—was the holy land of the post-1960s folksong revival, the epicenter of cultural aspiration, the site of resolution between town and gown, between populism and idealism, the seed bed where organic intellectualism nourished and was nourished by manufactured organic society. Precisely in its verisimilitude, *Breaking Away* found and exploited the hidden vein that had nourished post-1960s idealism.

If the core modality of dance was desire and resolution, *Breaking Away* appropriated this motif to assert the preeminence, in the end, of conflict and conquest. I am certain I was drawn also to this salient motif, enjoying its poetic justice, the pseudo-populist triumph of the four youths against whom Tesich set all odds. But it is only after Dave forsakes his guise and loses the capacity for creative resolution that he resorts to the purity of conflict. Ethnic utopia in the beginning is existential redemption; in the end it is a cute joke. Here the film etched the cultural arc of the 1980s, traversing the great divide between irony and mere irony that marked the transformation to postmodernism, to the necessity of conflict for authenticity, and to the incapacity of folklore.

Some veteran dancers would say that community dance, like *Breaking Away,* was afflicted by a similar erosion of cultural faith. "Supposing you were / someone else," began Dudley Laufman long ago, in a quatrain I have chosen as an epigraph. Here was the faith of the dance, the projection of hope of resolution of the complex of affections—from Eros to agape—onto a generalized other, the mantra with which the other was invented and resolved in endless reverberation as a core motif of liberal populism. This was the urgency of music and dance, an encounter with the covenant of tradition in an America far beyond the pale of cultural inheritance as it was then understood.

33  BLUE SPRUCE

I remember vividly my arrival in Bloomington. To get to Bloomington by car, one had to leave the interstate system and travel some fifty miles over picturesque two-lane state roads—my route from the east traversed the "hills o' Brown County." Along the roadside, modest homes of every vintage seemed eager to oblige the pastoral imagination. Many were punctuated by some artistic shrine, a fragment of their occupant's creative spirit that would have been frowned upon in the suburban neighborhood where I was raised. Almost archetypically, the material culture of the region seemed to embody the antithesis of postwar America.

The most striking to me was the blue spruce, which in its scarcity seemed to add to the landscape a hue that jolted the imagination without exactly seeming unnatural. These trees were all imported, of course, planted long ago in a gesture of commitment to the semiotics of the roadside. Against the boundless backdrop of yellowish native maples and poplars, the spruce was an abrupt self-contradiction, nature that could not be naturalized, poetry that refused to be assimilated into prose.

The pastoral ideal of the Brown County artists had not alienated the locals at all but instead had inspired a widespread movement of public

art. These emblems of domestic creativity represented in part a cultivated self-as-other, a display of staged authenticity that nourished the
regional stereotype and the "tourist crop." But there was also a measure
of exposure, a piece of home and self laid bare for casual visitors. This
nourished not regional stereotype but cultivated public trust, a quality
which I found in abundance in southern Indiana and which I came to
admire very, very much. It is ironic that Hohenberger preferred people
to things, yet his invented caricatures obscured the very "things" by
which, in their ambiguity, the boundary between public and private was
routinely traversed.

It was a searing hot August afternoon, a Wednesday, in 1976. I had
recently left the U.S. Navy with a comfortable savings account, three
years of GI Bill benefits, and a small remnant of aplomb, all of which I
would devote to graduate school at Indiana University. I had heard
about the Wednesday Night Dance in Norfolk, Virginia, from Mark
Russell, who had come from Bloomington to take a six-week guitar-
building class at Ramblin' Conrad's Guitar Store and Folklore Center.
When I visited Indiana earlier that summer, I had stayed with Mark
and his family in their primitive cabin in Greene County. During this
earlier visit they took me to a party at the country home of some friends,
and I recall being overcome by the serene pace and posture of all their
lives. But now I had living quarters waiting and a car filled with all my
belongings. When I arrived, I unloaded, had dinner, and headed out for
the Wednesday Night Dance. In my memory, that night was a blur of
awkwardness: it was some distance, I would learn, from the U.S. Navy
to the Wednesday Night Dance.

From that vantage, my endearing experience with the dance reverberated with the perplexing historical status that postwar folksong revival performance had accumulated. Postwar folklorists learned to recoil
from folksong revival not so much because of its populist ideals, which
many shared, but because of its means. It was too often a floating,
idealized, siren-song discourse ill suited to the mundane, relentless demands of place that characterized "real" folklore. It professed to honor
home and place and commitment but, in fact, accommodated mobility
and media and absentee power. Arriving in southern Indiana that autumn, I heard that message, not only in Richard Dorson's seminars but

also in the music and dance itself. The dance, after all, was carved not from the rootless imagination of the media but from localized self-consciousness at a particular stump in 1972. Like the blue spruce, its very perseverance put it out of place in its own place, at once an epiphenomenon and an epiphany.

This was incongruous until I began to see the dance as a discourse *on* place—a much different kind of thing than a folk club, a festival, or concert. It was relentless and mundane, shunning publicity. It was a conscious crafting of a collective subjectivity, nourished by routine co-presence and sunk deep in the prevailing semiotics of locality. If conventional folksong revival was ironic—setting overdetermined textual and textural features against a backdrop of conventional performance practices in order to "revive" qualities of the remote past—the dance, in contrast, was transgressive. It reversed the polarity of the trope, localizing and authenticating its self-consciousness against what became an ironic local archetype, so vividly depicted in the dreary masculine world of the Stohler and the Prozor households. Yet, where the Stohler and Prozor sons sought refuge in the ephemeral discourse of youth, the dance drew from the enduring strength of tradition. Receiving this covenant, the dance extracted transcendent values from antique customs, setting both against the very idea of conventional locality. Refracting imagined community through the lens of tradition, the dance shone a bright light on locality itself, exposing the illusion of locality as unreflective social organization. It was across this ironic distance that one could view *Breaking Away* naively, as something absurdly fictional, whose capacity to intrude upon the environs of the dance was unimaginable.

It was in this distinction that the dance was the dance group, fusing context and text around a dizzying expanse of social complexity. There was a reverence for textuality, a sense that stable texts—contra or square dances or fiddle tunes—were being re-created. But their re-creation was measured by the effects—social, spiritual, emotional—that they were thought in their historical foundation to be able to achieve. The overarching moral imperative, the social template for performance, the totality of the achieved music and dance experience—were all matters of great concern. They could not be so easily negotiated away as Italian cycling was for Dave Stohler. Where Stohler was without cultural allies, however, the texts of old-time music and dance connected musicians and dancers to one another and to their counterparts across space and time. Text was brought into being as a covenant, received from tradition. Its performance was a conjuration, uniting present and past, self and other. It was to imagine and then transcend self and other, but also to imagine and transcend all that constituted otherness. If its weakness was in affirming quaint and impractical social customs, its strength was in engaging the aspirations of all who dared imagine the impractical. To perform together was to leave the prosaic, detached present and establish an existential foothold in the timeless aspirations of others who danced and played and sang in similar articulations of imagined community.

It can be seen as a most curious thing that during the course of the 1980s, during the celebrated eclipse of authenticity, there was an explosion in the popularity of dance groups. In 1972, even in 1980, the Bloomington dance was an island in a sea that stretched vast distances. Today, however, even as the apocryphal stump recedes from the historical imagination, it is surrounded by a sea of dances which dance gypsies navigate with unprecedented fervor. A CDSS directory of affiliates from not too long ago—an apt measure of the spread of dance, said Mary Dart (1995: 12, and who wouldn't agree?)—listed dance groups of some sort in forty-five states and several international locales. There is no need for a stump as a point of origin when old-time dance seems to originate from all points at once.

Of course, this list is not merely a yardstick, but very much also a road map that dancers use to guide their travel. One might well also consult any of the web pages or e-mail lists that dance groups have devised or the dance camp directories that someone compiles each spring. Yet these suggest not merely that dance has exploded: it has also inhabited the cultural devices of that explosion. If yesterday's dances were about gardens, field recordings, and illicit swims, today's are more concerned with web pages, liability insurance, and boards of directors. This is the cruel and intractable dilemma that some veterans perceive. Music and dance is thriving, bringing genuine satisfaction and social intercourse to unprecedented numbers of people. But the covenant of tradition that gave the movement mystique and charisma—that set friendship above democracy, good will above security, natural morality above preemptive justice—has eroded. Veteran dancers grope for a way to understand the profound shift in the character of dance that can seem so imperceptible in its tangible exterior.

Responding to statements by veteran dancers, Mary Dart mapped this as a change in community—from organic to accidental. Where once the dance stood *in* the community, now it stands *for* the community. There is less contact outside the dance event; dancers anticipate an event more and more as a physical or social challenge, less and less as the focal social event of a cohesive, ongoing group. Some veterans nationwide loosely aligned with these concerns even organized a computer discussion group whose purpose is to "support discussions of locally-oriented, socially-centered community dances" and to promote "loyalty to local talent and events" (see Kermiet 1996). In old-time music circles, the conservative impulse leads to experiments eliminating sound amplification, restricting chord progressions, and promoting squares, especially those common in the old-style "house dances." The term "dance gypsy," not long ago an uncontroversial badge of honor, has become emblematic of this arena of contention, signifying for some the most sincere and passionate posture toward dance and for others the cavalier and rootless disregard for community.

Meanwhile, without anyone having much to say about it, community happens. This is certainly the view of community scholars, who engage with irreverence the cyclical clamor over the loss of community. The most recent complaint was Robert Putnam's best seller, *Bowling Alone* (2000). Putnam analyzed membership data and demonstrated dramatic declines in participation in voluntary associations over the course of the twentieth century, many showing their deepest drop at the onset of the 1960s. Most of these associations, it turns out, featured the kind of bureaucratic exoskeleton that enabled statistical tracking of members over much of a century. Putnam's chief contention is that participation in these organizations forms a kind of "social capital" that, cumulatively, is a measure of the social welfare of the nation. The counterculture, of course, fled in droves from organizations of this sort. Were Putnam to have counted, say, potluck dinners, he would have come up with differ-

Old–Time Music and Dance

ent results. More importantly, he would have identified a different sort of social capital and a different vision of the social welfare of the nation.

As for the relentless assault by instruments of mediation (e.g., sound amplification, sound recording, representative democracy, money as the medium of exchange and the measure of value, and excess value or professionalism among musicians and callers), examples are legion, in popular fandom, for example, where genuine moral community is fashioned around the most egregiously impersonal artifacts of the commercial culture industry (in commercial country music, for example, see Ellison 1995). That is to say, communities of "dance gypsies"—despite their mobility, despite their homogeneity—are no less genuine, no less rooted, even without the kind of deliberate fashioning of community that so characterized the 1970s dance groups like Bloomington. And foremost, the dance gypsy phenomenon is itself local. That is to say, the transformation in community dance is not a matter of the local versus the mobile, not even in Bloomington, but rather it is a matter of what it means to be a community and what community has to do with place.

What, then, is the point in this book in constructing a narrative of loss when there is no loss, in devising a historical other that is not truly other? Folklorists, I could begin by saying, are notoriously fond of marginality, of culture situated outside the bounds of dominant discourse. My ongoing attachment to Bloomington always has had to do with its willful and methodical fashioning of a distinctive and coherent idea of artistic community—with the astute sensitivity to context by which its participants, almost instinctively it seemed, would stand behind the most minute subtleties of a system they profoundly knew and loved. So, what I have sought to celebrate here is the capacity to distinguish and nurture those cultural artifacts whose social qualities resist the influence of prevailing cultural atmosphere. My historical narrative is offered not as a surrender to tragic loss but as a renewal of the historical other and of the self freed from the bonds of the eternally present.

In this respect, there was, over the course of the 1980s, a discursive closure in the dance and in Bloomington that has been the primary impetus for this book. It is in this way that *Breaking Away* was a prelude to the apocalypse. But it is not merely that after it, local pizzerias sprouted "Cinzano" umbrellas on their patios and with them a taste for

Blue Spruce

Euro-chic and with that a taste for "tasting" as experienced ethnicity. There were also decisive shifts away from sustained commitment to organic society. Many communes that operated in the early 1970s ceased to operate. The impressive gains in rural areas in the 1970s were abruptly halted in the 1980s, yet the city of Bloomington retained its rate of growth. Rural Orange and Greene Counties actually declined in population in the 1980s after double-digit 1970s gains; in rustic Brown County the growth rate dropped from 37 percent in the 1970s to 14 percent in the 1980s. From 1980 to 1990, the number of rental housing units in Monroe County that rented for less than $300 dropped from 12,000 to 2,100, while the number that rented for more than $300 jumped from 2,000 to 13,000. In Bloomington, the rooms above the stores that faced the south side of the courthouse square were gutted, remodeled, and reopened as a mini-mall of upscale shops, with the immaculate John Waldron Arts Center as the centerpiece. There some had lived cheaply throughout the 1970s and early 1980s, preserving the economic and cultural viability of a downtown that entrepreneurs at the time had abandoned. This south-side renovation was, of course, a genuine "revitalization" that all of Bloomington enjoys. The Waldron Arts Center, Scott Sanders wrote, was a "token of a vibrant community" (2002: 9). Still, as a consequence, the different sort of "vitality" that once nourished the dance was in some small way eroded by these changes.

More compelling, in fact, were structural changes in other local institutions that, like the dance, featured some tangible manifestation of structural coherence. In the mid-1980s, Bloomington's member-owned cooperative natural food store, located throughout the 1970s in a back alley near the campus so as to accommodate "foot traffic" (and thereby discourage the use of motor vehicles), opened a spacious satellite store in a suburban shopping center and eliminated its "working memberships" whereby members contributed work for an extra layer of discounts. Around the same time, the campus public radio station, citing ratings statistics that favored stylistic continuity across program blocks, canceled the Thursday night folk music program that had run continuously since it was begun in the 1950s by Bruce Buckley—even though the program was perennially exceptional in attracting member donations. After a fire leveled the theater next door, a favorite counterculture breakfast establishment abandoned its homely, intimate environs with mismatched, recycled tableware for a glitzy setting, with a bar and a grand piano, easily four times the size.

It was not that the proprietors had betrayed an ideal, for they had merely become successful at what all along they enjoyed doing. What *was* lost, and what *was* a betrayal for some of their clientele, was that, like the dance, they had once provided a mildly illicit pleasure for a community allied to a variety of progressive causes. It was precisely their rough-hewn, labor-intensive quality that made them inaccessible to conventional tastes. Once, they nurtured an atmosphere of studied alienation and thereby kept the conventional world at bay. Much the same happened with the food co-op: it was for lack of volunteers that working memberships had to be dropped. It took extraordinary communal will power to sustain these institutions, driven by a compelling sense of purpose that seems incredible today. When Hugh Gardner concluded that Americans have "trained incapacities for communal experience" (1978: 251), it is probably something like this that he had in mind. On occasion, a concrete image of some long past event flashes in my memory, and I am filled with a rush of emotion of a time so vastly different than now.

Dancers who had operated organic farms—Jim Johnson, Nancy McKinley, and Allen Paton—sold their land and took other jobs. With Mary Beth Roska, Frank Hall bought a house on the west side of town, bringing an end to the "Boys' Club" as a center of activity. In 1987, after nearly a decade, I gave up my $95-a-month rental log house, and no one in the dance wanted to take it over. When the Sugar Hill Serenaders disbanded that same year, not a single old-time music band responded to the advertisement Young Audiences placed in the Indianapolis newspapers calling for a replacement, nor did any from the Bloomington dance rise to the occasion. Those who had come to Indiana University on the tail end of the "folk boom" and lingered for years—some nurtured by the dance—all seemed to leave at once.

At the dance, bands began using the elevated stage, having once insisted on playing from the floor. Around 1990 an irreconcilable dispute arose over the price and quality of beer that split the after-dance gathering into two groups, and some reported to me a chilling atmosphere of exclusion at the gatherings. At about that time also, a committee from the group drafted bylaws so that the group could incorporate and raise tax-exempt funds, partly with the hope of starting a dance camp. Offices were created that corresponded to roles that had theretofore been informally passed on to interested new dancers—publicity, band and caller scheduling, booking out-of-town bands, Sugar Hill coordinator. Officers were elected annually; each held a voting seat on the group's new board of directors. One early board action was to devise an official membership status that was purchased by annual subscription. From this a mailing list was devised, and regular mailings began alerting subscribers to upcoming events and regularly scheduled bands and callers. The Orange Sheet still listed the wide circle of friends that had been important over the years, but official members were now identified with an asterisk. In 1992, there was a general referendum that at last established, by a convincing margin, admission charges and pay for bands at the Wednesday Night Dance.

I mean by this only to illustrate the ascendancy of a new discursive apparatus and certainly not to inject foreboding into a movement that was widely supported. "It's time for a change," I heard more than once—even from conservative veterans—as various of these items were being considered. And indeed, the dance is a stronger one. Attendance is high, support enthusiastic, music and calling plentiful, social mobility readily accessible, and elections a popular event. Dramatic acoustic improvements have made the hall a vastly pleasanter place to dance, and relations with the landlord have never been better. And foremost, it is the prevailing machinery of locality that has brought the dance into harmony with the new mood of its residents. Surely this is the spirit that grew from that stump in 1972.

What, then, does this historical phantasm have to offer? The type of social group that blossomed as "intentional community" at the end of the 1960s was susceptible to precisely the type of ideological drift that I have described. These were free, open societies, each with its own particular mission, which teetered precipitously on the will of its adherents on the one hand and on economic and cultural conditions of the outside

Old-Time Music and Dance

world on the other. They are assessed by way of "commitment theory" because commitment—not coercion nor necessity nor commercial value nor civic affiliation—was their means of stability. By definition, "commitment" referred to unconventional ideas from which there was always the possibility and freedom of retreat. Precisely by way of this vulnerability, they are dismissed as extravagances, just as ethnic utopia was in *Breaking Away*. This is why I have taken the alternative view, to view them as emblematic of a choice all people aspire to have.

When change came, sometimes in imperceptible increments, it indeed came as choices, measured fairly against attractive options, in moments of clarity, of presence. History arose as the non-present, the detritus, the excess, of these choices. Reclaiming it, as I do here, is not to raise doubt and nostalgia, but to reunite with the ambitions and purposes that flash before us in a "moment of danger." Those who played and danced long ago did so as an "urgent task," as Roszak put it, seeking "an enduring mode of life" that would safeguard "greater expectations of life." They took their cue from a historical other whose spiritual aspirations exceeded their material needs, whose pleasures and struggles were intertwined as an emblem of their ideals.

There is much to suggest an enduring presence of these ideals. New dance group leaders have emerged who have grasped the spirit of the dance in insightful ways. David Ernst, for example, solved the intractable problem of the after-dance gathering site by initiating a turn-taking system for choosing it. Bill Baus, with help from Barry Kern and other dance-group carpenters, built a new west-side house with a spacious living room to hold informal dances. After three decades, Ted Hall still hosts the weekly B-band meetings, now renamed "Monday night music group." The meetings have inspired a fierce attachment among the participants, so much so that fiddler Lee Mysliwiec painted portraits of each musician and gave them to the subjects as gifts. Easy Street has reissued *Money in Both Pockets* on CD and gives occasional reunion concerts. A new old-time band, the Monks—with Sam Bartlett, Claudio Buchwald, Abby Ladin, and Frank Hall—has taken up their role as the group's primary musical emissary. Mark Feddersen expands the Bean King song by one verse every year and has never missed singing it each January. Tom Morrison and his family still make the logistical arrangements for Swing into Spring each year. These represent considerable efforts, yet they seem so trivial on the surface. By many standards it would be much easier not to do these things, but in the community they are essential, meaningful, and purposeful. They are acts of commitment that, reciprocally, enable and are enabled by an atmosphere in which "greater expectations of life" can be achieved.

There is a vein of moral philosophy which holds the relation of self and other as its core component, and it is this theme to which my assembled narrative seems always to return. The cultural environment within which old-time dance revival emerged was one of radical reconfiguration of all aspects of self-other relations. Global politics, interpersonal relations, and psychological well-being all were thought to emanate from a single ontological source, and at the time all were in grave disarray. It was to this environment that folksong appeared as a potent symbol, one which incorporated the most radical political and cultural elements of the idea of the other. In this context, community music and dance arose as one of the foremost means by which folksong ideals penetrated the recesses of the lives of its participants. Moreover, the emergence of community music and dance was enabled by an important transformation in this symbol, one where otherness ceased to be a tangible object and became instead a vivid uncertainty—a thing that cannot exist but, as a moral necessity, must exist.

Yet, if rituals of imagined community, asserting the unity of all things as a communal ideal, emerged against a backdrop of objective certainty, how curious that now it is unity and interconnectedness—radical individualism—that drives the economic and political machinery of the dominant global discourses—as well, some think, they should. Beyond necessity and basic opportunity, however, there is a sense that difference must intervene in radical equality, that it is a necessity of freedom, that at some level human strivings have no common currency. Today, it is not objective certainty but cavalier irony that occasions the cause of modest utopias such as I have described here. And where every claim to authenticity can be deconstructed, one can do much worse than look to those sovereign moments of serendipity, of benefaction, of invitation—a chance meeting at a stump, or a possibly unpresumptuous call to be other. This book is about the Bloomington that lives in us all, as other to the self and to the community we can inhabit but not imagine, as an other yet to come, announcing itself as an epiphany, as a beckoning, "Supposing you were / someone else . . ."

Blue Spruce

REFERENCES

Alden, Ray, producer. 1985. *The Young Fogies.* 33 rpm LP. Galax, Va.: Heritage Records, 056.

Anders, Jentri. 1990. *Beyond Counterculture: The Community of Mateel.* Pullman: Washington State University Press.

Bealle, John. 1987. "A History of the Bloomington Old-Time Music and Dance Group." Distributed regionally as an attachment to the annual Sugar Hill Calendar. Reprinted verbatim in Bealle 1988: 295–345.

———. 1988. "American Folklore Revival: A Study of an Old-Time Music and Dance Community." Ph.D. dissertation, Indiana University.

———. 1993. "Self-Involvement in Musical Performance: Stage Talk and Interpretive Control at a Bluegrass Festival." *Ethnomusicology* 37: 63–86.

Benford, Mac. 1989. "Folklorists and Us: An Account of Our Curious and Changing Relationship (with More Personal Reminiscences)." *Old-Time Herald* 1(7): 22–27.

Bernhardt, Jack. 1986. "The Hollow Rock String Band." *Bluegrass Unlimited* 21(6): 74–81.

Blaustein, Richard. 1975. "Traditional Music and Social Change: The Oldtime Fiddlers Association Movement in the United States." Ph.D. dissertation, Indiana University.

———. 1994. "The Oldtime Fiddlers Association Movement: A Grassroots Folk Revival." *Southern Folklore* 51: 199–217.

Bloomington Old-Time Music and Dance Group. Web site. http://www.bloomington.in.us/botmdg/.

Bluegrass Breakdown. 1992. CD. Newport Folk Festival Classics (series). Santa Monica, Calif.: Vanguard Records.

Bluestein, Evo, et al. 1992–93. "A Tribute to Sweet's Mill: Same Old Man Living at the Mill." *Old-Time Herald* 3(6): 32–41.

Bradley, Sandy. 1979. *Potluck and Dance Tonite!* 33 rpm LP. Waterbury, Vt.: Alcazar Records, 202.

Burns, Thomas A., and Doris Mack. 1978. "Social Symbolism in a Rural Square Dance Event." *Southern Folklore Quarterly* 42: 295–327.

Bustin, Dillon. 1982a. *If You Don't Outdie Me: The Legacy of Brown County.* Bloomington: Indiana University Press.

———. 1982b. " 'The Morrow's Uprising': William Morris and the English Folk Revival." *Folklore Forum* 15: 17–38.

———. 1983. *Dillon Bustin's Almanac.* 33 rpm LP. Whitesbury, Ky.: June Appal Records, JA-045.

———. 1988. "New England Prologue: Thoreau, Antimodernism, and Folk Culture." In Jane S. Becker and Barbara Franco, eds., *Folk Roots, New Roots: Folklore in American Life,* 1–6. Lexington, Mass.: Museum of Our National Heritage.

———. 1990a. "Lotus Dickey and His Music." *Country Dance and Song* 20 (March): 1–5.

———. 1990b. "The Virtues of Lotus Dickey: 'Sitting at the Feet of Lotus.' " *Country Dance and Song* 20 (March): 7–13.

———. 1995. " 'His Ceaseless, Ever Changing Song': The Creative Life of Lotus Dickey." In Nancy C. McEntire, Grey Larsen, and Janne Henshaw, eds., *The Lotus Dickey Songbook,* 5–19. Bloomington: Indiana University Press.

Bustin, Dillon, and Richard Kane. 1981. *Tough, Pretty, or Smart: A*

Portrait of the Patoka Valley Boys. Documentary film. Bloomington: Indiana University.

———. 1982. *Water from Another Time.* Documentary film. Alexan-
dria, Va.: Kane-Lewis Productions.

———. 1984. *Add and Mabel's Punkin Center.* Documentary film. Wa-
tertown, Mass.: Documentary Educational Resources.

Camp, Charles, and Timothy Lloyd. 1980. "Six Reasons Not to Produce Folklife Festivals." *Kentucky Folklore Record* 26: 67–74.

Canby, Vincent. 1979. "A Comedy in Which Class Tells." *New York
Times,* September 2, p. 13.

Cantwell, Robert. 1996. *When We Were Good: The Folk Revival.* Cambridge, Mass.: Harvard University Press.

Cauthen, Joyce H. 1989. *With Fiddle and Well-Rosined Bow: Old-
Time Fiddling in Alabama.* Tuscaloosa: University of Alabama
Press.

Christmas Country Dance School. 1988. *Christmas Country Dance
School, 1938–1988.* Berea, Ky.: Christmas Country Dance
School, Policy Committee.

Claus, Jeff, and Doug Crosswhite, producers. 1977. *An Anthology: Old
Style, Old Time Fiddling.* 33 rpm LP. Huntsville, Ala.: Tennevale
Records, TV-004.

Cockrell, Dale. 1997. *Demons of Disorder: Early Blackface Minstrels and
Their World.* New York: Cambridge University Press.

Cohen, John. 1964a. "Adapted and Arranged in the Public Domain."
In John Cohen and Mike Seeger, eds., *The New Lost City Ramblers Song Book,* 33–38. New York: Oak Publications.

———. 1964b. "Introduction to Styles in Old-Time Music." In John
Cohen and Mike Seeger, eds., *The New Lost City Ramblers Song
Book,* 10–21. N.Y.: Oak Publications.

———. 1975. *Musical Holdouts.* Film. New York: Phoenix Films.

———. 1996–97. "Conversation with Chad Crumm and Keith Brand
of the Hix." *Old-Time Herald* 5(6): 22–29.

Cohen, Ronald D. 2002. *Rainbow Quest: The Folk Music Revival and
American Society, 1940–1970.* Amherst: University of Massachusetts Press.

Collins, Jim. 1996. "Who Still Follows the Pied Piper of Canterbury?" *Old-Time Herald* 5(4): 10–13.

Conway, Cecelia. 1995. *African Banjo Echoes in Appalachia: A Study of Folk Traditions*. Knoxville: University of Tennessee Press.

Costonis, Maureen Needham. 1986–87. "The War of the Quadrilles: Creoles vs. Americans, 1804." *Bulletin of Research in the Humanities* 86–87: 63–81.

Culbertson, Anne E. 1986. "Music and Dance at the John C. Campbell Folk School in Brasstown, North Carolina, 1925–1985." D.Mus.Ed. thesis, Indiana University.

Dalsemar, Bob. 1982. *West Virginia Square Dances*. New York: Country Dance and Song Society.

———. 1988. "Community Feelings: Center Set Syndrome." *Country Dance and Song Society News,* issue 82 (May/June): 10.

Daniel, Wayne W. 1990. *Pickin' on Peachtree: A History of Country Music in Atlanta, Georgia*. Urbana: University of Illinois Press.

Dart, Mary. 1995. *Contra Dance Choreography: A Reflection of Social Change*. New York: Garland Press. Revision of Ph.D. thesis, Indiana University, 1992.

Day, Douglas. 1995. "Folk Dance in the Early Years of the John C. Campbell Folk School." In Susan Eike Spalding and Jane Harris Woodside, eds., *Communities in Motion: Dance, Community, and Tradition in America's Southeast and Beyond,* 179–90. Westport, Conn.: Greenwood Press.

Dunford, Pat, and Art Rosenbaum. 1964. *Fine Times at Our House: Indiana Ballads and Fiddle Tunes*. 33 rpm LP. New York: Folkways Records, FS-3809.

Easy Street String Band. 1980. *Money in Both Pockets*. 33 rpm LP. St. Louis: Prairie Schooner Records, PSI-104.

Eells, Eleanor. 1986. *Eleanor Eells' History of Organized Camping: The First 100 Years*. Martinsville, Ind.: American Camping Association.

Ellison, Curtis. 1995. *Country Music Culture: From Hard Times to Heaven*. Oxford: University of Mississippi Press.

English Folk Dance and Song Society (EFDSS). 1949–67. *Community Dances Manual*. Vols. 1–7. London.

————. 1968. *Community Dances Manual*. Vol. 3. Reprint, London: English Folk Dance and Song Society.

————. 1973. *Community Dances Manual*. Vol. 1. Reprint, London: English Folk Dance and Song Society.

Erikson, Dave, and Sarah Day. 2003. *The Summer of a Lifetime: Wisconsin Summer Camps*. Film. Lone Rock, Wis.: Ootek Productions.

Feintuch, Burt. 1981. "Dancing to the Music: Domestic Square Dances and Community in Southcentral Kentucky (1880–1940)." *Journal of the Folklore Institute* 18(1): 49–68.

Fiore, Robert, and Richard Nevell. 1976. Film. *Country Corners*. New York: Phoenix Films.

"The Folksmiths." 1958. *Sing Out!* 8 (Spring): 17.

"Forgotten Dances Revitalized." 1972. *Bloomington Courier Tribune* 96(221; July 2): C-2.

Fuzzy Mountain String Band. 1972. *The Fuzzy Mountain String Band*. Notes by Bill Hicks, with assistance from Alan Jabbour. 33 rpm LP. Somerville, Mass.: Rounder Records, 0010.

————. 1973. *Summer Oaks and Porch*. 33 rpm LP. Somerville, Mass.: Rounder Records, 0035.

Gardner, Hugh. 1978. *The Children of Prosperity: Thirteen Modern American Communes*. New York: St. Martin's Press.

Gerrard, Alice. 1992. "Colby Street to New York and Points South: The Highwoods Stringband." *Old-Time Herald* 3(4): 26–33.

————. 1995–96. "Shared Passions—Art Rosenbaum & Friends." *Old-Time Herald* 5(1): 22–27, 32–34.

Gibson, George R. 2001. "Banjo History: Mountain Banjo History— Bluegrass Instruments Reflect the Diversity of America." i-Bluegrass.com. http://www.ibluegrass.com/bg_posting3.cfm?p__a=featu&p__i=1115&p__r= (accessed 14 July 2004).

Green, Archie. 1993. "The Campus Folksong Club: A Glimpse at the Past." In Neil V. Rosenberg, ed., *Transforming Tradition: Folk Music Revivals Examined*, 61–72. Urbana: University of Illinois Press.

Greenstein, Mike. 1979. "New York Stringbands: The Highwoods and Cranberry Lake." *Bluegrass Unlimited* 13 (February): 36–41.

Grogan, Eddie. 1984. "The Indiana Contra Dancer's Lament." *Country Dance and Song Society News* 60 (September–October): 4.

———. 1986. "Won't We Look Pretty in the Ballroom?" In *Back Home Again in Indiana: Contra at the National Square Dance Convention, Indianapolis,* p. 6. Booklet published for the 35th National Square Dance Convention. Indianapolis: National Square Dance Convention.

Hallman, Kirk. 1997. "The Indiana Fiddlers' Gathering—Battle Ground, Indiana, June 27–29, 1997." *Old-Time Herald* 5(8): 30.

Herman, Janet. 1995. "Music in a Dance Context: The Case of Contra in Los Angeles." *UCLA Journal of Dance Ethnology* 19: 6–13.

Hicks, Bill. 1991. "A Remembrance: In Honor of a Reunion of Middle-Aged Old-Time Musicians." *Old-Time Herald* 2(8): 25–26.

———. 1995. "Where'd They Come From? Where'd They Go? A Brief History of the Fuzzy Mountain String Band." *Old-Time Herald* 4(6): 20–24.

Highwoods Stringband. 1973. 33 rpm LP. *Fire on the Mountain.* Somerville, Mass.: Rounder Records, 0023.

———. 1975. *Dance All Night.* 33 rpm LP. Somerville, Mass.: Rounder Records, 0045.

Holden, Rickey. 1955. *The Contra Dance Book.* Newark, N.J.: American Squares.

Hollow Rock String Band. 1968. *Traditional Dance Tunes.* 33 rpm LP. Kanawha Records, 311.

———. 1972. *The Hollow Rock String Band.* 33 rpm LP. Somerville, Mass.: Rounder Records, 24.

Hulan, Richard. 1969. "The 1st Annual Country Fiddlers' Contest." *Devil's Box* (15 March): 15–18.

Jabbour, Alan. 1971. Notes to *American Fiddle Tunes from the Archive of Folk Song.* Washington, D.C.: Library of Congress, AFS L62, 33^1/$_3$ rpm phonodisc.

Jackson, Ken. 1995. "Seedstock for the Future: Larry MacBride and Marimac Recordings." *Old-Time Herald* 4(7): 25–28.

Jamison, Phil. 1987–88. "In the Old-Time Days: The Beginnings of Team Clogging." *Old-Time Herald* 1(2): 18–19.

———. 1988. "The Green Grass Cloggers." *Old-Time Herald* 1(5): 22–24, 39.

———. 1989. "Community Dances in the Eighties: Dare to Be Square!" *Old-Time Herald* 1(6): 21–24, 35.

———. 1991. "Make 'em Want to Dance! How to Play for a Dance." *Old-Time Herald* 3(1): 10–11, 52.

———. 1993. "Southern Appalachian Big Set Square Dancing." *Old-Time Herald* 3(8: 8–10, 52.

———. 1995. "The Green Grass Cloggers: The Appalachian Spirit Goes International." In Susan Eike Spalding and Jane Harris Woodside, eds., *Communities in Motion: Dance, Community, and Tradition in America's Southeast and Beyond,* 169–74. Westport, Conn.: Greenwood Press.

———. 2004. "Old-Time Square Dancing in the 21st Century: Dare to Be Square!" *Old-Time Herald* 9(3): 8–12.

Jennings, Larry. 1983. *Zesty Contras.* Cambridge, Mass.: New England Folk Festival Association.

Katz, Ruth. 1973. "The Egalitarian Waltz." *Comparative Studies in Society and History* 15: 368–77.

Kent, Dot. 1997. "A Visit with Mark Gunther of the Chicago Barn Dance Company." *Old-Time Herald* 6(1): 10–14.

Kermiet, Chris. 1996. "The Future of Community Dance." *Old-Time Herald* 5(3): 10–13.

Klassen, Teri. 1987–88. "A Hoosier Outpost for Old-Time Music." *Old-Time Herald* 1 (Winter): 25–26.

Krassen, Miles. 1973. *Appalachian Fiddle.* New York: Oak Publications.

———. 1974. *Clawhammer Banjo.* New York: Oak Publications.

Krause, Rhett. 1991. "Morris Dance and America Prior to 1913." *Country Dance and Song* 21: 1–18.

———. 1992. "Morris Dance and American Prior to 1913, Part II." *Country Dance and Song* 22: 20–35.

Laufman, Dudley. 1971. "Down the Outside: Dances of New England Today." *Country Dance and Song* 4: 3–7.

———. 1972. Notes to *Canterbury Country Dance Orchestra.* 33 rpm LP. Plymouth Union, Vt.: Farm and Wilderness Records, F-72-FW3.

———. 1974. Notes to *Swinging on a Gate*. 33 rpm LP. Vorheesville, N.Y.: Front Hall Records, FHR-03.

———. 1981. *A Dancing Master's Diary: Poems and Five Dances*. Canterbury, N.H.: Dudley Laufman. http://www.laufman.org (accessed 18 June 2004).

Leary, James P. 1980. "Recreational Talk among White Adolescents." *Western Folklore* 39: 284–99.

Leftwich, Brad. 1986. "What's in a Name." *To Be Announced*, January, 13–15.

———. "A Reader's Forum on Tradition." *To Be Announced*, March, 19–20.

Lockridge, Larry. 1994. *Shade of the Raintree: The Life and Death of Ross Lockridge, Jr*. New York: Viking.

Lomax, Alan. 1959. "Bluegrass Background: Folk Music with Overdrive." *Esquire* 52 (October): 108.

Loomis, Ormond H. 1980. "Tradition and the Individual Farmer: A Study of Folk Agricultural Practices in Southern Central Indiana." Ph.D. dissertation, Indiana University.

Lucas, Bob. 1990. "Last Chorus: Lotus Dickey—Songwriter/Fiddler." *Sing Out!* 34(1): 33.

Madison, James H. 2002. "Old Times and New Times in Bloomington." In Will Counts, James H. Madison, and Scott Russell Sanders, eds., *Bloomington Past and Present*, 19–44. Bloomington: Indiana University Press.

Mangin, Julie. 1995. "The State Folk Dance Conspiracy: Fabricating a National Folk Dance." *Old-Time Herald* 4(7): 9–12.

Marcus, Greil. 1997. *Invisible Republic: Bob Dylan's Basement Tapes*. New York: Holt.

Matthews, Gail V. S. 1983. "Cutting a Dido: A Dancer's-Eye-View of Mountain Dance in Haywood County, N.C." M.A. thesis, Indiana University.

McEntire, Nancy C., Grey Larsen, and Janne Henshaw, eds. 2005. *The Lotus Dickey Songbook*. Rev. ed. Bloomington: Indiana University Press.

Milnes, Gerald. 1999. *Play of a Fiddle: Traditional Music, Dance, and*

References

Folklore in West Virginia. Lexington: University Press of Kentucky.

Morris, Dale. 1987. Review of *Old Time Music* by Chicken Chokers and Tompkins County Horse Flies (Rounder Records, 0213). *Old-Time Herald* 1(1): 31–32.

Nelson, Paul. 1964. "Newport: The Folk Spectacle Comes of Age." *Sing Out!* 14 (November 1964): 6–11.

Nevell, Richard. 1977. *A Time to Dance.* New York: St. Martin's.

Nevins, Richard. 1968. Notes to Fred Cockerham, Tommy Jarrel, and Oscar Jenkins, *Down To the Cider Mill.* 33 rpm LP. County Records, 713.

———. 1972. Notes to *DaCosta Woltz's Southern Broadcasters.* 33 rpm LP. County Records, 524.

———. 1973. Notes to *The Skillet Lickers, Volume 2.* 33 rpm LP. County Records, 526.

———. n.d. Notes to *The Bogtrotters.* 33 rpm LP. Biograph Records, RC-6003.

Page, Ralph. 1973. "The History of Square Dancing: Part IV—Direct Ancestors." *Square Dancing* 25 (April): 59–60.

———. 1976. *Heritage Dances of Early America.* Colorado Springs, Colo.: Lloyd Shaw Foundation, Century One Press.

Powell, Rasby Marlene. 1997. "Creating Community: An Ethnography of Old-Time Dance Groups." Ph.D. dissertation, Florida State University.

Putnam, Robert. 2000. *Bowling Alone: The Collapse and Revival of American Community.* New York: Simon & Schuster.

Reuss, Richard. 1965. "So You Want to Be a Folklorist?" *Sing Out!* 15 (November): 40–43.

Rosenbaum, Art. 1968. *Old-Time Mountain Banjo.* New York: Oak Publications.

Rosenberg, Neil V. 1985. *Bluegrass: A History.* Urbana: University of Illinois Press.

———. 1993. "Introduction." In Neil V. Rosenberg, ed., *Transforming Tradition: Folk Music Revivals Examined,* 1–25. Urbana: University of Illinois Press.

————. 1995a. "Neil V. Rosenberg." In Ronald D. Cohen, ed., *Wasn't That a Time!" Firsthand Accounts of the Folk Music Revival,* 71–78. Metuchen, N.J.: Scarecrow Press.

————. 1995b. "Picking Myself Apart: A Hoosier Memory." *Journal of American Folklore* 108: 277–86.

Roszak, Theodore. 1969. *The Making of a Counter Culture.* Garden City, N.Y.: Anchor Books.

Sanders, Scott Russell. 1991. *In Limestone Country.* Boston: Beacon Press. Originally published in 1985 as *Stone Country* (Bloomington: Indiana University Press).

————. 1995. *Writing from the Center.* Bloomington: Indiana University Press.

————. 2002. "Loving This Place." In Will Counts, James H. Madison, and Scott Russell Sanders, eds., *Bloomington Past and Present,* 1–17. Bloomington: Indiana University Press.

Sannella, Ted. 1982. *Balance and Swing: A Collection of Fifty-Five Squares, Contras, and Triplets in the New England Tradition with Music for Each Dance.* New York: Country Dance and Song Society of America.

————. 1986. "The New England Tradition: An Interview with Ted Sannella." By Tom Phillips. *Country Dance and Song* 16: 24–28.

Seeger, Mike, with Paul Nelson. 1964. "Some Thoughts about Old-Time Music." In John Cohen and Mike Seeger, eds., *The New Lost City Ramblers Song Book,* 22–29. New York: Oak Publications.

Seeger, Pete. 1961. *How to Play the 5-String Banjo.* Rev. ed. Beacon, N.Y.: Author. Originally published 1948.

Shapiro, Bruce. 1997. Review of *Invisible Republic: Bob Dylan's Basement Tapes* by Greil Marcus (1997). *Nation* 265 (August 25/September 1): 44–46.

Smith, Harry. 1952. *Anthology of American Folk Music.* 33 rpm LP. New York: Folkways Records.

Snyder, Eugenia. 1986. "Joe Wilson: A Bluegrasser at the Helm of the NCTA." *Bluegrass Unlimited* 20(10): 77–82.

Spalding, Susan Eike. 1993. "Aesthetic Standards in Old Time Dancing in Southwest Virginia: African-American and European-American Threads." Ed.D. thesis, Temple University.

St. James, Jana. 1995. *Memories of Madison County: The True Story of My Romance with Robert James Waller*. Beverly Hills, Calif.: Dove Books.

Stanton, Gary. 2000. "We Were a Family." From "WFIU: 50 Years of History and Memories." http://www.indiana.edu/wfiu/50history-gstanton.htm (accessed 3 November 2003).

Sundell, Jon. 1981. "Rural Square Dances in East Tennessee: A Personal Account of Visits to Four Communities." *Country Dance and Song* 11/12: 53–64.

Sutherland, Pete. 1982. *Eight Miles from Town*. 33 rpm LP. Crown Point, Ind.: Marimac Recordings, 9031.

———. 1989. "A Trip with Lotus Dickey." *Sing Out!* 33(2): 12–19.

———. 1991. "Beware of Old-Time Music Revivals! The Henry Ford Story." *Old-Time Herald* 2(7): 33–37, 50.

Taylor, Gordon Rattray. 1972. *Rethink: A Paraprimitive Solution*. New York: Dutton.

Thom, James Alexander. 1976. "Indiana's Self-Reliant Uplanders." *National Geographic* 149 (March): 341–62.

Titon, Jeff Todd. 2001. *Old-Time Kentucky Fiddle Tunes*. Lexington: University Press of Kentucky.

Tolman, Beth, and Ralph Page. 1937. *The Country Dance Book*. New York: Farrar & Rinehart.

Twork, Eva O'Neal. 1982. *Henry Ford and Benjamin B. Lovett: The Dancing Billionaire and the Dancing Master*. Detroit: Harlo Press.

Tyler, Paul L. 1991–92. "Voices from the Villages." *Old-Time Herald* 3(2): 32–34, 56.

———. 1992a. " 'Sets on the Floor': Social Dance as an Emblem of Community in Rural Indiana." Ph.D. dissertation, Indiana University.

———. 1992b. "The True Story of 'Dickey's Discovery': Thoughts on Lotus Dickey's Fiddling." Notes to Lotus Dickey, *Fiddle Tunes from Orange County, Indiana*. Cassette. Crown Point, Ind.: Marimac Recordings, 9029–30.

———. 1995. "Square Dancing in the Rural Midwest: Dance Events and the Location of Community." In Susan Eike Spalding and Jane Harris Woodside, eds., *Communities in Motion: Dance, Community, and Tradition in America's Southeast and Beyond*, 35–46. Westport, Conn.: Greenwood Press.

U.S. Congress. House. Subcommittee on Census and Population of the Committee on Post Office and Civil Service. 1984. *A Bill to Designate the Square Dance as the National Folk Dance of the United States: Hearings on H.R. 1706*. 98th Cong., 2nd sess. Serial 98-51.

Vittek, Jenny Cleland. 1988. "A Summer in Fat City." *Old-Time Herald* 1(3): 22–24.

von Schmidt, Eric, and Jim Rooney. 1979. *Baby, Let Me Follow You Down: The Illustrated Story of the Cambridge Folk Years*. New York: Anchor Press. Reprint, Amherst: University of Massachusetts Press, 1994.

Waller, Robert James. 1992. *The Bridges of Madison County*. New York: Warner.

Whisnant, David E. 1984. *All That Is Native and Fine: The Politics of Culture in an American Region*. Chapel Hill: University of North Carolina Press.

Wiggins, Gene. 1987. *Fiddlin' Georgia Crazy: Fiddlin' John Carson, His Real World, and the World of His Songs*. Urbana: University of Illinois Press.

Wilfert, Ed. 1989. "Pinewoods Fifty Years Ago." *Country Dance and Song* 19: 1–37.

Wilson, Joe, and Lee Udall. 1982. *Folk Festivals: A Handbook for Organization and Management*. Knoxville: University of Tennessee Press.

Wolfe, Charles. 1980. "Dave Freeman and County Records." *Bluegrass Unlimited* 15 (December): 50–55.

———. 1989. "The Legend That Peer Built: Reappraising the Bristol Sessions." *Journal of Country Music* 12: 24–35.

———. 1995. "Rounder Is 25! The Early Days of Rounder: Vol. I." *Old-Time Herald* 4(8): 35–37, 60.

———. 1997. *The Devil's Box: Masters of Southern Fiddling*. Nashville,

References

Tenn.: Country Music Foundation Press and Vanderbilt University.

Woolf, Andrew. 1971. "Notes from a Fiddler." *Country Dance and Song* 4: 35–40.

Wyatt, Marshall. 1999. "A Visit with Joseph E. Bussard, Jr." *Old-Time Herald* 6(7): 12–17, 34.

References

INDEX

Ramblin' Conrad's Guitar Store and Folklore Center (Norfolk, Va.), 303

Randall, Zoe, *82*

rapper sword dance, 182

Rapp's Pizza Train, 78, 100, 149, 208, 211, 224

RCA-Vintage Records, 243

realism of particulars, 170, 175, 191

record collectors, 13–14, 17

recordings: active vs. passive listening practices, 60, 245, 248–49; as articulation of community, 150–51; cassettes, 245–50; Dry and Dusty "lost" recording, 63, 65; dubbed 78s, 14; formality vs. informality in, 56, 59; "homegrown" studios, 247–48; "invitational" recordings, 148; of jam sessions, 58, 234, 245; liner notes, 18–19, 55, 244; live vs. multi-track recording, 56, 246; as material culture, 241–42, 249; reel-to-reel (quarter inch) tape recording, 245. *See also* field recordings; LP records; "poor substitute" phenomenon; record collectors; reissues; 78 rpm records

Redbud Records, 185

rediscoveries, 15–16, 75

Reed, Henry, 58, 60

reel-to-reel (quarter inch) tape recording, 245

Reese, Anne: as dance performer, 177, *179*, 203; gardening by, *110*; as musician, 79, *80;* at New Harmony, *233;* wedding, 97–98

Re-evaluation Counseling, 101

reissues: *Anthology of American Folk Music* compared to, 13, 17, 20; expansion of, 21–22; jazz as model for, 17, 18; liner notes, 18–19, 244; sales/distribution network, 22, 244

religion, 107–108

repertoire, 57–58, 66, 142

representative democracy, 132, 139–40, 307, 310. *See also* capitalization

Restle, Kathy, 36, 49, 68, 69, *70,* 97

retributive justice, 115

Reuss, Richard, 6

Rice, Eileen, 111

Rice, Emma, *121*

Rice, Mitch, 111, 211, 291

Ritchie, Gene and Margaret, 211, 213

Ritchie, Mark, 212

Roane Mountain Hilltoppers, 233–34

Roberts, Doc, 73–75

Robertson, Eck, 26

rock music, 91, 145, 241–42

romance: arbitrary dyadic encounter and, 133–35; dance camp romance, 155, 157; dance group romances, 88–91, 94–96; dance group weddings, 96–99, 177–78; flirting, 103; folk revival as basis for, 92–94; waltz and, 90, 276–77

Roos, Sara, *220*

Rosenbaum, Art, 27–34, 41

Rosenberg, Neil, 6–10, 13

Rosenthal, Mark, 181–82, 203, *204*

Roska, Mary Beth: as caller, 198, 211; at camps/weekends, *222;* as dance performer, *204, 225;* at social gatherings, *121;* wedding, 96

Ross, Cindy, 81

Roszak, Theodore, 43, 311

Rothfuss, Helen, 210

Rounder Records, 22, 55, 59–60, 243–46

Roznak, Theodore, 43–44, 311

rumor, 100, 139

Russell, Mark, 303

Ryan, Bill "Pigweed," 118

Ryan, John, 295

Rygas, Jana, 203–204, 216

Sacred Harp singing, 80–81

Sanders, Scott, 112–13, 295, 308

Sannella, Ted, 35, 98, 173, 191, 255

Schmid, Ewan, 120, *121,* 179

Schmid, Lee, *79,* 96

Schneider, Mark, 177, *179*

Schwarz, Tracy, 207

Scotch on the Rocks, 259

Scruggs, Earl, 49

Second Story, 224

secrecy, 103

Seeger, Mike, 12, 14

Seeger, Pete, 27–28, 30, 254

serendipity: Bean King ritual and, 120–21; convergence of values as, 105; cultural genealogy of, 87; as folk revival motif, 5; freedom and, 125–26; in Mateel settlements, 44–45; public performances and, 1–2, 10, 64–65. *See also* spontaneity

set dance: as aesthetic vs. social, 134–35; arbitrary dyadic encounter, 123, 128–32, 194, 199–200; dyadic jargon in, 88, 131, 192; eye contact, 88; "giving weight," 88, 127; structural rigidity of, 125–26, 130. *See also* contra dance; square dance

Tanner, Gid, 19
tape recordings. *See* cassettes; field recordings; recordings; reel-to-reel (quarter inch) tape recording
Taylor, Gordon Rattray, 45
technology, 22–23, 84, 307. *See also* "poor substitute" phenomenon
Tesich, Steve, 292, 297
Thatcher, Bill, 72, 185, 233–34
therapeutic talk, 101–104
Thompson, Bobbie, 58
Thompson, Tommy, 58–59, 60
Thompson, Uncle Jimmy, 164
Thoreau, Henry David, 39–40
Titon, Jeff Todd, 21
Tolman, Beth, 37, 128, 192, 198
Tomkins County Horse Flies, 185, 257–58
Tough, Pretty, or Smart (Bustin and Kane), 281
town-gown corridor: depiction in *Breaking Away*, 300–301; description of, 3–4, 51–52; Jukebox relation to, 71; map, *4;* 1980s changes to, 308. *See also* cultural geography; Indiana University
tradition: popular music and, 241–42; rational choice in, 42; simplicity in, 169–70; utopian vs. commercial aspiration in, 13, 17–21, 164
Transcendentalism, 39–40
travel: band touring, 146, 149–50; dance group network and, 157, 174–75, 183, 305; dance group performances, 138; to festivals/camps/weekends, 26, 113–14, 143; group vacations, 87; morris dance tours, 181. *See also* festivals
T-shirts, 83, 105, 207, 215, 216
twirl (dance movement), 129–32, 273
Tyler, Paul: arrival in Bloomington, 186–87; at Battleground, 234; as caller, 189, 198, 219; as dance performer, 179, 182, 203–204, *204;* Lotus Dickey and, 287, 290; as musician, 211, 225, 228, *288;* at social gatherings, *82,* 120, *121*

Ungar, Jay, 156
Unitarian Universalist church (Bloomington dance site), 208
Upper Cascades Park (Bloomington dance site), 268
utopian society: appropriation of, 299–301; Bean King party and, 122; capitalization and, 132–33; communes

and, 42–43, 45; cooperative labor, 111, 113–14, 216–19; cooperative living arrangements, 112; dance as articulation of, 37–38, 131–32; ethnic utopia, 293–96, 298, 301, 311; old-time music as, 13, 17–21, 146–48; open access and, 123, 124–25, 138, 140, 199; political action and, 43–44, 47; public trust and, 302–303; society/polity convergence in, 139; sport and, 296; utopian feminism, 130; wry humor and, 139–40. *See also* community; natural morality

values: acceptable articulation of, 105, 114–16; cooperative labor, 111, 113–14, 217–19; food preparation and, 110; gardening as expression of, 108–109; household values, 112; prices at events and, 114, 124, 218; religious values, 107–108; in romance, 90–91; saturation of calendar and, 107. *See also* community
VanAuken, Margie, 207, 215
Vanguard Records, 243
vegetarian cooking, 110–11
Vetco Records, 22
Vietnam War, 3, 8, 23, 42–43
vintage clothing, 111–12
vintage dance, 171
volleyball, 81–83, *82,* 85–86, 95
voluntary primitivism, 45
Voyager Records, 22

Wagner, Michael, 78, 215, 216
Wallace, Andy, 40–41
Waller, Robert James, 92–95
waltz, 90, 170, 275–77
Warner, Frank, 12
Water from Another Time (Bustin and Kane), 282, 285
Watson, Willard, 201
weddings, 96–99, 177–78
Weirhake, David, 211
Wells, Herman B, 5, 7
Welty, Doc, 216
WFIU (Bloomington's National Public Radio affiliate), 6, 159, 250–51, 308
What Color Is Your Parachute? (1971), 107
Wheatland Folk Festival (Remus, Mich.), 204
White Springs Folk Festival (Fla.), 149
Whole Earth Catalog, 45
Wild Asparagus, 171, 252–53

Index

John Bealle has written extensively on folksong revival with an eye to its deep-rooted connections to American cultural history. His previous book, *Public Worship, Private Faith: Sacred Harp and American Folksong*, traced the fasola singing movement through its various encounters with American religious and musical culture. He is an exceptional old-time fiddler, and plays in a dance band with fellow travelers Eloise Clark and Jim Johnson. John and his wife Eloise and daughter Josie live in Cincinnati.

Dee Mortensen, Sponsoring Editor for this book, went to her first BOTMDG dance in 1983. Sharon Sklar, Book and Jacket Designer, attended her first BOTMDG dance in 1974. Miki Bird, Managing Editor and Project Editor for this book, first danced with BOTMDG in 1991. The cover art by Margie VanAuken originally appeared as an early BOTMDG t-shirt design.

This book uses Water-Titling and Adobe Caslon for typefaces. The book and jacket were printed by Thomson-Shore.